Happy 21st Birthday Philippa,

We wish you every happiness in the years ahead and may all your dreams come true.

With love,
Ian and Sylvia.

June 1998.

PORTUGUESE GARDENS

PORTUGUESE GARDENS

HELDER CARITA

ANTÓNIO HOMEM CARDOSO
Photographer

MIGUEL ESTEVES CARDOSO
Preface

ANTIQUE COLLECTORS' CLUB

Published for the Antique Collectors' Club
by the Antique Collectors' Club Ltd.

Design and Coordination
Helder Carita
Composed in fine Garamond by Planitipo Artes Gráficas
Colour selection: Reproscan, Reproducão Gráfica, Lda.
Printing: Resopal
Translator: David Kirkby

British Library CIP Data

Carita, Helder
  Portuguese Gardens
  1. Portugal. Gardens
  I. Title II. Cardoso, Homem III. Jardins em Portugal ● *English*
712.6'09469

CONTENTS

THOSE WHOSE VALUABLE HELP
contributed to the making of this book
PERSONAL THANKS

Personal thanks to those architects who where most closely involved in the making of this book: João Paulo da Conceição, João Cabral, Maria Luciana Miguel, Raul Veríssimo and Tiago Braddel.

The authors would also like to express their appreciation for the contributions of:

Armanda de Meirelles
Arquivo Histórico da Cidade de Lisboa
Arquivo Histórico do Ministério das Finanças
Arquivo Nacional da Torre do Tombo
Biblioteca da Academia das Ciências
Biblioteca Nacional de Lisboa
Câmara Municipal de Évora
Câmara Municipal de Guimarães
Condes de Campo Belo
Condessa de Mesquitella
Condessa de Santar
Condessa de Sibour
Condessa de Vilalba
Convento da Cartucha de Évora

D. Dinis de Sotto Mayor
Directora do Palácio Nacional de Queluz
Directora do Paço de Sintra
Dr. Francisco Jácome de Vasconcellos
Arq. Frederico George
Fundação da Casa de Bragança
Fundação da Casa de Mateus
Hemeroteca de Lisboa
Dr. José Maria de Mello
Dr. Júlio Basto
Dona Maria del Carmen d'Almada
Dona Maria Teresa Teles da Sylva
Maria Peixoto Villas-Boas
Maria Hermínia Silva de Oliveira Paes
Maria Margarida Cancela de Abreu
Maria Ribeiro da Cunha
Museu Nacional de Arte Antiga de Lisboa
Dr. Pedro Canavarro
Presidência da República
Raul Sousa Coutinho Empis

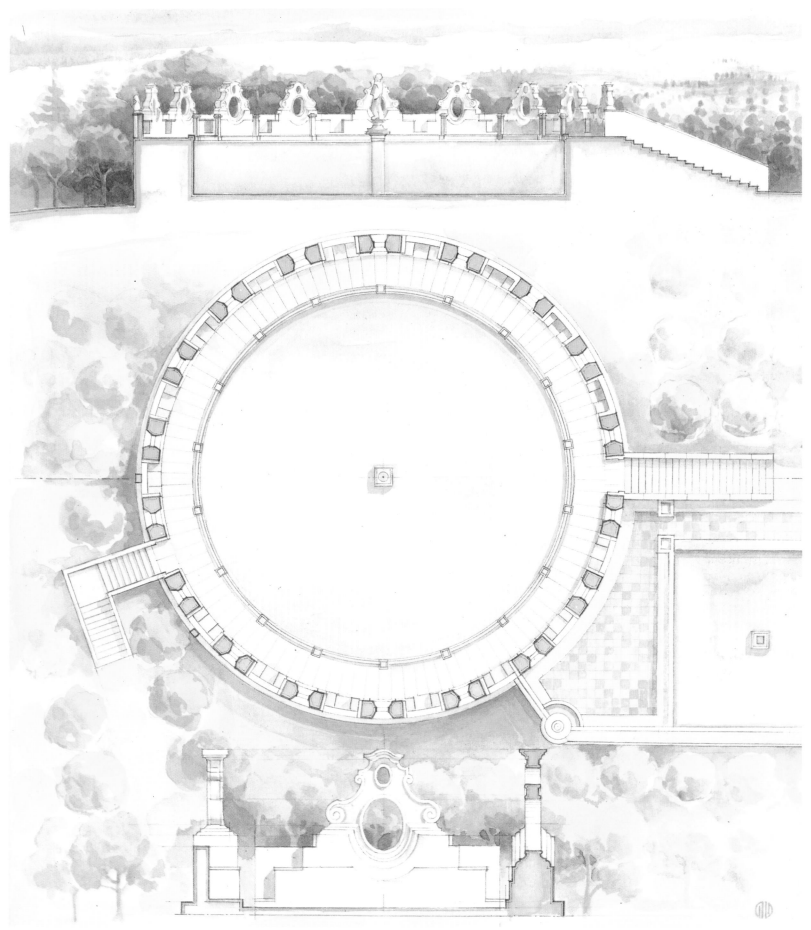

Plan, cross-section and detail of the water tank of the gardens of
the Mitra Palace, Valverde — Evora.
Drawing by Raul Verissimo

PREFACE

This book is a garden. In it, I learnt that a garden is a difficult thing, a human thing, an idea that people have of a place.

This book is a garden and one can stroll through it, stop and breathe in the atmosphere, walk around with one's eyes open or closed. But it is more than this. Just as a garden is more than that which one sees. A garden becomes part of us in many ways. It has a temperature, music, breath. One lives it in a very particular way.

This book sets us thinking. It presents us with the unsettling idea of a Portuguese garden, walled-in, made for staying inside, full of smells and peace. The lost gardens are always those that appeal to us the most, but we should resist the temptation to cry over them and resurrect them.

In this book I learnt that a garden is alive, something which owes its existence to man and which reflects, as far as possible, the heights to which he can rise. If countries have characters, tendencies and tastes in specific measures and combinations that distinguish them one from another, then the relationship between gardens and cultures, independent of the changes brought about by the passage of time, is very pertinent. The idea of a universal and ideal garden is beautiful and exists as long as our dreams and faith keep it alive, but it doesn't exist in this world. Each one of us has our own idea of paradise and the paradise of everyone can be the garden of no one.

This book is like looking after a garden in that it is concerned with care, patience, good taste and perfection, as well as the way in which gardeners (the author and photographer) have subjugated themselves so as not to distract or dazzle the reader. The photographs of António Homem Cardoso show, as always, the way in which he has overridden his personality in order to emphasise the importance of the image he is going to capture permanently. The care and elegance of the work of Helder Carita restores in all its detail much that has been lost. His sensitive approach expresses the civilised anger he feels at the stupid and barbaric attitudes which are today reflected in the state, condition and use of our gardens.

This book, unlike those decorative volumes which only serve to fill the gaps in book cases or to put on the table of the living room, is like a visit to a garden that we linger over so we can enjoy it to the full. To produce it took a lot of time, knowledge and patience, just as if we were creating a peaceful garden where we could learn and live and enjoy the experience to the full.

This book is a garden. And like those gardens where one can spend a lifetime without once thinking how something like it could be created, there is a heart beating away inside. It is the heart of the world. And, of course, it is a Portuguese heart.

Miguel Esteves Cardoso

THE CONCEPT OF
THE GARDEN
IN PORTUGAL

INTRODUCTION

The garden, the image of a lost or promised paradise coupled with the desire to bring order to nature, is a universe protected from the uncertainties of climate and geography. Although it appears to be a simple space for recreational or social purposes, the garden contains within itself the means to fulfil the profound need of the human soul to create a paradise on earth.

Portuguese gardens were less influenced by outside forces than was architecture, and for centuries they remained closely connected to the way of life and the imagination of the Portuguese soul. While stylistic transformations seem to have affected only the surface of decorative forms, Portuguese gardens reveal permanent characteristics, at a profound level, of a spatial concept of a particular way of feeling about and living in this small universe that is the garden.

Ever since the fifteenth century, foreigners who visited Portugal came across recreational traditions that did not coincide with their own. The references and observations that they left behind in diaries and notes on their journeys, although frequently uncomplimentary, reveal that Portuguese gardens were somewhat removed from their own ideas of gardens. The Portuguese attitude to European culture, coupled with the writers' own cultural pride, frequently prevented them from accepting the differences or else led them simply to classify the differences as exotic and influenced by the Orient and Islam.

While in the majority of cases the writers did not perceive the special significance of fragrance in the Portuguese garden when they referred to the strong presence of orange trees and lemon trees, or to the intimacy and privacy conferred by high surrounding walls, their descriptions become valuable documents in the analysis of the Portuguese concept of a garden.

Throughout the centuries the garden has been closely connected with architecture and domestic life. High walls, flowerboxes, benches, summer houses, tile-work and brick paving are defined as elements of a space that is essentially one of leisure, and which Courtils defined extremely clearly when he visited Mafra: '*It is more a room of greenery than a real garden.*'

Profoundly dependent on dry and excessively warm summers, the garden is closed in on itself in a small, green, cool universe. Finally, tile-work and shell-work, introduced as Indo-Portuguese art, give these refined spaces an ambience of magic and intangible beauty, which radically distances them from the natural surroundings.

It is this concept of architectural garden and leisure garden that separates Portuguese gardens from the landscapist trend of northern Europe, where the surrounding natural landscape is invited to be a part of the overall layout of the garden. More architectural than landscapist, the Portuguese garden is somewhat dependent on the geography of the country, facing inwards on itself in an atmosphere of sophisticated intimacy which is better seen on the inside than to be admired from the outside.

Opposite page. *Detail of the gardens of the Palace of the Marquises of Fronteira.* São Domingos de Benfica. Lisbon.

THE GRAECO-ROMAN TRADITION

CHAPTER I

One cannot truly speak of the art of landscaping in Portugal, in the recreational sense, prior to the Roman occupation.

No works involving landscaping are known to have been carried out by the cattle-herding peoples who occupied the Iberian peninsula four thousand years before Christ and who had spread over Europe as far as the Baltic sea.

Later on, with the establishment of settlements, contacts were made with the more urban and organised cultures of the eastern Mediterranean.

Both the Greeks and Romans were also of tribal origin and, in the first few centuries of their cultures, demonstrated a total lack of knowledge of the more sophisticated customs of the imperial courts of Egypt, Mesopotamia and Persia.

In Greece, it was the Stoics whose voices were raised loudest in protest when the first work to beautify outside spaces was undertaken. Chrysippe openly criticised fixing grape vines to trellises, planting myrtle bushes and rearing animals such as peacocks, pigeons, partridges and nightingales for simple pleasure or enjoyment.[1]

The art of gardening came late to both Greece and Rome, after the great conquests and cultural contacts with the eastern Mediterranean. In Rome, there were those who defended the simplicity of the customs of the Republic, and Cato (234-149B.C.), for example, praised the simplicity of life in the countryside. Later, Varro (116-27B.C.) highlighted recent changes in taste when he stated that the Romans of his time think that theirs is not a true villa unless it is adorned with Greek names such as 'peristylon' (colonnade), 'ornithon' (aviary), 'peripteros' (arbour) or 'oportotheca' (orchard)'.[2]

It was, however, Varro who, at the end of his life, constructed a villa near Casinum and described his aviary there in such great detail and with such precision that it would be possible to reconstruct it: *'The aviary is next to the banks of a stream, along which runs a path, three metres wide, which is open to the skies. Off this path, and facing the open fields, is the site on which the aviary is constructed, this being enclosed on both sides, on the right and left, by high walls. The aviary, in the shape of a writing slate, topped by a dome at the far end, is between these walls, the quadrangular area being sixteen metres wide and twenty-four metres long, while the dome is nine metres in diameter. Pointing towards this, as if it were drawn on the lower edge of the slate, is an open path which might have been an entrance. On both the left and right of this entrance are colonnades of stone columns, alternating with dwarf trees; while the space between the top of the wall and the architrave of the colonnade is covered with hemp netting which also hangs from the architraves to the ground. These colonnades are full of birds of all species'.[3]*

The aspect that stands out most from an analysis of the spatial structures of Varro's aviary, is the idea of a vault-like space which resembles the concept of the peristyle of the Roman villa. Only really studied this century, the Roman villa has no façade: instead it faces completely inwards on to the atrium and peristyle, like a space closed up on itself and surrounded by high walls.

The Varro aviary is the oldest detailed description of an outdoor space in Roman literature and Pliny the Younger (A.D.61-113), in his letters to Gallius, provides us with what is perhaps the most important document on the art of landscaping in Roman times.

Opposite page. *Detail of water spouts in the peristyle of a Roman villa.*
Conimbriga. Coimbra.

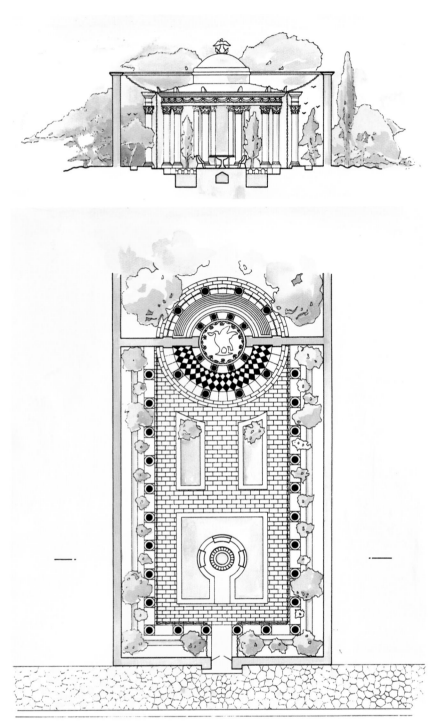

From the detailed description by Varro, it is possible to reconstruct his aviary. Surrounded by high walls, the aviary shows features seen in the spatial concepts of Portuguese gardens up to the eighteenth century.

Raised cross-section and plan of the Varro's aviary.

The luxury and complexity of Pliny's two villas testify, however, to the conflicting radical changes of the time. The gardens assume a fundamental importance, with windows being let into the surrounding walls. *'Here begins an almost completely covered arcade almost as big as a public building. It has windows on both sides, more on the side facing the sea, while on that facing the garden there is only one in every other opening. In front is a perfumed terrace with violets. When the sun shines, the temperature of the arcade rises, and not only are the direct rays of the sun shut out, but the effects of the north-east wind are also greatly moderated, with the result that the arcade gets as hot in the front as it stays cool in the rear. It is sheltered from the south-west, and is thus able to diffuse the strength of winds from opposite directions, first with one, then with another of its sides; it is pleasant in the winter, but even more so in the summer when the terrace in the mornings, and the area of the path and the part near the gardens in the afternoons, remain cool, this being dependent on the amount and position of shade and whether the day is dawning or drawing to its close.'*[4]

Besides the views, there is a prominent self-contained colonnaded recreational area.

Other areas are described in great and precise detail: *'A covering of young and shady vines with a soil that is soft and gentle, even for unshod feet'.*[5]

Pliny's writings show us that the Romans were aware of how to control the wind and use the heat of the sun. They were also well versed in making use of the available water both for watering and recreational purposes, and the numerous aqueducts, thermal springs and spas which covered the empire are good examples of this. Water, of course, in a Mediterranean region with hot, dry summers, is essential for the maintenance of a complex landscaping system.

Pliny complained of the lack of running water in the gardens of his Villa Laurentina, while in those of his Villa Toscana *'everything was watered by small streams which never ran dry'.*[6] These streams fed groups of fountains, water spouts and swimming pools.

In the Villa Toscana, he also described the most sophisticated forms of topiary: *'A terrace, bordered by boxwood hedges trimmed into different shapes, which sloped downwards with figures of animals facing each other on both sides'.*[7]

The art of topiary was invented, according to Pliny the Elder, by Gaius Matius, a friend of the Emperor Augustus. In his *Natural History*, Pliny the Elder refers to the introduction of this custom: *'In our time, the cypress is cut so as to form thick walls or columns with smooth surfaces'*,[8] and he continues with a description of hunting scenes, animals and other objects cut out of bushes.

If topiary appears to have been introduced as a means of substituting or varying the method of decorating gardens with statues, then it very soon acquired an aesthetic expression of its own, combining a sculptural aspect in the use of cut-out shapes, and a more architectural aspect in dividing and structuring outdoor shapes.

Neither temples nor grottoes are mentioned at Pliny's two villas. We know, however, that in the Villa Alticus there was a large artificial grotto with a sculpture representing the life of Zeus. Such grottoes were an integral part of the Greek tradition of sacred and mysterious places. Pliny the Elder stated that they were formed from volcanic rocks brought from the south of Italy.

In Portugal, the ruins of Conimbriga have revealed villas whose complexity of plan and refinement of decorative elements suggest highly sophisticated buildings. One of the main granaries of the empire, the Hispanic peninsula was the object of special attention from Rome. Although they do not possess the same sense of luxury and beauty as the large villas built by the emperors on the outskirts of Rome, there were villas on the Iberian peninsula of the same type and grandeur. The villas of Conimbriga have, therefore, to be seen in the perspective of villas in a provincial city which lay mid-way on the route between Olisipo (Lisbon) and Bracara Augusta (Braga).

The water systems with water spouts, which can still be seen today in the peristyles at Conimbriga, together with the sophisticated treatment of these peristyles where pools are shaped into patterns forming flower beds, are examples of the way in which the appreciation of and liking for domestic architecture spread throughout the region.

As regards country villas outside the city, which were known all over the empire and which Pliny describes, few remains are to be found either in Portugal or in what was the Roman empire.

Their privileged location in places with abundant water, protection from the winds and good land for cultivation, were, without doubt, decisive in such villas being salvaged and restored after the fall of the empire. The Islamic occupation of the peninsula — not long after the fall of the Roman empire — and its civilised customs, meant these villas were used as recreational estates.

From recent studies, it has become evident that old properties in the south and centre of the country, which until today were considered to be from the Manueline period, were in fact ancient Roman villas which were occupied in the Islamic period and restored during the Manueline era. This is the case of the Mitra estate, in Valverde, near Evora, and the Palace of Sempre Noiva, while it is not difficult to imagine that the Palace of Agua de Peixes, which possesses one of the largest sources of water in the Alentejo region, was used for recreational purposes.

* * *

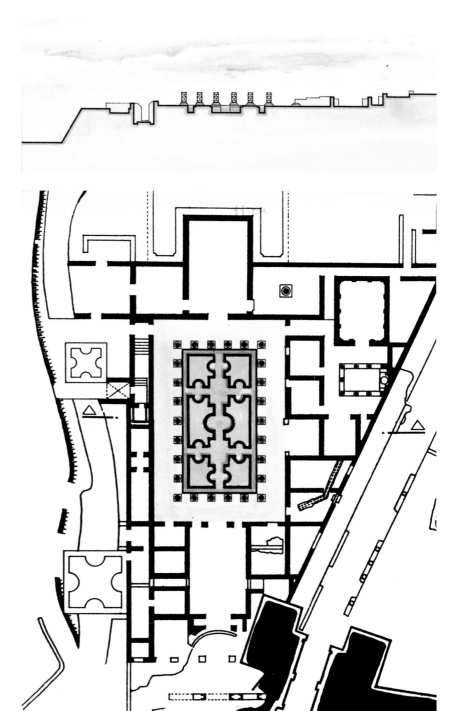

Cross-section and plan of the Roman villa complex at Conimbriga.

Left. *Details of pavements in the Conimbriga Museum.*

Following pages. *View of the ruins of a villa at Conimbriga.*

THE TRADITION OF THE 'WALK'
and spatial structure

From an analysis of the different descriptions of the gardens and ruins of the Villa Adriana, one finds that the gardens were bordered by high walls, thus establishing a clear contrast between interior space and exterior space. The clearest example of this is, without doubt, the Varro aviary which reveals a close tie with the concept of vault-like space of the peristyle of the Roman villa. Thus, just as the Roman villa seems to close itself off from the outside, while opening itself up on to the atrium and the peristyle, so too do the gardens seem to protect themselves, although windows, which Pliny describes in detail, open on to the landscaped scene.

When the Italian Renaissance brought about a revival of the ancient Roman gardens, like those at the villas d'Este, Medici and Lante, it only borrowed decorative elements from Rome, as it did with architecture. The structure of the architectural space and the design of the façades of the new palaces reveal a total dissimilarity with Roman villas where façade design was practically non-existent.

If the Villa Adriana is more than an imperial villa (it is a complex of 160 acres which virtually resembles a small city), the structure of its layout is completely different from that of the exterior spaces of Renaissance Italy which, paradoxically, wanted to revive both the architecture and spirit of Roman times.

Few detailed descriptions of the Villa Adriana remain which allow us to determine the shape of its gardens with any precision. However, the ruins reveal a large colonnade laid out in the shape of an 'ambulatio', about 230 metres long, and a 'canopus', a type of long pool, the whole terminating in a semi-circular colonnade. Both the 'ambulatio' and the 'canopus' were limited in size by walls and colonnades, permitting strollers, depending on the season of the year or the hour of the day, to take advantage of the

Above and right. *Detail of Roman villa at Conimbriga.*
Opposite page. *Labyrinth, which would be used as a theme in gardens from the sixteenth century onwards.*

Conimbriga Museum, Coimbra.

22

shade or else enjoy the warmth of the sun while being protected from the wind at all times.

These elements show themselves to be independent of the overall structure, being individual parts of the whole, reserved for a quiet, meditative walk. This recreational feature seems to have had its roots in the Greek tradition of 'peripaton'. Aristotle, at his school of philosophy near Athens, strolled along the 'peripaton' (an avenue lined with plane trees) while discoursing with his pupils. His disciples adopted the name of Peripatetics. Theophrastus also had a 'peripaton', and the Stoics took their name because of their custom of discussing while strolling along the great 'stoa' (colonnade) of Athens.

Later, when Adrian gave the name Poecile to the colonnade at his villa, he was no doubt inspired by the Stoic Poecile at Athens.

With this diversification in the exterior spaces of Roman villas, 'ambulatio' were divided up into much more simple forms of colonnades, pergolas and trellises, while still retaining the characteristics of meditative walkways.

The confined space of the Roman garden, surrounded as it was by high walls, together with the organic nature of the structure of the exterior spaces, were features which were prevalent in Portuguese gardens for centuries in a more or less concealed form.

The permanency of this tradition was undoubtedly connected with the Islamic culture. Occupying the peninsula two centuries after the fall of Rome, Islamism retained certain characteristics of the Romano-Hellenic culture while introducing certain characteristics of its own.

In the eighteenth century, the majority of Portuguese gardens were still surrounded by high walls with windows looking on to the exterior, in the manner of the Villa Laurentina or the Varro aviary.

At the same time, the concept of the 'ambulatio' space and its independent character in terms of the overall space structure, while revealing a vision of organic space, also continued in Portugal until the eighteenth century.

It is within the context of this tradition that one can better understand and appreciate the Galeria do Lago (Lake Gallery) of the Quinta da Bacalhoa, the great trellis of the Palace of Vila Viçosa or, later on, the Galeria dos Reis (Kings' Gallery) and the Terraço da Capela (Chapel Terrrace) of the Palace of Fronteira, which were still called 'walks' in the eighteenth century.

NOTES

1 — Christopher Thacker. *The History of Gardens*. London 1979. Page 16.
2 — Idem. Page 19.
3 — Pierre Grimal. *Les jardins Romains*, Paris, 1943. Page 75.
4 — Pliny the Younger. *Les lettres de Plinte le Jeune*. Paris, 1938. Page 68.
5 — Idem. Page 70.
6 — Idem. Page 69.
7 — Christopher Thacker. *The History of Gardens*. London 1979. Page 23.
8 — Idem. Page 23.

THE ISLAMIC TRADITION
and the birth of the Portuguese garden

CHAPTER II

With the break up of the Roman empire in the west, the cultural life of the northern Mediterranean underwent a radical transformation. In the crude, tribal customs of the invaders from the north of Europe, there was a factor which proved profoundly devastating to the Romano-Hellenic culture: a radically different view of the conception of the world with its attendant repercussions in the way of seeing and sensing space.

Later on, this factor would play an extremely important role in the cultural and aesthetic evolution of Europe and, in particular, the creation of the distinctive character of Portugal.

The centre of European culture, which spread to the Mediterranean, gravitated to the north and took on a Franco-Germanic aspect.

During the period which developed out of the so-called Holy Roman Empire, the Iberian peninsula was occupied by peoples converted to Islam coming from the north of Africa and, in consequence, found itself generally cut off from the cultural evolution taking place in the rest of Europe.

Unlike the barbarians from the north of Europe, the Islamic peoples were culturally much closer to the Hellenic civilisation and their rapid growth was quickly followed by the subjugated population absorbing the Islamic culture and transforming it, albeit in a veiled way, into the great continuation of the Hellenic tradition of the Mediterranean.

The cultural and religious tolerance of the first centuries of Islamic rule, and particularly that of the caliphates of the Iberian Peninsula, was to bring, in its turn, the Jewish elite of Europe and north Africa to the area. Between the seventh and thirteenth centuries, the high standard of the Islamic universities on the peninsula, together with a parallel development in the arts and poetry, was very different from the cultural environment in the rest of Europe.

Much later, in the fifteenth century, when there was a renaissance in the art of landscaping in Portugal, this appeared to be deeply rooted in the Hellenic-Islamic tradition, which had apparently been diluted by the occupation of the Catholic population in the north of the peninsula.

The permanency both of the Islamic and, especially, the Jewish communities, as well as the court's preference for the southern cities of Lisbon and Evora, helped to preserve the Portuguese Mediterranean tradition which reached its peak in the first gardens of the fifteenth century.

We must not forget that although the conquest of the Algarve occurred in the thirteenth century, the caliphate of the peninsula was only overcome at the end of the fifteenth century, and this ensured that luxury and sophistication would continue to influence the courts of the Iberian kings.

However, when the Yemen and Caidio Arabs arrived on the peninsula, they did not possess the culture or the special qualities which would manifest themselves centuries later. Their attitude towards the indigenous cultures was always to take the local traditions and combine them with their own.

Their first monuments were constructed with materials removed from ancient temples and palaces, but with none of the individuality and exoticism of the original buildings, and this makes it difficult to classify the Islamic legacy to Portugal. Even today, one can detect columns and capitals from ancient Hellenic-Roman temples in numerous mosques, including that of Cordoba and the great mosque at Damascus.

The horseshoe arch, a slightly simplistic example of traditional Islamic architecture, was never systematically used by the Arabs. In many buildings on the peninsula, one can see the use of ogival and half-circle arches, together with the horseshoe arch, which was also used prior to the Islamic occupation in Byzantine chapels, such as that of St. Frutuoso or Lourosa.

Opposite page. *The Swan Courtyard seen from the interior of the Water House.*
Sintra Palace.

Originating with the nomads, who knew neither forests nor stone, clay was for thousands of years the principal building material of Islamic cultures.

The Arabs felt no affinity for large trees such as chestnuts and oaks, and consequently took no special measures to protect them, the result being that they only exist in small numbers nowadays, particularly in the south of the country.

In contrast, orange and lemon trees, which were exotic and rare in Roman times, are to be found throughout the peninsula. According to Abu-Zacaria, they originated in India.[1]

One of the consequences of the rapid spread of the Islamic culture on the Iberian peninsula was the introduction of numerous plants and trees to enrich the gardens, as Abu-Zacaria describes in his twelfth century agricultural treatise.

Sugar cane, from Asia, and rice, from India, were introduced at this time. Although the latter was known in the time of the Greeks, following the campaigns of Alexander the Great, it is to the Arabs that the Portuguese owe the cultivation of rice for they brought both it and cotton from the Nile delta.

Their knowledge of the cultivation of fruit trees was a determinant factor in agriculture. They knew the process of grafting as well as other methods of reproduction, and introduced to the peninsula date palm groves and the damson which they grafted on to almond trees. The jasmine, however, appears to have been introduced for the first time.

The Islamic poetry of the peninsula is rich in references to these and other flowers, which suggests that they were quite common at the time.

The Swan Courtyard seen from a window in the Swan Room.
The direct link between the house and the lake, by means of
double windows that go down to the floor, are evidence of an
Islamic way of life and spatial concepts.

Sintra Palace.

THE WHITE LILY

The hands of spring are walled in behind
the stems of the castles of white lilies
Castles with silver battlements, where the defenders
grouped around the prince have swords of gold.

Ibn Alcacetali[2]

THE ORANGE TREE

Is it the fiery-coloured oranges that show on the
branches their bright colours
or faces that emerge
between the curtains of the litters?
Are they branches which sway or delicate shapes
for whose love I suffer what I suffer?
I see the orange tree which shows us its fruits
which appear to be tears coloured red
by the torments of love.
They are frozen but if they melted they would be wine.
They are like balls of red coral on topaz branches
and in the hand of the west wind are hammers to strike
them.
Sometimes we kiss the fruits
other times we smell their fragrances

*and so they are alternately
the faces of maidens or perfumed breasts.*

Ibn Sara [3]

Although the orange tree is cultivated over an extensive area, it always enjoyed a mythical and sacred significance as the symbol of the tree of Paradise, and as such it is regarded as being one of the fundamental elements in the Islamic garden. The Los Naranjos courtyard of the Cordoba mosque is an example of this, it being the oldest Islamic garden on the peninsula, although the paved surface is of a later date. Islamic literature regularly refers to gardens symmetrically planted with orange trees, and Ibn Khagan refers to the Hair-al-Zajjal garden in Cordoba: *'The court-yard is of the purest white marble: a narrow water channel crosses it, undulating like a snake. There is a tank into which the water falls. The roof* [of the pavilion] *is decorated in gold and blue, as are the sides and various parts. The garden has rows of systematically aligned trees and the open buds of the flowers seem to be smiling. The foliage of the garden prevents the sun from seeing the ground and the breezes that blow day and night fill it with fragrant perfumes'.* [4]

WATER
in the Islamic world

Water is the essential element of the Arab house, its importance coming from a tradition of thousands of years of living in the desert. Even today, property in the desert is defined not in terms of the surface area in square metres but by the number of wells and springs it possesses. A land without water is of no value at all. Thus, for the Islamic world, water was the original element which generated life and made the earth fertile.

In a hot, dry and sterile environment, the unexpected appearance of water was regarded as an act of divine favour, and the special attention the Arabs attributed to the existence of water led them to develop channelling, watering and storage techniques.

The scoop wheel for drawing up water was introduced for the first time and these are still to be found throughout the country. Muhammad Al-Edrissi, a geographer who lived in the twelfth century, wrote in his *Description of Spain: 'Silves, whose territory is renowned for its well-laid out gardens...and Santarem, a town built on a very high mount...have many gardens which produce fruit and vegetables of all kinds'.* [5]

The 'marhifal' was also introduced, this being an instrument for levelling the land which permitted greater control and economy of use of water in each watering operation.

Forest springs and small waterfalls were unknown to the Islamic world. Desert water issues from the ground to fill the pools of the oases, and the result is that the water of Islamic

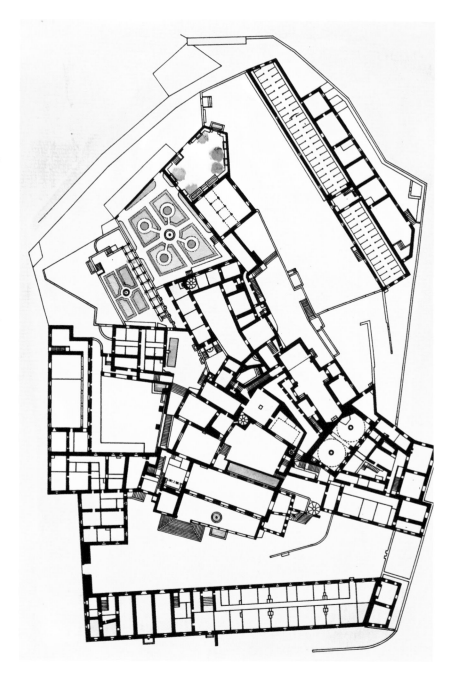

Plan of the palace at the end of the nineteenth century, prior to the restoration that would significantly destroy the large entrance courtyard and the relationship between the palace and the outside spaces.

Sintra Palace.

27

Despite successive transformations, the ancient Ladies' Courtyard still suggests the concept of the Islamic garden-courtyard. Intimately connected with a specific zone of the house, these garden-courtyards were reserved for an individual or a specific group (princess, princes, ladies, queen).

Lion's Courtyard. Palace of Sintra.

gardens has the appearance of a large water-mirror. This trend can be seen not only in the well-known gardens of Alhambra or Generalife, but also in many earlier gardens. Ibn Bardin, in his Al-Maqqari chronicle, describes how *'al-Ma'nun, the king of Toledo, constructed a lake, in the centre of which was a crystal kiosk upon whose roof water was directed so that it fell down the sides like artificial rain'.*[6]

Recent excavations in the Medina Al-Zahar Palace reveal the existence of a large garden comprising four pools which surround a central pavilion.[7]

Also long disappeared are the palace and gardens of the Alcazar of Cordoba on the banks of the Guadalquivir river, which were described by Ibn Said as being *'of great magnificence and possessing an enormous lake of water-lilies'.*[8]

THE IMPORTANCE OF FRAGRANCE

as a feature of Islamic space

From the descriptions which have come down to us, and from the existing remains of Islamic gardens, we are able to perceive a concept of space that is eminently crypto-sacred in nature. Surrounded by high walls, the gardens are like secret places that have been removed from all contact with the outside. The grandeur of the Villa Laurentina, with its hippodrome, colonnades, rows of plane trees and laurels, is in sharp contrast to the Islamic garden with its somewhat reserved atmosphere of courtyards and water-mirrors. The Arabs disliked tall trees and topiary, preferring small flowers and orange trees symmetrically laid out.

This feeling of sacredness in the composition of Islamic gardens can be directly linked to the violent contrast between the inhospitable and lifeless desert and the green and perfumed garden. The Koran tells us that Paradise, like any Islamic garden, was closed off with doors and guards. Four rivers are also mentioned in Sura XLVII.

The Islamic garden is thus clearly the symbolic image of the promised Paradise.

Along with the symbolic character of the Islamic garden goes its spatial structure; this is linked to a special perception of space which radically differentiates the Islamic culture from others. We know today that the perception of space is part of the education of an individual in a given society. These perceptive models vary from culture to culture and become permanently ingrained in the character of the people in an unconscious way. The sense of smell of an individual in the Arab world is of decisive importance in his personal relationships. Temperament and moods are related to the smell of a particular individual, so much so that a bride can be refused in a marriage contract if *'she doesn't smell good'*.[9]

The sense of smell, which was studied in great detail by the anthropologist Edward Hall, is of decisive importance in the understanding of Islamic space.

The extremely high olfactory sensitivity that exists in the Islamic world contributed to the perfumes of the gardens being contained in relatively reduced spaces surrounded by high walls.

Equally, a garden's spatial structure was organised to provide a calmer and more peaceful olfactory and visual perception. In the Paradise described in the Koran, the Chosen ones *'reclined on soft cushions'*. The Islamic descriptions of gardens are full of references to the olfactory qualities of the place: *'and the breeze, blowing day and night, fills it with fragrant perfumes'; 'in the chosen corner, the garden comes to us carrying its presents on the perfumed hands of the breeze'*.[10]

With the resurgence of secular architecture and the art of garden making in the fifteenth century, the Aguas de Peixe Palace marked a reintroduction of ancient Roman and Islamic traditions. To the Roman tradition of the trellis was added the lake water-mirror directly connected to the house. These elements continued in Portuguese gardens until the seventeenth and eighteenth centuries.

Aguas de Peixe Palace. Viana do Alentejo.

THE CONCEPT OF THE GARDEN
and Islamic space

A symbolic image that is closed in on itself, each Islamic garden is like a unique space with its own special characteristics. Pietro Moreno, a few years after the conquest of Granada by the Catholic kings at the end of the fifteenth century, describes this aspect of the gardens of Generalife: *'It is composed of a series of enclosed spaces, each of which has its own particular ambience... each part possesses its own particular shapes and proportions which are determined by the recreational purpose for which it was conceived'.*[11]

And to the typical crypto-sacred character of the Islamic garden is added the special quality of absolute discontinuity.

Each garden is normally connected to the next by means of a small side gate, gallery or steps, which is not an integral part of the garden.

Another spatial characteristic which radically separates the Islamic courtyard garden from the medieval Catholic kitchen-garden is its relationship with the house which, in the Portuguese case, can be seen in the origins of fifteenth and sixteenth century gardens. The Islamic garden reveals its sacred character by occupying the centre of the house, while in the medieval kitchen-garden the house occupies the centre, rising up like an all-conquering symbol, the symbol of a dominion over the landscape. When, at the end of the Middle Ages, the European political and cultural centre moved from the cathedral to the castle-palace, the additional space expanded progressively, so much so that by the Baroque period it encircled the whole of the building, this continuing to be the command centre of the whole. The Islamic palace, on the other hand, extends over the ground in an organic series of pavilions, which open up on to courtyard-gardens.

* * *

An analysis of the spatial qualities of the Islamic garden clearly shows the Islamic character of the courtyard-gardens of the Paço da Vila de Sintra (Royal Palace of Sintra).

Although the unstable life of the first Portuguese kings did not allow them to show any great interest in their palaces and gardens, we do know that many of these were not abandoned or completely destroyed. On the king's visits to the city, he installed his court in the old Moorish palace of Lisbon. The Moorish palace of Evora, today known as the Palace of the Counts of Basto, was

The fact that the water tank of the Torre de Ribafria predates the sixteenth century building and tower suggests the possibility, due to the architectural affinities in the two groups of buildings, that the water tank of the Amoreira da Torre Estate *is much earlier than the buildings and the sixteenth century tower.*

Amoreira da Torre Estate,
Montemor-o-Novo. Alentejo.

ceded by Dom Afonso Henriques to the military order of St. Bento of Calatrava[12] and Dom Fernando inhabited it with his wife, which indicates that the palace had not lost the grandeur that was required to house a royal family.

When, in the reign of Dom Dinis, the country went through a period of peace, the king contracted a Moorish master, Muhammad Alaufa[13], to be the architect of his palaces, a fact which attests to the prestige and influence of Islamic culture in the peninsula.

It was also Dom Dinis who bought the Agua de Peixe Palace from Judas Navarro *'with an orchard, vineyard, water-mill and houses...',*[14] a palace which, because of its architectural features, suggests it was a possible country retreat of the Moorish alcaide of Viana do Alentejo.

The Palace of Sintra must have undergone repairs at this time since the four great Gothic arches of the ancient entrance court-yard are earlier than the work that Dom João I carried out at the beginning of the fifteenth century.

Of a very similar design are the arches of the inner courtyard of the Palace of Belas. Its geographical location in a low area next to the Ribeira de Belas indicates it was not built for defence or to dominate the landscape, and thus suggests it is pre-medieval.

But it is the Palace of Sintra where we see the clearest example of the continuity of the Islamic tradition in Portugal.

Both the Queen's Fountain *and the high wall of the gardens with cylindrical buttresses provide evidence of the importance of the outside spaces of the house and a continuation of sophisticated living habits in the sixteenth century.*
The Queen's Fountain and a buttress on the wall of the gardens.

Amoreira da Torre Estate.
Montemor-o-Novo. Alentejo.

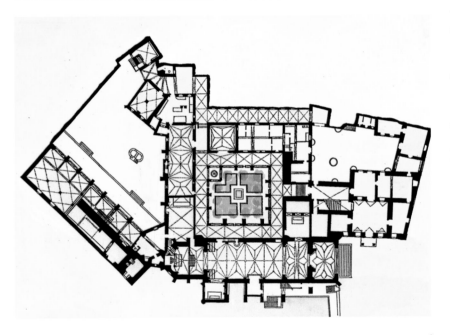

The orange tree was the predominant element in all cloisters and gardens in the fifteenth century.
The preference given to it reveals a garden tradition in which visual value was substituted by the concept of a perfumed garden.

Plan and detail of the Loios Cloister. Evora.

THE AWAKENING OF THE PORTUGUESE GARDEN

in the fifteenth century

The uncertainty about the so-called Manueline style and its Islamic affinities has been mainly explained by a superficial revivalism confined to the Alentejo area and by influences from the south of Spain and north Africa.

This theory is mainly based on an analysis of lines and decorative values, such as the horseshoe arch, twin windows, capital, frame, portal, and demonstrates a clear lack of knowledge of the spatial values that are the basis and essence of Islamic architecture.

The gardens and architecture of houses clearly show that the essential spatial values were a permanent feature in Portugal and were due neither to revivalism nor momentary cultural influences. When the Manueline and proto-Manueline styles — styles restricted to the reign of Dom Manuel I — adopted decorative elements with an Islamic influence, this was a continuation in Portugal of an ancient and indigenous tradition which was not interrupted in medieval times, as has been suggested.

From the fifteenth century onwards, the exterior spaces of country retreats and palaces in the region of Lisbon and the Alentejo tend to be in the form of pleasure orchards, and their characteristics reflect both a Mediterranean ambience and recreational customs which cannot be dismissed as being mere aesthetic influences. These customs were rooted to such an extent in the Portuguese concept of space that, together with the changes brought about by the evolution of style, they became a permanent fixture of gardens up to the eighteenth century.

Although considered to be an exception in terms of Portuguese civilian architecture, the Palace of Sintra is the only royal palace with significant work from the fifteenth and sixteenth centuries which has survived.

The palaces of Evora, Ribeira, Almeirim, Salvaterra, Santos-o-Velho, Estaus and the Alcaçova (fortress) of Lisbon, to name only the more important, are all now lost.

The description of Secretario Alexandrino, in 1571, of the Palace of Alcaçova, is not much different from that of the Palace of Sintra: *'A labyrinth of interior steps and staircases which, with the galleries and balconies, complicates the whole internal structure'.*[15]

Equally, the illuminated manuscript of Antonio de Holanda, in the *Genealogy of the Kings of Portugal*, shows the Palace of Santos-o-Velho in the Manueline era with an exterior form and structure very similar to that of the Palace of Sintra.

Profoundly altered after the reign of Dom João I, the Palace of Sintra retained part of the pre-existing Islamic structure, thereby establishing an aesthetic continuity which was maintained until the fifteenth century.

The Páteo dos Cisnes (Great Courtyard of the Swans) continues to be the nucleus of the whole of the architectural programme. The so-called Sala de Banho (bath room), one of the most curious outbuildings of the palace, which tradition says is also from the Islamic era, opens on to it. All the present ornamentation is eighteenth century except for the three arches which connect it with the Great Courtyard of the Swans.

The 'Curious Pilgrim' who travelled around Portugal during the reign of Dom Sebastião, described this Sala de Banho: *'All golden and decorated with paintings of grapes and other fruit, and when the Prince was there, thin jets of water emerged from the grapes to form a small pool, and when the jets of water were turned off, the water in the pool drained away, so that it was as if there had never been water there, and it gave pleasure to the Prince'.*[16]

Along with the refined architectural taste that is evident in the Sala de Banho are the large twin windows of the Sala dos Cisnes which go down to ground level and open directly on to the water-mirror so that people seated on the cushions placed on the floor in the Arab tradition could look out on to the courtyard. This relationship with the courtyard conveys all the refinement and sophistication of customs found in traditional medieval Catholic architecture.

Along with the restoration of the Palace of Sintra and the work carried out on it, we find from the fifteenth century onwards a growth in the construction of country residences and palaces by both the royal family and the nobility.

This trend, which also occurred throughout the whole of Europe, took on certain forms in Portugal that were influenced by both local tradition and historic events.

Following the taking of Ceuta, the impact caused by direct contact with the Islamic cultures of the north of Africa was another significant factor in the development of a liking for elegant buildings and an enjoyment of recreational activities in outdoor spaces. The impression which the Portuguese had of the sophisticated Islamic dwellings was commented on by Zurara in his chronicle of the taking of Ceuta: *'Large houses covered with floor tiles of various colours and...ceilings made of wood of the olive tree, with beautiful terraces surrounded by walls of very white and polished marble...We, on the other hand, are wretches who, in Portugal, walk through the fields gathering in our crops, getting tired with the effort we put into our work, and, at the end of the day, have no other place to rest our weary bones except for our poor houses which, in comparison with these, seem to look like pig sties'.*[17]

The growing interest in their dwellings naturally extended to gardens and the treatment of outdoor spaces.

For the gardens of his new palace at Evora, King Dom João II sent in 1494 for a famous gardener from Valencia, a fact which was registered in the records of Dom Manuel's Chancellor: *'Desiring that the kitchen-gardens of our palaces in our city of Evora were planted with noble and beautiful trees and grasses, we had the gardener Gomes Fernandez Valemcyano sent from Valencia so that we could be informed of what he knew and was able to do well'.*[18]

And there is no doubt that due to the impact of the presence of the sophisticated caliphate of Cordoba in both Portugal and Spain, an unmistakable Islamic influence made itself felt in gardening arts.

Unfortunately, gardens are infinitely more susceptible than architecture to changing trends in taste and living habits.

Little information has been handed down about fifteenth cen-

'This city (Evora) has no castle and only possesses two renowned palaces, one episcopal and the other belongs to the Duke, the brother of the King. The house adjoins the church, the front of which is elegantly constructed and it has next to it a pleasant orchard of trees and bushes'.
Leo de Rosmital. 1465 [1]

Detail of the Castros' Palace orchard. Evora.

Besides orange and lemon trees, fifteenth and sixteenth century documents frequently refer to cypresses. The way in which they are set out, constituting highly shady places, is seen in the small pleasure orchard of the Grijó Convent, which retains a strong medieval atmosphere.

Grijo Convent. Oporto.

Right. *Cypress surrounded by garden shrubs, a detail from the painting 'Virgin with Child'.*

Portuguese school of the sixteenth century.

tury gardens which allows us to define their spatial qualities and features with any certainty. Consequently, it is only through historical documents and the reports of some foreign visitors that we are able to reconstruct their characteristics.

If the architectural structures show themselves to be closely connected to a Mediterranean and Islamic tradition, then the way in which use is made of the outdoor spaces reveals a similar connection. Unlike the medieval European kitchen-garden, planted with small flowers and medicinal plants, Portuguese gardens took on the form of pleasure gardens, to which other sweetly-perfumed plants were added.

THE ORCHARD-GARDEN

in the early Portuguese garden

In 1494, Dom João II was having lunch with Jerónimo Müncher in his new garden, next to the Royal Palace. In his itinerary on Portugal and Spain, Müncher wrote: *'One day, the king was having lunch in a garden at the foot of the castle which was bordered by orange trees...this garden, where he was lunching, was new, since he had planted it and surrounded it with a cane fence only four years previously'.* [19]

The idea of enjoyment featured in this new orchard-garden is clearly seen in Muncher's description.

In the chronicle he wrote about his journey through Europe between 1465 and 1466, during the reign of Dom Afonso V, Leo de Rosmital also mentions a pleasure orchard in Evora, albeit in the episcopal palace: *'In this city, one of the principal in Portugal, we find the King with his court. This city has no castle and only possesses two notable palaces, one being episcopal and the other that of the Duke, the brother of the King. The episcopal house adjoins the church, the front face being elegantly constructed, while next to it is a delightful orchard of trees and bushes'.* [20]

The fact that the term 'garden' only appears in the reign of Dom João III, and then in an erudite form, throws new light on the regular mention in ancient documents of orchards and kitchen-gardens beside rural residences and palaces, the word not having the same meaning as it has today.

A document in the Torre do Tombo (National Archives) in the second book of the Royal Rights of King Dom Dinis, refers to the purchase by Dom Dinis of the Palace of Agua de Peixes with *'orchards, vineyards, a water mill and houses'* from Judas Navarro.

A document from the reign of Dom Afonso V, copied by Júlio Castilho,[21] setting out the terms of the rental contract of the Paços do Arcebispo (Archbishop's Palace) in Lisbon Castle, not only mentions orange and lemon trees in some detail but also refers to cypresses and goes on to itemise both the number and type of tree to be planted and the work to be carried out so that they would flourish.

'and he the priest will further plant in the referred to orchards twenty cypresses, six orange trees and three lemon trees: of these, sixteen cypresses and four orange trees are for the orchard at the far end and two lemon trees in the top orchard...'
Lease contract for the Archbishops' Palace in the Fortress of Lisbon, 1477. [II]

Garden orchard of the Castros' Palace. Evora.

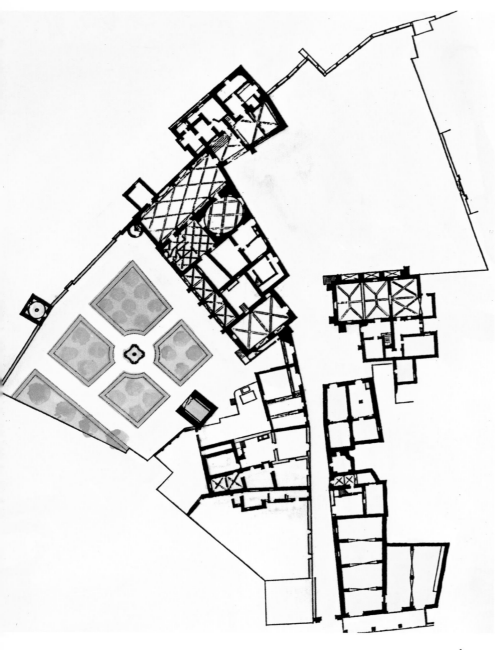

Plan of the Castros' Palace. Évora.

The number of cypresses is significant for an area as small as the orchards of the Paços do Arcebispo. These cypresses would, in principle, be distributed in continuous lines in order to form avenues as was the custom in Mediterranean and Islamic gardens. Even today, in the Convent of Grijo, near Oporto, there is a small grove of orange trees and cypresses surrounded by old walls, with a form of porch at the entrance which has steps bordered by protective rails of medieval design. The flowerbeds, benches and fountains reveal decorative features of the eighteenth century when large-scale improvements were undertaken at the convent, but the atmosphere and the individuality of the structure clearly take us back to the descriptions and documents of the fifteenth and sixteenth centuries.

In the sixteenth century, the extensions which Dom Manuel initiated in the Palace of Sintra carried over into the gardens, more specifically to the Pomar da Rainha (Queen's Orchard) and the Pomar do Sol (Orchard of the Sun).

The account book of the Royal Treasurer, André Gonçalves, in the Torre do Tombo, shows us not only how much was spent on these orchard-gardens, but also on what, as well as following the progress of the work, and at the same time providing us with a detailed picture of how these spaces were treated at that time. In 1507, the Royal Treasurer paid *'Pero of Carnyde for twenty-five days' work laying slabs where the orange trees had dried up'*.[22] It is known that orange trees had been in place for some time and that the area was not totally paved over, since later on Gonçalves made payments to a man called Lourenço, among which was one for *'digging holes to plant orange trees in the Orchard of the Sun'*.[23]

These holes would, in principle, be for planting the orange trees which ran around the walls, as is still the case today in the Pátio dos Tanquinhos, this being a common practice right up to the seventeenth century.

Later on, Gonçalves had a large wall erected around the Orchard of the Sun. Windows were let in to this wall, which explains why the Count of Sabugosa stated that the Orchard of the Sun was the present-day Pátio dos Tanquinhos, even though it was transformed afterwards by new work carried out on the orders of Dom João III.

The present Manueline windows of the Pátio dos Tanquinhos have lost their shutters, but the apertures they slotted into are visible today in the armillary spheres of the present windows.

As regards the Queen's Orange Grove, we find no expenses recorded for window bars, which perhaps explains the fact that what is now the Lindaya garden has windows from the time of Dom João I, or at least prior to Dom Manuel.

The work carried out was mainly concerned with the purchase and grafting on and setting out of *'orange trees, peach trees and fourteen cedars'*.

The improvements to the place also included the construction of a 'new house' in stone, in the tradition of country retreats, such as that in the Duke's garden in Vila Viçosa. For this, the Royal Treasurer paid *'the masons and carpenters their wages in wine and fruit to shore up the walls of the new house in the orchard'*.[24] From the payments and expenses we learn that a *'storm destroyed some arches in the Queen's Orchard'*,[25] and that *'walls of the new house...fell down,'*[26] and that André Gonçalves sent *'a message to the king in Almeirim'*.[27]

'one day, the king was lunching in the garden
bordered by orange trees at the foot of the
castle...this garden where he was having lunch
was new, having been planted and surrounded
with a cane fence four years previously...'

Jeronimo Müncher 1494 (III)

'Dixit mihi rex prandens in horto de aranciis septo circa castellum
in Ebora... item his hortus, in quo pransens finit, erat et citra
quatuor annos plantatus in cancellas arundineas'.

Garden orchard of the Castros' Palace. Evora.

'the Royal Treasurer gave and paid to the above-mentioned Pedro Annees for six days work spent repairing the railings of the 'çoteia do soll' (sun terrace)... and he also bought three sets of hinges and joints for the aforementioned railings...'

André Gonçalves. 1508 (IV)

'From the Royal Treasurer's expenses, one can see that both the Queen's orange grove and that of the 'çoteia do soll' were walled in, and at this time improvement work was carried out on them'. Detail of the surrounding wall and sections of the ancient Queen's Orange Grove, later on the Prince's and the Lindaya Garden.

Sintra Palace.

Because of the changes it underwent in the time of Dom João III, the Queen's Orange Grove is not exactly like the present Lindaya garden, although the site is the same. As regards the 'new house', it disappeared when the Galé room was built.

Orchards and kitchen-gardens framed by cane fencing can be seen in detail in Portuguese sixteenth century paintings. Although the painting of the time was somewhat stereotyped in character and followed strict standards of composition and iconographic rules, the naturalistic feeling for certain details is undeniable. This is how the small cane fence appears to us in the painting 'Jesus in the Kitchen-garden', by Santos-o-Novo and in the 'Virgin and the Child...', both in the National Museum of Ancient Art. More refined is the detail of 'Virgin with Child' attributed to Gaspar Vaz, in the church of São João de Tarouca. The fence is composed of a double trellis up which roses are climbing. This custom must have been common in other centuries, for William Beckford, on his visit to the Palace of Palhavã gardens, referred to it as he left the Maze Garden: *'I came out of it and approached areas where irrigated kitchen-gardens were to be found and where aromatic herbs grew, the whole being encircled by cane fencing covered with the freshest and most perfect roses'.*[28]

Returning to the account book of the Royal Treasurer, André Gonçalves, we find that he also *'bought canes for the fencing around the Queen's Orchard'*[29] and *'rushes to tie the canes of the ... orchard together'.*[30]

Other characteristic elements of these pleasure-orchards and kitchen-gardens were flowerbeds and benches. For his Evora Palace, Dom Manuel made payments via his treasurer for *'works undertaken by Luis Gomes and Gil Fernandes in the residences of the young Princes: twelve flowerboxes and twenty benches to be set out in the new kitchen-garden at a cost of 7,900 reis, and made by Braz Martins'.*[31]

THE WATER-MIRROR
as a structural element of the garden

Closely connected with the presence of water, which was the reason for the existence of the property, and in true Islamic fashion, a large water-mirror tank was a fundamental element of the exterior space.

In the book which records the rewards and favours bestowed by Dom Manuel, the King gave André Gonçalves the *Herdade de Laranjeiras do Tanque em Cintra* (literally Orange Grove of the Tank Estate at Sintra).[32]

This estate, which later became the Quinta da Torre da Ribafria, belonged to the royal house. It already had houses and a tank which, due to its size, was to give it its name. However, while some have dated the estate to the time of André Gonçalves, it does in fact date back further. The inherent character of the great recreational tank appears to be related to those of the Quinta da Amoreira da Torre, Montemor, of the Palace of Aguas de Peixe, Viana do Alentejo, of the Quinta do General, Borba, and to that of the Palace of Vila Viçosa, on the outskirts of the town of the same name (medieval), and this leads us to believe that all these estates were formerly country retreats of the alcaides in Islamic times.[33]

If these great water-mirror tanks cannot be traced back with any accuracy to Islamic times, nevertheless an influence from this period can be seen in them.

Retaining the water in order to distribute it depending on the needs of the season of the year, especially in the summer, the water-mirror tank, due to its privileged situation and decorative treatment, is put on the same symbolic level as the gardens and life itself.

Instead of being regarded purely as a large reservoir, the tank-lake was seen as a place of recreation, creating around itself areas of leisure and relaxation which made use of its cool waters. Thus benches appeared at the foot of walls covered with lattice-work, so that relaxation could be made more enjoyable. In more sophisticated cases, a summer house was located next to the tank, as is the case at the Quinta do General at Borba (covered later on with decorative tiles from the end of the seventeenth century), and the Pleasure House at the Palace of Dom Jaime, in Vila Viçosa, at the edge of the Bosque Garden and next to the Tritão Lake. These houses were often made of wood which accounts for the fact that they no longer exist. Dom Manuel I had one such at the bottom of the orange grove which extended from the Palace of Santos to the banks of the Tagus: *'In the year 1513, King Dom Manuel was in Santos-o-Velho, signing official documents in a wooden house which was at the end of a pier, standing in the water'.*[34]

'...the aforementioned Royal Treasurer also bought on the third day of February twenty-six orange trees on the banks of the Pera Lomga...and he put them in the Queen's orchard...'

André Gonçalves. 1508 [V]

The regular references to orange trees in gardens, in documents of the time, are evidence of the permanence of Islamic traditions in the resurgence of landscaping art in Portugal. Ancient Orange Grove of the Queen (the Prince's and Lindaya Garden).

Sintra Palace.

'The aforementioned Royal Treasurer gave and paid to Pero of Carnide...for placing stone slabs on the ground of the Sun orange grove from which the dried up orange trees were removed'.

André Gonçalves. 1508. (VI)

The Tanquinhos Courtyard, formerly the Sun Orange Grove, transformed into a courtyard by Dom Manuel.

Sintra Palace.

From an analysis of documents, the Portuguese garden was revived from the fifteenth century onwards, being closely connected with an Islamic-Mediterranean tradition, both in terms of its spatial containment characteristics and its interrelationship with the house by means of the verandas, landings, staircases and galleries, and in terms of the ambience in which the orange tree was on a level with the great water-mirror tank.

These characteristics became progressively less noticeable, although they were much more evident to Europeans who travelled around Portugal and who were confronted with recreational gardens and habits profoundly different from their own.

THE GREAT TANK

of the Torre da Amoreira estate,
Montemor-o-Novo

The oldest known document relating to this estate dates back to 1321, in the reign of Dom Dinis, *'as a possession of the Chapter of Lisbon Cathedral'*. Later on, in 1437, it was the property of a governess of Infanta Dona Isabel, daughter of Dom João I. In its gardens, a delicate Arrabida stone fountain of Gothic-Manueline design recalls the past greatness and elegance of the house.

The great tank which extends along the length of the present façade overlooking the gardens is of the same type as the tank at the Palace of Agua de Peixes and the Quinta da Torre da Ribafria in Sintra. From documents written by Dom Manuel, we know that the latter tank was of an earlier age than the tower and that it lent its name to the estate which Dom Manuel gave to André Gonçalves (*'my estate of the Laranjeiras do Tanque'*), and, consequently, we can infer that the tower of the Quinta da Amoreira is not the original nucleus of this estate.

The great age of the house is also seen in the high wall of cylindrical buttresses which marks the limit of the gardens and orchards, which have now almost disappeared. These buttresses, with their Islamic influence, have been classified as being from the Manueline period. There are no documents or archaeological studies which prove them to be prior to the Manueline period, and this classification is based on documents that are not completely reliable.

On the other hand, its privileged position, four kilometres from the village of Montemor-o-Novo, on the right bank of the Almancor river, suggests that the summer retreats of the Islamic alcaides were established here.

* * *

EXTRACTS FROM DOCUMENTS ON WORK
*carried out on the Queen's Orange Grove
and the Sun Orange Grove
at the Palace of Sintra*

"Item deu e pagou o almoxarite ao dito pero de carnyde de vinte e cynquo dias que serujo nestas obras em asemtar lageas no laramjall do soll homde tiraram as laramjeiras que secaram

Item deu e pagou o almoxarife ao dito pero de carnjde de duzemtos e corenta e seis peças de cunhaees emxillares de pedraria pera a obra do çerco dos coelhos e pera a casa da fazenda de que a daver por cada hua peça a vinte e oyto reaes qm que momta seis mjll e oytoçemtos e oytenta e oyto reaes a quall pedraria deu mestre boitaca ao sobredito pello dito preço que he pella taxa de ssamta maria da pena.

Item majs deu e pagou ao dito pero de carnyde de seis degraaos de pedraria que laurou e asentou na varanda da Rainha por avemça trezemtos reaes.

Item majs comprou o dito almoxarife em tres dias do mês de feuereiro vimte e seis laramgeiras na Ribeira de pera lomga .a saber. a João pirez e ao azambujo e aluaro annes canavall e a maria pirez e a maria annes e a aluaro pirez e a pero afomso perrynho e a vicente fernandes e afonso nunez e a joham perrynho e a joham diaz e a esteuam Lourenço a duzemtos reaes cada laramjeira em que amomta çymquo mjll e duzemtos reaes as quaes se poseram no pumar da Rainha.

Item majs comprou o dito almoxarife de Emxertos pera o dito pumar coremta emxertos artur Rodriguez E a joham doliuença e a gaujnha E a pero annes da bemposta e a outras pessoas .a saber. a coremta reaes cada huum por serem gramdes em que amomta mjll e seis cemtos reaes.

Item majs comprou o dito almoxarife aos sobreditos de emxertos pera o dito pumar coremta a trimta reaes cada huum em que amomta mjll e duzemtos reaes.

Item comprou majs o dito almoxarife de pesegueiros durazios pera ho dito

'...more than two miles of cane that he bought for the cane fence of the Queen's orchard...he also bought string to tie the canes of the aforementioned orchard together...'.

André Gonçalves. 1508. (VII)

Crossed cane fencing, which is seen in sixteenth century paintings was an old custom and continued till the eighteenth century.

Detail from 'Jesus in the Kitchen-garden'. Mestre de Santos-o-Novo. Sixteenth century. M.N.N.A. (National Museum of Ancient Art).

In the fifteenth century, the Portuguese garden developed out of indigenous Islamic-Roman traditions. The garden is regarded as an absolutely private space, an architectural extension of the house — a concept that continued into the nineteenth century.

Courtyard-cloister of Dom Jaime.
Vila Viçosa Palace. Alentejo.

pumar coremta a doze reaes cada huum amomta quatro çemtos e oytenta reaes

Item majs comprou o dito almoxarife de çedreiras pera o dito pumar aluaro annees e a outras pesoas ...·

Item majs comprou o almoxarife em lixboa de cestos de verga pera as ditas obras pera a terra que se cauou pera o emtulho do pumar da Rainha e asy pera as ditas obras do dito çerco dos coelhos çemto e quatorze reaes.

Item majs de dous mjlheiros de canas que comprou pera a canycada do pumar da Rainha com o carreto duzemtos reaes.

Item majs comprou de jumco pera atar a canycada do dito pumar vimte reaes.

Item majs comprou de laramgeiras pera o pumar da Rainha duas que veeram da Ribeira de peralomga que custaram quatroçemtos e cymquoemta reaes.

Item majs comprou de canas pera a canjcada do pumar da Rainha dous mjlheiros por duzemtos reaes com o carreto.

Item majs deu e pagou a hua besta daluger por trazer çestos e cordas e pregadura pera as ditas obras coremta reaes.

Item majs deu e pagou aluaro annes daçenha por hyr buscar e comprar as duas laramgeiras oytenta reaes.

Item majs comprou de caruam seis sacos pera o mestre dos quanos do chumbo pera fumdyr o dito chumbo pera fazer canos çemto e çynquoemta reaes a vimte e çynquo ho ssaco.

Item mais comprou de junco pera atar a canyçada do pumar da Rainha sesemta reaes.

Item majs comprou a fernam gill tres pereiras e huum pesegueiro durazio pera o pumar da Rainha por çem reaes com duzemtas e cynquoemta canas pera o dito.

Item majs comprou quinhemtas tachas pera as grades nouas da çoteia do soll por çem reaes.

Item majs comprou a fernam gonçalluez tres gatos pera as grades nouas que se asentaram na çoteia do ssoll

Item majs deu e pagou a gonçallo camello por leuar hua carta a El Rej almeirjm quamdo a tormemta derribou os archetes do pumar da Rainha duzemtos reaes.

Item deu de feria de vinho e frujta aos pedreiros e carpemteiros por escoirarem o cauouco da casa noua do pumar vinte e seis reaes.

Item majs comprou hua fechadura com hua aldraba gramde pera as grades da çoteia do ssoll duzemtos reaes.

Item majs comprou de machafemeas gramdes pera as ditas grades seis por trezemtos e sesemta a sesemta reaes por peça.

Item majs comprou pera as portas das ditas grades tres peças de machafemeas por çemto e cymquoemta reaes.

Item deu e pagou o almoxarife ao sobredito pedre annees de seis dias que serujo nas grades da çoteia do soll em as comçertar em outros serujços das ditas obras em que serujo na feria de tres dias do mês de junho ao dito preço em que a amomta trezemtos e sesemta reaes.

Item deu e pagou o almoxarife ao sobredito de dous dias que serujo na feria de tres dias do mês de junho em laurar madeira pera as grades da çotea do soll çem reaes ao dito preço.

Transcribed by the Count of Sabugosa. *O Paço de Sintra*. Lisbon. 1903. Pages 221-243.

(André Gonçalves and his methodical book on the accounts of the Palace of Sintra at the time of Dom Manuel I give us an accurate and precise picture of the spatial characteristics of the small gardens which surrounded the palace as well as the plants. It is also worth mentioning here the cane fencing that William Beckford would refer to in the eighteenth century.)

THE GARDENS OF THE ARCHBISHOP'S PALACE IN THE FORTRESS OF LISBON. 1467.

"Em nome de Deus Amen. Saybham os que este presente publico stromento de afforamento vyrem que no anno do nascimento de N. S. Jesu Christo de 1467 annos, aos oyto dias do mez de Junho, na muy nobre e sempre leal cidade de Lixboa, dentro nos paaços que som a par de S.ⁱᵒ Eloy do Reverendíssimo em Christo Padre o Senhor D. Jorge Arcebispo d'essa mesma, stando hy o dito senhor em presença de my notairo appostolico, e das testemunhas adyante nomiadas, pareceo hy Pero Machado Vigayro da Igreja de Santa Cruz d'Alcaçova da dita cidade; e logo per o dito Senhor Arcebispo foi dito que elle afforava e dava de foro ao dito vigairo por seis annos primeiros futuros, e mais nom, os seus paaços, e casas grandes e pequenas que som no cerquo da dita Igreja, com seus pumares e logradoyros... Coortará e alimpará todas as laranjeiras e arvores dos ditos pomares, e lhes deitará agua aos pees aos tempos quonvinháveis. E alguas outras arvores enxertará per guysa que todo seja acrecentado, melhorado, e nom pejorado. E elle dito Vigairo plantará em os ditos pumares vinte aciprestes, e seis laranjeiras, e tres limoeyros: convem a saber: dezasseis acciprestes e quatro laranjeiras no pomar do fundo, e dois limoeyros; e os quatro acciprestes e duas larangeyras e hum limoeyro no pumar de cima, per guysa que per todos os pés vinte e nove. E o dito Senhor Arcebispo haverá para sua casa dos dittos pumares as laranjas que lhe mester fezerem..."

Transcribed by Júlio Castilho. *Lisboa Antiga*. 3rd edition. Volume VII. Notes II. Pages 342-343.

(The document contains a description of two gardens and their plants and trees. Orange trees and cypresses are regularly mentioned in the descriptions.)

NOTES

1 Abu-Zacaria, the Sevillian, translated by José Banquieri. Madrid 1878.
2 António Borges Coelho — *Portugal na Espanha Árabe*. Lisbon 1975. Volume IV Page 314.
3 Idem. Page 352.
4 Cited by Christopher Thacker — *The History of Gardens*. London 1979, Page 36.
5. Muhammad Al-Edrissi — *Descrição de Espanha*. Madrid 1901.
6 Al-Maqqari — *History of Mohemmedan Dynasties*, translated by Pascual Gayangos. London 1840-1843, Volume II, Book VII, Chap. V, Page 263
7 Marquesa da Casa Valdés — *Jardins de Espanha*. Edições Aguiar. Madrid 1973, Page 30.
8 Idem. Page 30.
9 Edward Hall — *A dimensão oculta* . Ed. Antropos. Lisbon, Page 188.
10 Ibn Amar, transcribed by António Borges Coelho — *Portugal na Espanha Árabe*. Vol.IV, Page 375
11 Pietro Moreno — *Los jardins de Granada*. Madrid 1952.
12 Sousa Viterbo — *Dicionário dos arquitectos*. Vol. I, Page 62.
13 Túlio Espanca. *Inventário Artístico de Portugal, Concelho de Évora*. Lisbon 1966.
14 Book II of the Royal Rights, folio 200, A.N.T.T.
15 Transcribed by Alexandre Herculano — *Opúsculos*. Vol. VI, 4th ed., Page 81.
16 Transcribed by Conde de Sabugosa — *O Paço de Sintra*. Lisbon 1903, Page 171.
17 Zurara, Gomes Eanes de — *Crónica da tomada de Ceuta*.
18 Transcribed by Sousa Viterbo — *A Jardinagem em Portugal*. Coimbra 1906, Page 71.
19 Translated from the Latin by Basílio de Vasconcelos — *Itinerário do Dr. Jerónimo Müncher* (excerpts). Coimbra. 1931. Page 60-61.
20 Transcribed by C. Castelo Branco. *Um viajante em Portugal há 393 anos. O Mundo elegante*, 1858. V. 6.9.
21 Transcribed by Júlio Castilho — *Ribeira de Lisboa*, 3rd ed. V.III, Note III, Page 246.
22 Transcribed by Conde de Sabugosa — *O Paço de Sintra*. Lisbon, Page 224.
23 Idem. Page 226.
24 Idem. Page 240.
25 Idem. Page 240.
26 Idem. Page 240.
27 Idem. Page 240.
28 William Beckford — *Diário de W.B. em Portugal e Espanha*. Lisbon 1983, Page 43.
29 Conde de Sabugosa, ibid., Page 239.
30 Idem. Page 239.
31 Cited by Túlio Espanca — *Palácios Reais de Évora*. Cadernos e História e Arte Eborense. 1946, Page 42.
32 Chancellor's book of Dom Manuel I, Book II, folio 114, A.N.T.T.
33 This hypothesis was also raised by Campos de Andrade in the case of the Palace of Águas de Peixe, the Sempre Noiva Palace and the Mitra Palace — *A Antiguidade Árabe em Portugal* — and needs to be accompanied by archaeological reseach to ensure it has a more solid basis in reality.
34 Damião de Góis — *Crónica de El-Rei D. Manuel I*. Part I, Chapter XLVI.

Notes on Illustrations

  I. Transcribed by C. Castelo Branco. Ibid. N. 6.
 II. Transcribed by Júlio Castilho. Ibid. Page 246.
III. Transcribed by Basílio de Vasconcellos. Ibid. Page 60-61.
IV. Transcribed by C. de Sabugosa. Ibid. Page 241.
  V. Idem. Page 239.
 VI. Idem. Page 224.
VII. Idem. Page 239.

THE CONCEPT OF THE LEISURE-GARDEN

and the taming of nature in the sixteenth century

CHAPTER III

Perhaps one of the most outstanding peculiarities of Portuguese art is an absence of a period of theoretical reflection as can be found in the European Renaissance.

The Renaissance is regarded in Portugal as being more of a court fashion, an alteration of decorative elements rather than a style with values of its own. And while the pure Renaissance style of the Church of Conceição de Tomar and the Church of the Convent of Bom Jesus at Valverde, near Evora, is unique, it had no real influence over the aesthetic taste of Portugal. The spatial concept of gardens and outside spaces, the architecture of small village churches, the popular furniture, the popular and semi-erudite style of painting, the customs — all evolve out of the Gothic-Manueline tradition into the Baroque, without any indication of true Renaissance ideals.

During the fifteenth century, and throughout the sixteenth century, Europe passed through a period of self-doubt and concern about its concept of the world. Economic changes, the expansion of trade, the growth of the middle classes and contact with new worlds and civilisations gave fifteenth century man a taste for life that was incompatible with the symbolism so familiar to medieval man.

The *cathedral*, where a strong spirit of ecclesiastic scholarship and discussion and was to be found, gave way to the palace with an urban and courtly atmosphere imbued with this self-discovery.

Both Portuguese experimental humanism and Italian scientific rationalism, manifestations of a meridional spirit, appeared as opposites to the excesses of mystical pleasure displayed by the 'Gothic' man from the north of Europe.

The Italian Renaissance underlines the great differences between the 'Gothic' and the Graeco-Roman tradition. But Italy's adoption of the fundamental style and culture of classical antiquity for the new man who possesses a scientific spirit and philosophical outlook was quite different from the style and culture adopted by Portugal.

In the midst of the euphoria over the voyages of discovery, Portugal had neither the time nor the need to develop an attitude of theoretical reflection.

The activity generated by the discoveries was governed by a mysterious urge which was somehow connected to the religious spirit of the 'Gothic' period on the one hand, while it led to the development, on the other hand, of an empirical and scientific spirit based on a Mediterranean-Hebraic cultural tradition.

It is this aspect which enables Luis de Camões in the *Lusiadas* to maintain a peaceful coexistence between Christian sentiment and Pagan wonder.

For the Portuguese upper classes, nature and experience provided an explanation for everything, rather than the classical Graeco-Roman tradition which revealed itself to be increasingly incorrect and full of generalisations. Duarte Pacheco in *Esmeraldo* affirms: *'Experience permits us lives that are not coloured by the superstitions and fables recounted by some of the ancient cosmographers when describing the land and the sea'.*[1] At the same time, Garcia de Orta, in *Colóquios*, has his central character, navigator and sixteenth century man, speak out against the ancient wisdom: *'Don't try to frighten me with Dioscorides or Galen: because I will not say anything except the truth, and what I know'.*[2]

A new concept of the world and of life looked to nature to keep all things ordered and infinitely varied, and without doubt it was this attitude which set the Portuguese experience apart from the Italian Renaissance and its rationalist vision. It was an attitude which revealed itself in Portugal both in the arts and in garden design by an absence of the abstract concept of space. In the Italian Renaissance it was this abstract concept of space that created gardens which stem from a central point and develop into a rigorously pre-established series.

In Portugal the tendency was towards the taming of nature by

Opposite Page. *Perspective of the gardens seen from the west* loggia *of the house with the Lake House at the end.*

Gardens of the Quinta da Bacalhoa. Azeitão.

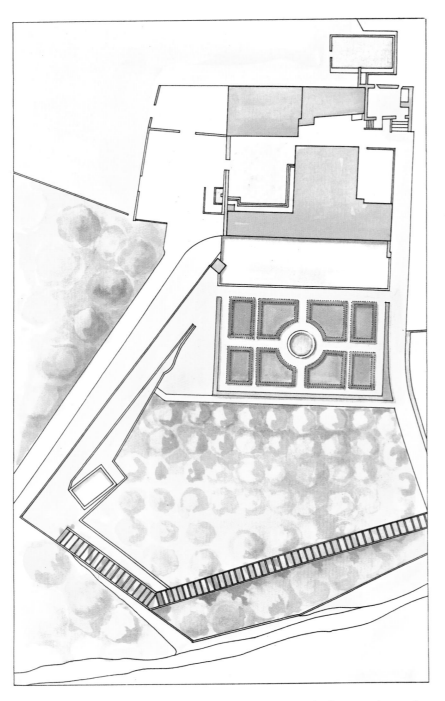

Plan of the estate showing the water-tank that predates the sixteenth century house constructed by André Gonçalves.

Quinta da Ribafria. Sintra.

maintaining gardens as organic spaces and developing them naturally in accordance with the taste and circumstances/situation of the individual residence.

Many of the gardens of the country retreats and royal palaces were changed for the better but never in terms of the whole. Dom João III, in a payment note to Johão de Castilho in 1541, refers to work in a royal palace: *'the decoration of the garden in the Santos palace'.*[3]

If, however, the idea of total renovation is not apparent, a more formal attitude can be seen in the renovation of the old garden of the Santos-o-Velho Palace where Dom Manuel had a simple walled orange grove which ran down to the banks of the Tagus: it is illustrated in the illuminated manuscript of Antonio de Holanda for the *Genealogy of the Kings of Portugal*, now in the British Museum.[4]

The change from a strongly naturalist sentiment in the fifteenth century and during the reign of Dom Manuel to a more formal attitude is also seen in the extension of the sixteenth century palace of Vila Viçosa. Dom Teodósio II, in a note to Manuel Ribeiro, refers to the payment being made for *'the great care that Manuel Ribeiro has taken with the work carried out in the service of His Excellency and for accompanying Father Bautista in the measuring and laying out of the orchard that His Excellency ordered for the Reguengo gardens and for other works to be undertaken in that orchard'.*[5]

THE PLEASURE-ORCHARD
and the Italian style garden

In 1533, Dom João III charged *'Nyculau Luys, clergyman, with the task of taking charge of and caring for the gardens of all my palaces and of carrying out in them the work he feels is best suited to them, as well as any other that I order be done there'.*[6]

The habit of surrounding the gardens with trellises was closely connected with pleasure-orchards and kitchen-gardens, as has been seen throughout the fifteenth century and in the reign of Dom Manuel.

At the time that the garden as an orange orchard was fashionable, one begins to see the appearance of Roman- or Italian-style gardens. Even the Manga Garden, undeniably Renaissance in conception, had, according to Father Jerónimo Roman, a central fountain *'isolated between four orchards that are separated by water channels which fill everything with their freshness'.*[7]

This was a deep-rooted practice, a similar development having taken place in the seventeenth century in the gardens of the Monastery of Jerónimos which Monconys described in this way: *'The dormitory is also very long and contains 72 rooms, some of which have a view over the sea while others have a view of a* great *walled garden planted with lemon and orange trees'.*[8] Monconys did not call them gardens but *grand clos,* indicating that the space was not only large, but also walled, thus reflecting the Portuguese spatial concept of the time.

To the planting of lemon trees and orange trees is added trellis work: this tradition had its origins in Roman times and continued in Portugal up to the eighteenth century. In their palaces in Lisbon, the Dukes of Braganza had, between the palace building and the orchards, a trellised courtyard, and it was here that the wedding feast following the marriage of Dom Teodósio I to his cousin Dona Isabel de Lencastre was held in 1578.[9] The trellises hung down, as was the custom, *'from stone pillars topped by a wooden frame with iron cross bars',*[10] according to a description of the palace of Alcântara, built between 1636 and 1643.

But the Italian style imposes itself as the standard of good taste of the time. Besides the orange trees, lemon trees and cypresses, and the hedges formed by crossed canes to which climbing roses were attached, there also appeared myrtle and thorn bushes shaped into topiary forms.

On his journey to Portugal in 1571, the secretary of Cardinal Alexandrino wrote about the gardens of the Palace of Vila Viçosa: *'The building is all closed in, with rows of houses which look out on to cool gardens, one of which is very spacious and is set out in the Italian style'.*[11]

Strange as it may seem to anyone who knows this palace, the

'Dom Manuel... to all who read this letter, we wish to make it known that we wish to bestow favour on André Gonçalves, our Lord Treasurer at Sintra, and here after he shall have possession of our Laranjeiras do Tanque Estate'.

Chancellery of Dom João II. Book 45, page 136, and Chancellery of Dom Manuel. Book II, folio 114.

This Crown estate is without doubt the Quinta da Ribafria. The fact that it bears the name 'orange trees of the tank' proves that the water-tank was prior to the house, and also suggests, due to its grandeur, a dignity and landscape framework that is of Islamic tradition.

Large tank and interior courtyard of the Quinta da Ribafria. Sintra.

*Fountain with renaissance lines in the courtyard, dated 1549.
Quinta da Ribafria. Sintra.*

secretary was referring to the orchard (also known as the Reguengo Garden — the Garden of the King — which we will deal with in greater detail in Chapter VI) since for the secretary a 'very spacious' garden could not be the Bosque (or Duqueza) Garden as this would appear small to someone used to the large Italian gardens of the time.

As regards the topiary, António de Oliveira Cadornega referred to it in his description of the palace: *'One can see two attractive and delightful gardens in front of the windows of the rooms and galleries of the palace. Both are very well looked after and have been laid out with many myrtles which have been shaped into artificial figures'.*[12]

The growing taste for luxury items which the new trade routes opened up in the country led to the placing of fountains, statues, niches and ceramic bosses in gardens. The fountain that André Gonçalves placed in the courtyard of his Laranjeiras do Tanque estate (later known as the Torre da Ribafria) is an example which has survived to the present day, and the date 1549, inscribed on a small tablet fixed to the inside of the small arched dome over the fountain, gives us a reference point for when changes in taste occurred.

The fountain in the Manga Garden is, however, the most elegant example that exists today. Its construction is set down in detail in the *Book of Income and Expenses of 1534-35*[13], and while mention is made of payments for *'etchings and carvings done in stone'* to the sculptors João de Ruão and Jerónimo Afonso, no one knows who actually designed it, although its spatial complexity is such that it has to be the work of an architect.

A sixteenth century (1589) description by a Spanish friar of the Order of St. Augustin states: *'Upon leaving the refectory, there is a staircase which leads to the Manga Cloister, which is very elegant and has a lot to show to those who visit the Monastery. Both the walls and the woodwork of the ceiling have been freshly painted, the latter being formed by smooth, flat boards, as is the custom in Portugal'.*[14]

It is interesting to note that, although Spain and Portugal were united at the time, the Spanish friar pointed out differences in the artistic customs of the two countries: *'The Courtyard of this cloister is not made up of slabs nor of garden, but of water, even though stone and greenery to make the work perfect are not lacking.*

'The centre is occupied by a fountain of such rare good taste that I hardly know how to describe it, it being isolated between four orchards, separated by channels which fill everything with freshness. Four richly carved stone staircases, each of which has seven steps, and which are guarded by a pair of pillars crowned with sculpted animal heads, lead to a very perfect and elegant plinth. A fountain of great elaborateness rises from it and its water falls into tanks where it is collected by secret pipes, so that it flows continuously, with no one knowing where it comes from nor where it goes to. Around it, above the water, there are four round chapels with arched domes, excellently worked in very beautiful stone, which are called the 'Ermidas', where the friars go to pray when they want to; and to ensure peace, those who go there can pull up a small drawbridge behind them, which also serves as a door, and can stay there as long as they like'.

The great cloister of Jerónimo would seem to be related to the Garden of Manga. Decorated with orange trees, it had,

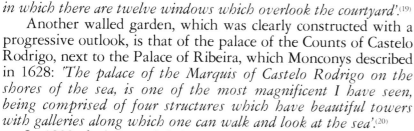

in which there are twelve windows which overlook the courtyard'.[19]

Another walled garden, which was clearly constructed with a progressive outlook, is that of the palace of the Counts of Castelo Rodrigo, next to the Palace of Ribeira, which Monconys described in 1628: *'The palace of the Marquis of Castelo Rodrigo on the shores of the sea, is one of the most magnificent I have seen, being comprised of four structures which have beautiful towers with galleries along which one can walk and look at the sea'.*[20]

In 1882, during work being carried out at the Navy Arsenal, the remains of a garden were discovered which Júlio de Castilho described: *'Ancient flowerboxes in the form of low right-angled walls set out in the shape of a square, with the remains of a circular tank in the centre. These small walls were about 1 metre in height and were covered with decorative tiles on the inner face,*

while floor tiles were laid on the ground'.[21]

These walls which enclosed the gardens were, for the most part, destroyed in the eighteenth and nineteenth centuries when their crypto-sacred symbolism had lost its meaning, even though both Beckford and Ruders frequently refer to high walls enclosing gardens at the end of the eighteenth century.

Following a visit to a farm on the outskirts of Lisbon, Ruders, who did not give it a name, said: *'A little away from the high walls which surround the garden and on the side opposite the avenues, separated by thick hedges of intercrossed canes, some lemon trees have been planted — some in flower, some with unripe lemons, others with fruit that is already ripe. On the inside are apple trees and orange trees, the latter bending under the weight of the fruit. And on every side, one can see beautiful beds*

53

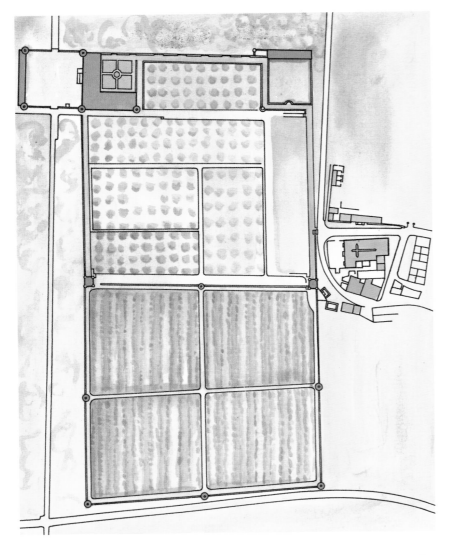

Plan of the estate and detail of the wall which separates the orchard from the vineyards. At the far end of the wall, the ancient dovecot.

Quinta da Bacalhoa. Azeitão.

of flowers and many species of trees, all giving off fragrant perfumes'.[22] It is often from foreign writers and travellers that we learn of certain typically Portuguese characteristics dating from the fifteenth century and still to be found in the eighteenth century. Crossed-cane hedges, pleasure orchards and avenues of trellises created an architectural climate which was Mediterranean in character but which would be lost in the nineteenth and twentieth centuries.

The Ducal Palace of Vila Viçosa is one of the few cases of a large palace retaining a walled-in garden — the Bosque (or Duqueza) garden. The walls which enclosed the Damas and the Buxo gardens were destroyed in 1946, transforming them into insignificant spaces. The book by Armando Lucena and António Belo, *The Gardens of the Vila Viçosa Palace,* confirms that *'at the time of writing, these gardens are isolated from each other by two walls three metres in height which are to be demolished in order to permit these two gardens to become part of the one whole'.*[23] Thus these spaces lost the architectural and aesthetic values which had, for centuries, expressed a specific architectural and aesthetic concept.

The Palace of the Castros underwent large-scale remodelling in the reign of Dom Fernando, the 1st Count of Basto. A vast veranda-gallery of Tuscan columns carved out of Estremoz marble looked out over a garden which today still has orange trees and cypresses in it. Despite the extensive view over Alentejan countryside, this garden is still enclosed by high walls containing two windows, just like the Queen's Orange Grove and the Orange Grove of the Sun, at the Palace of Sintra, or the Duchess's garden at Vila Viçosa.

These orange groves or kitchen-gardens, as they were called for some time, continued to be enclosed by high walls and were associated with a person or some other characteristic which gave them an identity. Such is the case with the Orchards of the Queen and the Sun Orchards, the Duchess's garden, and the Reguengo

orchard. To these we can also add the Damas garden at Vila Viçosa and the Caphião garden (a type of summer house) which still stands today, lined with late sixteenth century white and green tiles, at the the Pena Longa Convent in Sintra.

In terms of a concept of space, these gardens are far removed from the rationalist and programmed vision of the landscape layout of Italian villas such as Lante or Aldobrandini. They remind us more of architectural spaces designed for leisure purposes, clearly separated from each other and not forming a landscaped whole.

As a result of the two long visits that Braz de Albuquerque made to Italy, and because of his 'modern' taste, it is not difficult to see why his gardens in the Quinta da Bacalhoa are laid out in the form of an Italian-style box maze. A leasing agreement of the farm in 1674 *obliges the tenant of the farm to trim the bushes of the garden and paths twice a year and to clean out the vases in the flowerboxes*.[24] A wide path connects this garden laterally to the lake and the summer house. Set against the walls surrounding the garden were Della Robbia ceramic bosses. The skill and care with which these are made are evidence that the estate was extremely sophisticated for the time.

New to Portugal, although it in no way had any repercussions on the stylistic evolution of Portuguese gardens, is the the Quinta das Torres, which, like the Quinta da Bacalhoa, is in Azeitão.

Constructed in around 1570, the layout of this estate is different from any other of the time, with both the architecture and gardens reflecting the spirit of the Italian Renaissance.

The house's character was, without doubt, bestowed on it by its first owner, Dom Diogo D'Eça, a nobleman of great culture who spent many years out of the country in the south of Spain and Italy. In its metrical preciseness, in the symmetry of its façades, in the simplicity of its decoration, the Quinta das Torres suggests that it was constructed from plans brought directly from Italy.

View of the palace with its towers topped by 'orange- segmented' cupolas, prior to the works of Braz de Albuquerque.
Entrance courtyard and detail of the north loggia.

Quinta da Bacalhoa. Azeitão.

'...there stretches from the west, or garden...to the water tank a path, 3.50m in width, covered with tiles and flowerboxes and paved with bricks...'. Archives of 1630. (III)

This walk was also decorated with a set of Della Robbia ceramic relief bosses (sold to Italy) which were fixed there as a result of the pleasing stone bosses on the north loggia of the house.

Above. Path connecting the garden to the Lake House. Right. Loggia facing north with marble bosses, attributed to Nicolau Chantrene.

Quinta da Bacalhoa. Azeitão.

Because of the changes that the house has undergone over the centuries, the distribution of its outdoor space has been greatly modified. The great old trees which surround the large water tank were brought from Brazil at the end of the nineteenth century as a gift for the famous doctor who was the grandfather of the present owner.[25]

The large lake, with a small, classical temple in the centre, served as a water reservoir, and the gardens and orchards had to be developed in a way that was compatible with its beauty and magnificence.

While we cannot analyse the original layout of the gardens with any great accuracy, the lake is, without a doubt, its most significant element, since it clearly places the house, despite its individuality, within the Portuguese tradition.

THE QUINTA DA BACALHOA GARDENS
and the three fundamental elements of Portuguese gardens

The estate of the Lords of Infantado in the fifteenth century — the palace and the gardens of the Azeitão Estate — enjoyed a golden period in the sixteenth century under Braz de Albuquerque, with whom they will always be associated. The natural son of Afonso de Albuquerque, Braz de Albuquerque was, after the death of his father, raised by Dom Manuel to a high social and economic position. The legitimization of Braz de Albuquerque by the king in 1506 had its origins in his remorse for the treatment meted out to Afonso de Albuquerque. Due to intrigues in the palace, Dom Manuel believed that the victorious soldier wanted to declare himself independent and create a large empire in the Far East.

Made legitimate by Dom Manuel — there was no other son — and given the surname of his father, Braz de Albuquerque took the name of Afonso Braz de Albuquerque, received a large allowance from the king and was afterwards married off to a cousin of Dom Manuel — Dona Maria de Noronha, daughter of the Count of Linhares.

The great splendour of both the Casa dos Bicos (House of the Pointed Stones) and the Azeitão estate (only in the seventeenth century did it take the name Bacalhoa) was perhaps at the root of Braz de Albuquerque's desire to show himself to be better than the members of the high nobility to which he had been raised, but to which he did not belong by blood.[26]

In 1521 he was chosen to accompany the Infanta Dona Beatriz to Italy. The embassy which accompanied Dom Manuel's daughter spent some time in Italy[27] visiting various cities and it will have been there that Braz de Albuquerque's interest in the Italian Renaissance was born.

In his house in Lisbon, known later as the House of Diamonds (Casa dos Diamantes), Braz de Albuquerque opted for an unusual treatment of the façade, thereby compensating for the small amount of land compared with that of the enormous palaces of the nobility nearby (the Atouguias, the Lords of Belas,

'and the garden also has the aforementioned orchard on its western side, and, extending from the south to the north there is another path, which goes from the tank with its tiles and flowerboxes and, in the wall which lines it, there are niches with various figures..'
Archives of 1630. (III)

Besides the tiles and ceramic bosses in Della Robbia style, the walks were decorated with niches with busts while, the ends of the walls carried ball and pyramid decorations, some remains of which still exist.

Detail of the garden walk.
Quinta da Bacalhoa. Azeitão.

'...the aforementioned tank has five pleasure
houses with columns carved out of jasper and
which are covered in tiles all over and the
ceilings are plaster covered and painted to show
various stories and figures...'
Archives of 1630. (III)

*The paintings on the ceilings of the pleasure houses have
disappeared over the centuries, together with the bosses, niches,
busts and a large amount of the tile-work. These elements created
an atmosphere that was completely different at the time from
that now experienced.
A perspective of the gardens from the gallery of one of the
pleasure houses.*

Quinta da Bacalhoa. Azeitão.

the Counts of Linhares, and the Counts of Vila Flôr).

On his Azeitão estate, bought in 1528 from a cousin of his wife, known as the 'Condestablessa', Braz de Albuquerque was able to give rein to his imagination and his taste for luxury by improving both the palace and the gardens.

These had already enjoyed a certain splendour in the second half of the fifteenth century, under the Lords of Infantado, and in the sixteenth century, under the Supreme Commander of the Army, Dom Afonso, nephew of Dom Manuel. Both the loggia facing the north and the sectioned cupolas topped with small towers reveal an Arabic and Manueline style that predates the works of Braz de Albuquerque. Examples of Levantine tiles from the second half of the fifteenth century were found on the south tower[28] during restoration work carried out in 1937 by the then proprietor, Mrs. Scoville.

The sectioned cupolas on top of the walls surrounding the gardens would seem to suggest that the gardens had been laid out on two levels. The garden formed by the two wings of the palace was totally walled in, as the house register of 1630 mentions, and may also have been intended as a Pomar de Recreio (pleasure-orchard) in the same way as the Sun Orange Grove or the Queen's Orange Grove at the Palace of Sintra. Although there are no reports that any work prior to that of Braz de Albuquerque has been found in the Casa do Lago (lake house), one cannot discount the possibility of the great water tank predating Albuquerque's works. With the resurgence of civilian architecture in the fifteenth century and the beginning of the sixteenth century, we find at great estates, such as the Palace of the Aguas de Peixe, the Quinta do Tanque das Laranjeiras (later on the Torre da Ribafria), and the Palace of Vila Viçosa, that a large lake-tank for watering purposes appeared as a principal element of the external space. Also of interest, due to its archaic character, is the small walled-in garden which serves as an antechamber to the Casa do Lago. The fact that it has a door to the street explains its function as a transitional area between the outside world and the gardens. The reduced size of this area, surrounded as it is by high walls with flowerboxes, reveals an environment of spatial containment which is not compatible with the large size of the gardens, and this fact once more raises the possibility of earlier works near the Casa do Lago.

More traditional than archaic was the walled garden next to the west loggia. This garden, according to the land register of 1630, was surrounded by walls *'with citrons and lemon trees by the walls...'*,[29] a practice which may also be seen in other gardens, such as the Garden of the Duchess of Vila Viçosa, which Diogo F. Figueiroa describes: *'A large tank full of fish among the green shadows of the lemon trees which surround them'*.[30]

The Palace of Vila Viçosa still has some of these old lemon trees in the Jardim do Bosque (formerly Garden of the Duchess) but the large tank has disappeared. While the extensive orchard which decorated and still decorates the gardens of Bacalhoa had *'infinite orange trees, lemon trees and citrons'*,[31] the orange tree and the lemon tree were predominant, even in more important gardens, such as the walled garden next to the west loggia. This

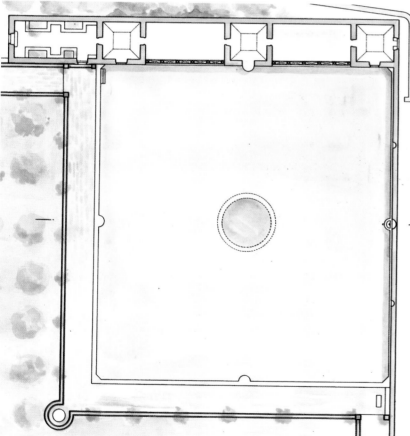

'...there is a water tank...from which is watered with water from the São Simão river, all the aforementioned orchard...and the water which falls into the tank, falls from the mouth of an artificial whale with a Triton on top...and with various figures in stone niches around the walls of the tank...'
Archives of 1630. (III)

Cross-section and plan of the lake complex.

Following pages. *View of the pleasure houses and lake and, at the far end, the west face of the house.*
Quinta da Bacalhoa. Azeitão.

garden, which today has a box maze, has lost the wall which separated it from the orchard, thereby diluting that Portuguese concept of spatial containment and discontinuity between the garden's different parts.

The Renaissance and Italian taste of Braz de Albuquerque was, as we have seen, on a more decorative level. The structure and spatial concept of the gardens remains imbued with the Portuguese tradition of spaces which are autonomous and independent of each other, with a preference for orange trees used in an architectural rather than landscaping manner, and which will continue to be popular in Portugal until the eighteenth century.

Braz de Albuquerque thus emphasised in his work a refined humanist trend and enjoyment of life, added to a personal taste for sophisticated decorative elements which would strongly influence Portuguese gardens in the seventeenth and eighteenth centuries. For decades, he ordered, from both the Portuguese and foreign markets, decorative tiles for the interior of the palace and especially for the gardens. Between 1540 and 1545 — the period during which the architectural work was finished — decorative tiles were ordered from the Triana workshops in Seville. Afterwards, and until the 1570s, decorative tiles were ordered from Portuguese manufacturers, these being of various types (in pattern and shape), and the best and most up-to-date produced at the time. To these decorative tiles, dealt with in great detail by Santos Simões,[32] Braz de Albuquerque added a notable collection of glazed ceramic bosses which had a border of fruits and flowers, and a bust in the centre, in the style of Della Robbia. These bosses are to be found distributed along the three gallery walks which are laid out between the palace and the Casa do Lago, between this and the Casa da India and, finally, between the Casados Pombas and the north wing of the palace.

Joaquim Rasteiro[33] found these bosses in a relatively bad state of conservation. The twelve bosses which were better preserved, and which were situated on the walk between the palace and the Casa do Lago, were sold to Italy at the beginning of the twentieth century and were classified there as being authentic Della Robbia.

Besides the glazed tiles and bosses, the walls along these walks had niches with masonry frames and were adorned with balls and pyramids which can still be seen today on the south facing wall and the end retaining wall of the lake.

Of interest in the history of Portuguese gardens is the significance given to the tank and the Casa do Lago and the three galleries laid out in the ancient Roman tradition of 'deambulato'. The emphasis placed on the walk is largely due to the large trellis, which is similar to that of the Reguengo Garden at Vila Viçosa. The flowerboxes and the benches, together with the glazed tiles, appear at regular intervals along these walks, these characteristically Portuguese elements in no way reflecting the rationalistic theory prevalent in Europe whereby the layout of the garden was organised around the walks. Instead, walks were created in certain areas of the gardens because their very nature, which reflected a

'A garden...with a fountain in the middle and water spouts around the garden, and with citrons and lemon trees against the encircling walls, and with tiles forming pictures that occupy half the height of a wall. The paths of the garden are tiled...' Archive of 1630. (III)

In accordance with the spatial concepts of the time, each garden was surrounded by walls which established different levels of privacy and ritual for each space. It should be mentioned that the garden was covered in tiles depicting figures, but these have since disappeared, and only a flowerbox with paintings in Renaissance style remains.
Above and on the opposite page. *The Box Garden.*

Quinta da Bacalhoa. Azeitão.

joy for living, made them special places for strolling, conversing or relaxing on small benches framed by flowerboxes.

Influenced by the Italian Renaissance, the Bacalhoa gardens clearly show a structure and spatial concept that is closely connected to the origins of the Portuguese garden. The whole, which comprises the Casa do Lago, the great watering tank and the walks laid out in the form of long galleries, was, therefore, a new expression of these fundamental elements, and the garden possesses a feeling that is both architectural and magnificent.

The large trellises with benches and flowerboxes, which are traditionally Mediterranean, here take on the character of more sophisticated galleries, being the future model for the walks of the Fronteira Palace, the Palace of the Count of Castelo Melhor and the Anunciada Palace. The summer house and the pleasure house which we see appear in gardens such as that of Dom Jaime (Bosque and Duqueza) in Vila Viçosa, or the Queen's Orange Grove in the Palace of Sintra, are also connected with the typical large water tank in a more magnificent and landscaped form, paving the way for the lake house of the Fronteira and Castelo Melhor gardens, and also, much later on, the music house on the great lake at Queluz.

Following the spatial tradition already defined in the fifteenth century and the beginning of the sixteenth century, the gardens of Bacalhoa favoured the following elements: the summer house, the lake-watering tank and the walk. They thus become the model for Portuguese gardens of the seventeenth and eighteenth centuries, with the above elements playing a central role.

* * *

Together with vast lake-tanks for watering purposes on the large estates, such as that of Bacalhoa, the tank was an almost obligatory element of the outdoor spaces of sixteenth century estates.

Above and right. *Terrace, plan and elevation of the outside of the Quinta da São Tiago. Sintra.*

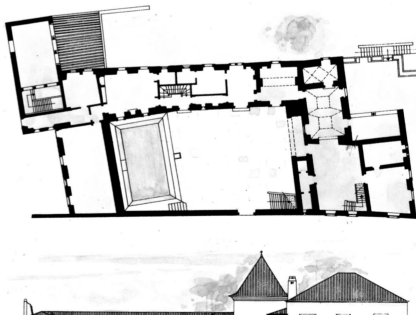

THE LARANJEIRAS DO TANQUE ESTATE

the future Ribafria estate

Although the estate has always been considered to be sixteenth century in origin, when work was undertaken by André Gonçalves, Superintendent of the Palace of Sintra, a letter from Dom Manuel proved it was, in fact, older. Owned by the crown till then, the estate was called Laranjeiras do Tanque (Orange Grove of the Tank), which indicates that the great lake-tank next to the house predates the sixteenth century tower which, by virtue of its architectural character, suggests an Islamic origin.

LETTER OF FAVOUR OF DOM MANUEL

Dom Manuel etc.ª. A quantos esta nosa carta virem fazemos saber que queremos nos fazer graça he merçee a andre gonçalves noso almoxarife de Syntra temos por bem he lhe fazemos merçee daquy em dyante da nosa erdade das laranjeiras do tanque da dicta villa asy he pella maneira que a tynha Johom Rodrigues filho do cosayro que ora faleceo he a nos pertence esto encanto nosa merçee for he porem mandamos ao noso contador da dicta comarqua que o metam em pose da dicta erdade he lha leyxem lograr sem lhe nisso ser posto embarguo por nos lhe fazermos della merçee como dicto he.

Dada em lixboa ao darradeiro dia de junho jorge fernandez a fez anno de myll b·xb anos

'that wood, those fountains, that island that seems to flaunt itself in the middle of the waters...and those thousands of birds inside an immense cage...'
A. Cabedo. 1578. (IV)

By the end of the sixteenth century, these famous gardens, constructed by Miguel da Silva, were in ruins.
Above and left. *Detail of the tank and plan of the estate.*
The Fontelo Palace. Viseu.

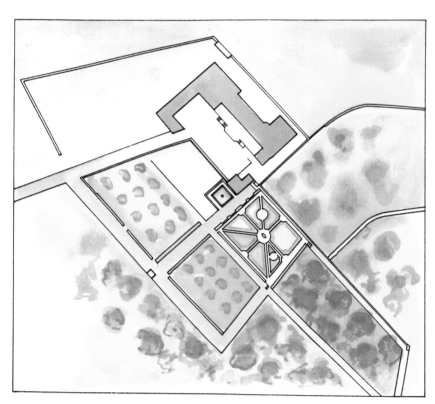

With its strict symmetry and rationalist aspect, the Quinta das Torres radically distances itself from the concepts of the era, suggesting an imported architectural plan. Main entrance.

Quinta das Torres. Azeitão.

A.N.T.T. Chancellery of Dom Manuel. Book 11. Folio 114V

Transcribed by Alice Estorninho.

(This Letter of Favour in which the King makes a gift of his Laranjeiras do Tanque estate, shows the estate is older than previously thought: it is usually simply described as being of sixteenth century origin.)

DESCRIPTION OF THE MANGA GARDEN IN THE SIXTEENTH CENTURY
by Father Jerónimo Roman

CAP.lo DE LAS MAS PARTES DEL MONASTERIO QUE TIENEN COSAS DIGNAS DE NOTAR, Y SER SAVIDAS

Ay, saliendo del Refitorio passado el angulo a se arrima a la pared una escalera q sube a otra claustra que llaman de la Manga, mui galana, y qué dá bien que ver a los q de nuevo entran en este Monasterio: llamasse de la Manga, porq quando se hazian las obras nuevas quando se iva introduciendo la observancia del Rey Don Iuan el tercero padre de los Portugueses trahia en la manga del sayo pegada la traza de lo q se iva edificando, y ali mirava como se edificava cada pieça, y como en este claustro se remiró mas que en las otras obras, y nó se ponia piedra que el nó pusiesse los ojos en ella; acudia al papel que tenia pegado a la manga para ver se iva conforme a la traza; y assi llamaron por esto la Claustra de la Manga: Tiene esta clauztra muchas cosas que notar, porq está toda pintada al fresco, y assi por las paredes como el techo, y maderam. to por ser de tabla lissa y llana, que es edificio mui ordinario de Portugal: El pattio que haze este claustro, nó es ensolado, ni hecho vergel, mas es de agua, aunq ay de todo algo para q la obra sea perfecta: Ay pues aqui una fuente en medio de este patio de el claustro trazada para ponerse alli de tan estrana manera, q nó sabria yo pintarla como ella es: tiene esta fuente para llegar a ella quatro arcos de piedra que estaá en medio de todas las quatros partes ó angulos del dicho claustro, tiene en sus porporciones sus calles adonde ay sus naranjos y jornas, y intermedio de cada una lleva lleva su rio ó arroyo q haze mas fresco lo que está dentro de manera que en este espacio ay quatro vergeles, y ocho rios, ó arroyos: en medio de estos jardines, y rios estan quatro escaleras ricamente labradas de piedra, y cada escalera tinne sette gradas acompanadas de unos bestiones bien labrados, y sobre estas quatro escaleras se arma un pattio octavado mui pulido, y galan, en medio del qual salé una fuente de gran artificio, porq el agua q cahe de ella sobre aquellos rios, buelve a recogerse por otros canos secretos, y assi ay agua continuamente sin q se sepa por onde viene, ni adonde vá. En este mesmo pattio con estremado artificio estan hechas quatro Capillas redondas, y de boveda labradaz ricamente de piedra mui hermosa, que hermosea todo este patio quasi todo de agua, las quales son llamadas las Ermidas adonde los Religiosos quando quiera q quieren se van a orar en ellas: y para estar quitos, el que alli se vá a recoger levanta una puente levadiça que ay para entrar que le sirve de puerta, y alli se recoge hasta que le parece: Son los Oratorios por de dentro mui bien labrados, con sus ventanas, y vidrieraz, que nó hay mas que dizer: Los Retablos, y altares estan dedicados a San Iuan Baptista, San Hieronimo, San Pablo primero hermitano, y a San Antonio, todos Principes de la vida solitaria:

Transcribed by Virgílio Correia. *A fifteenth century description of the Monastery of Santa Cruz de Coimbra.* Coimbra. Pages 27-28.

(This description shows us the Manga Garden at the end of the sixteenth century and once again makes special mention of the presence at the time of orange trees, which have now disappeared.)

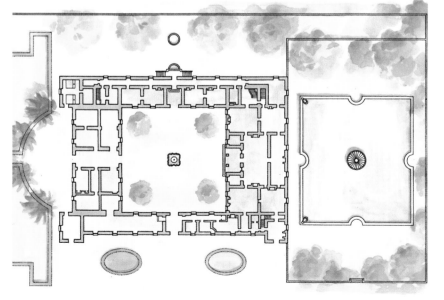

Despite the profoundly Italian character that Dom Diogo D'Eça wished to give his estate, the great tank was an omnipresent element of the gardens, and this, together with the decision to opt for a design based around a courtyard, reflects much more the Portuguese way of life of the sixteenth century.
Inner courtyard and plan of the estate.
Following pages. *The Great Lake with a small temple in the centre.*

Quinta das Torres. Azeitão.

DESCRIPTION OF THE BACALHOA GARDENS

Extract from the Morgado Archives of 1630

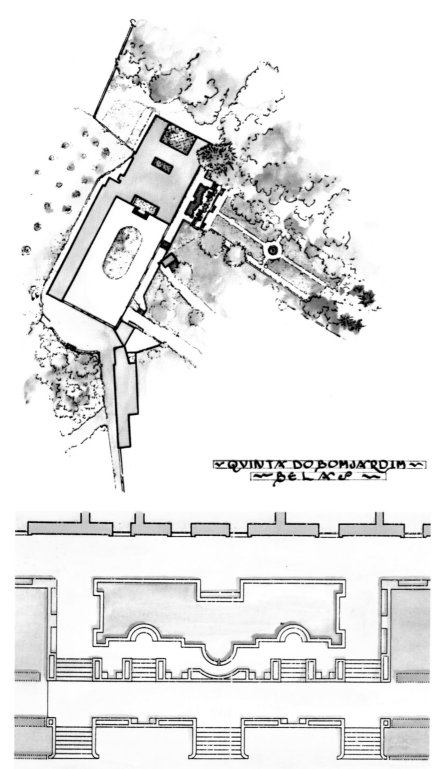

Plans of the estate and the lake. Watering tank for the gardens.

Quinta do Bom Jardim. Belas.

"Umas casas muito grandes e muito nobres, edificadas com muito primor, com varandas de todas as partes e casas, e muitas salàs, camaras, recamaras, como abaixo se declarará especialmente e o numero d'ellas, postas da parte do norte e do levante, ficando a quinta e pomar com seus jardins da parte do sul e poente, e tem o sitio das ditas casas em circuito pela extremidade da parte de fóra a saber:

"Da banda do nascente, indo do norte a sul, de extremo a extremo do edificio e assento das casas, tem, trinta e quatro varas e meia, e cada vara de cinco palmos, dos que falla a ordenação d'este reino.

"E da parte do norte, de nascente a poente, de extremo a extremo, tem trinta varas e meia.

"E da parte do poente, em ponta que o edificio faz, tem quatorze varas e meia, e vindo da parte do poente para o nascente contra o sul, tem vinte e seis varas, e voltando de norte a sul, pela banda do poente, na ponta que o sitio das casas faz para o sul; tem vinte e quatro varas e, n'este vão, ao longo do edificio das ditas casas, está um jardim com uma fonte e casa de agua no meio, do que se faz a declaração e medição seguinte:

"E pela parte do sul de nascente a poente e pelo extremo da ponta, que as ditas casas fazem para a dita parte do sul, tem, de canto a canto, as ditas pontas, que fazem as ditas casas para o poente e sul, e tem cento e trinta e sete varas, que são juntas as medições atrás declaradas.

"Tem mais estas casas tres cubellos nos tres cantos, que se fazem para fóra contra o norte, dois ao norte e um ao sul, com que ficam muito realçadas e lustrosas, e a entrada, que está em um pateo muito grande com seus portaes, cerrado de muro, em que se correram e podem correr touros, está uma escada toda de pedraria com uma volta, toda com seus balaustres de marmore, que formosca a entrada da primeira sala. As quaes casas têem de salas, camaras, recamaras, retretes e antecamaras dezoito em numero, todas espaçosas e todas ladrilhadas e com azulejos pelas paredes, altura de mais de um covado e alguns retretes todos lavrados de azulejo e os tectos lavrados de bordo e com mulduras, e pintados de diversas e agradaveis pinturas, e por baixo outras muitas casas e officinas e almarios, que respondem ás casas superiores, mas repartidas em muito maior numero.

"Tem mais duas varandas com seus arcos de jaspe e columnas do mesmo, uma para a banda do poente e outra para o norte com suas grades de ferro até ao meio, com seus azulejos até meio das paredes com figuras. Tem a varanda da parte do poente de comprido onze varas e meia e de largo quatro varas. E a varanda da parte do norte, em que não ha grade de ferro, tem uma meia parede de pedra lavrada, com seus azulejos por dentro, sobre que armam as columnas, tem de comprido dez varas e de largo quasi tres varas. E os portaes de todas estas casas são de pedraria de jaspe, com suas portas de bordo e muito bem lavradas e com suas chaminés de pedraria e todas as mais pertenças respondentes á qualidade do edificio.

PATEO

"Item um pateo defronte das ditas cass cercado de muro com dois meios cubellos, com duas portas, por que se éntra e sáe á estrada publica e é commum a todos e feito em quadro. Tem do norte a sul trinta e cinco varas, e de nascente a poente trinta e cinco e meia, e para a parte do nascente tem uma varanda de columnas de jaspe, que serve entre as casas terreas e gasalhadòs de creados, e tem um chafariz de agua a uma parede da banda do norte.

JARDIM

"Um jardim, que fica entre as duas pontas das casas atrás medidas, com o qual fica o sitio das ditas casas em quadriangulo. Tem de norte a sul pela parte do poente e por onde confronta com o pomar, que se segue, vinte e quatro varas e de poente a levante outras vinte e quatro, e pelos outros dois lados confronta com as casas, com uma fonte ao meio e em roda com seus canos de agua e pelas paredes cidreias e limoeiros, com meias paredes de azulejo feito em quadro. É arruado e ladrilhadas as ruas.

'the noble estate of Bom Jardim with a small chapel of the Good Jesus...which belongs to Senhor Thome de Sousa, Count of Redondo: there is a good Palace with a large courtyard and there are orchards of fruit-bearing thorn bushes, vines, kitchen-gardens which are watered by seventeen fountains of crystalline waters...'
Carvalho Costa. 1712. (V)

The term orchard was synonymous, at the time, with a pleasure-garden in which orange trees and lemon trees traditionally predominated, especially in the fifteenth and sixteenth centuries.

Quinta do Bom Jardim. Belas.

It was the custom in country retreats for the north façade to face the gardens. The lake-tank for watering purposes was, because of its serpentine shape, behind the original layout of the house and is perhaps seventeenth century. It was almost certainly completely covered with tiles.
Entrance, and view of the lake-tank.

Quinta do Bom Jardim. Belas.

TITULO DO POMAR

"Item um pomar contiguo ás casas e jardim, que lhe ficam para a parte do levante, todo plantado de infinitas laranjeiras em ordem, limoeiros e cidreiras com todo o mais genero de fructas, mui espessas e plantadas em ordem e fileiras, o qual está todo cercado ao redor de um muro mais de doze palmos em alto e pela parte de dentro com suas ruas de azulejo, que abaixo se declaram. Tem do nascente, ou jardim, atrás declarado, até ao tanque de agua por uma rua cercada de azulejos e alegretes e ladrilhada de largura de mais de tres varas, oitenta e quatro varas e n'este canto, que o dito pomar faz para o poente, está um tanque de agua, ladrilhado por baixo, que cobre um homem, cercado de pedraria e de azulejos, feito em fórma quadrada; tem vinte e nove varas de canto a canto e fazem em circuito cento e dezeseis, do qual se rega todo o pomar atrás declarado com agua do rio de S. Simão, de que lhe pertence toda a dita agua quatro dias naturaes e tres horas cada nove dias.

"Tem o dito tanque, na cabeceira pela parte do sul, cinco casas de prazer armadas com columnas de jaspe e forradas todas de azulejos e os tectos pintados em estuque com varias historias e figuras, e ao lado das ditas casas de prazer, para a parte do nascente, tem um jardim com seus alegretes na distancia e largura das mesmas casas.

"E a agua que cáe para o dito tanque, cáe pela bôca de uma baleia artificiosa com um Titão em cima, que formoseia muito o dito tanque e casas de prazer, e com figuras varias em nichos, feitos de pedraria pelas paredes do dito tanque.

"Tem mais o dito pomar pela parte do poente, começando do sul e norte, outra rua, que vae do dito tanque, da mesma largura e feito com seus azulejos e alegretes e pela parede seus nichos com varias figuras, que tem cento e dezeseis varas, e no remate do canto de baixo, da banda do norte, tem uma casa quadrada com quatro janellas, em que estão pintadas sobre estuque as historias da India, com as quatro cidades principaes conquistadas pelo grande Affonso de Albuquerque, pae natural de Affonso de Albuquerque, instituidor d'este morgado.

"Tem esta rua, da parte do poente, uma porta, que sáe para a igreja e freguesia de S. Simão, pouca distancia de portal a portal, da qual igreja é costume sair a procissão da Resurreição de Christo Nosso Salvador e correr as ruas do dito pomar e tornar-se a recolher pela mesma porta á mesma igreja.

"Tem o dito pomar do dito canto da casa da India, atrás declarada, de poente a nascente, pela banda do norte, cento e trinta e sete varas, que tambem servem para medição da vinha abaixo declarada, que confina com o dito pomar pela banda do norte e do canto, que o muro faz para a banda do nascente até ao jardim, d'onde esta demarcação e medição começa, subindo de norte a sul, tem cento e seis varas, ficando no meio a ponta que as casas fazem para o parte do poente, que se mettem entre o jardim e o pomar. Pela parte d'onde a dita demarcação d'elle começou, em o dito canto de baixo, está uma casa, que se chama *das Pombas,* com um bofete de jaspe ao meio. E da dita casa, na largura d'ella, que corre de norte a sul, como se diz atrás, até ás ditas casas principais, vae uma rua de ladrilho com seus alegretes de azulejo na fórma das outras ruas atrás declaradas.

TITULO DA VINHA

"Tem mais uma vinha pela parte do norte, que dos lados fica dentro dos muros do pomar atrás confrontado e dividida do dito pomar pelo muro menos principal. Tem do sul ao norte, pela parte do nascente, cento e trinta e tres varas e de nascente a poente, pela parte do norte, cento e quarenta e duas varas e meia, e pelas outras duas partes tem a mesma medida de varas por estar em fórma quadrada.

Transcribed by Joaquim Rasteiro. *Quinta e Palácio da Bacalhoa em Azeitão.* Lisbon. 1885. Pages 62-64.

(Although seventeenth century this description, taken from a document relating to the dividing up of some property, not only describes the house and the gardens in great detail but also refers to the garden next to the loggia with high walls covered in glazed tiles. These walls, which have now disappeared, indicate a spatial structure quite different from that which we find today.)

NOTES

1 António Sérgio. *Breve intervenção da história de Portugal.* Portugal. Lisbon 1972, page 85.
2 Idem. Page 85.
3 Transcribed by Anselmo B. Freire. *Arquivo Histórico Português.* Document 770, Chancellery of Dom João III, Letter of Discharge from Debt, 1541.
4 This ornamental manuscript has been studied in detail by Júlio Castilho, Ribeira de Lisboa, Vol. V. 2nd ed., page 72
5 José Teixeira. *O Paço Ducal de Vila Viçosa.* Document II, page 120.
6 Chancellery of Dom João III, book 19, folio 245. A.N.T.T.
7 Transcribed by Virgílio Correia — Uma descrição quinhentista do Mosteiro de Santa Cruz de Coimbra, page 27.
8 Monseiur de Monconys. *Journal de Voyages.* 3rd part. Lyon. 1666, page 46. B.N.L.
9 D. António Caetano de Souza. *História Genealógica da Casa de Bragança —* Provas. Volume VI, page 46.
10 Transcribed by Júlio Castilho. *A Ribeira de Lisboa,* 3rd ed. Vol. III. Note III. Page 246.
11 Report of the journey of Cardinal Alexandrino, written by João Baptista Venturino, transcribed by Alexander Herculano in *Opúsculos,* Volume VI. Lisbon, 1884, pages 49-93
12 António de Oliveira Cadornega. *Descrição de Vila Viçosa.* Introduction by Heitor Teixeira, 1983, page 88.
13 Virgílio Correia. Ibid. Page 27.
14 Idem. Page 263.
15 M. de Monconys, Ibid., page 48.
16 Arquivo Pitoresco. Volume VI, page 79.
17 Idem. Volume VI, page 250.
18 Padre António Reis. *Corpus Illustrium Poetarum Lusitanorum.* Lisbon. 1745.
19 Francisco Moraes Sardinha. *Do famoso e Antiquíssimo Parnaso...* Manuscript work, pages 58-59. B.N.L.
20 M. de Monconys. Ibid., page 15.
21 Júlio de Castilho. *Ribeira de Lisboa.* 3rd ed., Vol. IV, pages 43-44.
22 Carl Israel Ruders. *Viagem a Portugal* (1798-1802). Lisbon. 1981, page 50.
23 Armando Lucena e António Belo. *Jardins do Paço de Vila Viçosa.* Fundation da Casa de Bragança. 1955, page 25.
24 Joaquim Rasteiro. *Quinta e Palácio da Bacalhoa em Azeitão.* Lisbon. 1885, page 31.
25 Information obtained from the late Dr. Bento de Sousa, father of the present owners of the estate.
26 For a biography of Braz de Albuquerque the following books are recommended: *Brazões da Sala de Sintra.* Braamcamp Freire. Vol. II, page 203. *Biblioteca Lusitana.* Diogo Barbosa Machado. Vol. I, page 25.
27 Garcia de Resende. *Ida da Infanta dona Beatriz para Saboya.*
28 J. Santos Simões. *Azulejaria em Portugal nos sécs. XV e XVI.* Lisbon. 1969, page 55.
29 Joaquim Rasteiro. Ibid. Page 63.
30 Diogo F. Figueiroa. *Ipitome das Festas...* Évora 1633, page 7.
31 Joaquim Rasteiro. Ibid. Page 63.
32 J. Santos Simões. *Azulejaria em Portugal nos sécs. XV e XVI.* Lisbon. 1969.
33 Joaquim Rasteiro. Ibid. Pages 35-38.

Notes on Illustrations

I. M. de Monconys. *Journal des Voyages.* III Part. Lyon, 1666. Page 48.
II. Virgílio Correia. Ibid. Page 27.
III. Transcribed by Joaquim Rasteiro. Ibid. Page 63.
IV. In Corpus Illustrium Poetarum Lusitanorum. Lisbon 1745. B.N.L..
V. A. Carvalho Costa. *Chorografia Portuguesa.* Lisbon 1712. Page 52.

THE HIGH POINT OF THE CRYPTO-MAGIC GARDEN

and the oriental mannerism of the seventeenth century

CHAPTER IV

The defeat at Alkacer-Kibir and the consequent loss of nationhood brought many significant changes to the economic and social life of the country. For many years, the nobility was obliged to sell its jewels, tableware and gold to pay the cost of war and to ransom members of their families imprisoned in Morocco.

Integrated into the Spanish Empire, Portugal was also obliged to sever links with almost the whole of Europe on account of the Counter Revolutionary wars in which Spain was involved. These wars, besides calling for a large military contribution, impoverished the country at all economic levels.

This period saw the beginning of the decline of the royal Palace of Evora. The object of successive work by Dom João II, Dom Manuel and Dom João III, its gardens extended over a vast area which Dom João II had annexed from the lands around the Convent of São Francisco.

On his visit to Evora in 1616, Filipe III authorised the holy brothers of São Francisco to use: *three rooms in the convent building, for the health of the holy men.*[1] Meanwhile, he moved into the Palace of the Castros, since the royal palace was not in a fit state to house him.

The subtle petition of the brothers of São Francisco transformed the palace into a 'stone quarry' for the convent works with the result that one of the most interesting examples of civilian architecture in the fifteenth and sixteenth centuries was lost for ever.

High-ranking families which had occupied important administrative and military positions in the frail structure of the empire, withdrew to their rural domains, far from the court which, for its part, had practically disappeared.

This was a time of crisis and pause, before the country found itself and its own resources and abandoned the practice of importing artists and works of art from Europe.

This self-discovery may possibly have contributed to the episodic character of the Renaissance in Portugal, reducing it to a series of works, without any true continuity in the evolution of art or the spatial concept of Portuguese architecture.

Church officials maintained their rights and luxurious lifestyles, being integrated in a religious community where the concept of nationality was of secondary importance. Always in contact with the luxury of Rome, the bishops did not lose their interest in their palaces and country retreats. In 1583, three years after the loss of the country's nationhood, Dom Afonso de Castelo Branco initiated the work on his Palace of São Martinho, on the outskirts of Coimbra, next to the banks of the Mondego. The description by his biographer, Almeida Soares, is very clear *'...the estate, so sumptuous and royal that it seems to be more a dwelling of princes than a bishop's retreat; the gallery of the houses and their pomp, the harmony, the courtyards, the shell-work, the gardens, the fountains, the orchards, orange groves and other numerous magnificent things'.*[2] The magnificence of the place is, however, not unconnected with the fact that Dom Afonso was appointed Viceroy of Portugal at the time of the Spanish occupation.

The Bishop of Oporto, Dom Frei Marcos de Lisboa, also initiated works on the Prado estate which Dom Rodrigo da Cunha described in 1632: *'The bishop ordered that on this estate some very famous fountains be constructed, that orchards be planted as well as shady and cool groves of trees'.*[3]

Opposite page. Integrating Italian influences in a Portuguese aesthetic tradition of tile-work, shell-work and a particular concept of space. The Oratory Walk in the gardens of the Fronteira Palace is a unique example of a series of garden plans constructed in Portugal in the second half of the seventeenth century.

Detail of the Chapel Walk of the Palace of the Marquises of Fronteira. São Domingos de Benfica. Lisbon.

Monconys, who was in Lisbon in 1628, writes in his book *Journal of Journeys*: 'the retreat of the Count of Faro in this city is very pleasant, having a quantity of gardens, woods, walks, and an infinite number of fountains, but what is most notable is a table made of valuable imported stone in the shape of well-known personalities'.[4] From this description, the gardens certainly seem to have been splendid, but the strange thing is that nothing at all has remained of them. The Counts of Faro belonged to the ranks of the nobility which supported the Filipine dynasty of Spain and who were disgraced after the restoration of the Braganzas to the throne.

The Palace and estate of Alcantra became part of the property of the royal house as a result of the debts of the Milanese nobleman João Baptista Rovellasco, who was ruined by the pepper trade, though neither the palace nor the gardens underwent significant transformation during either the Filipine period or after the restoration.

The official archives of this estate, which refer to the period between 1636 and 1645,[5] tell us of the trellised walks, the summer houses made of wood, the large water-mirror lakes, the seats lined with glazed tiles — still without the sophisticated shell adornments — the balustrades and the statuary of these gardens in the middle of the seventeenth century.

They appear to be linked to a sixteenth century tradition with a strong Mediterranean flavour. Corsini refers to this atmosphere, in 1669: *'The garden, which is not very large, is formed by various small gardens, situated on various levels, which are joined together, the only interesting thing being the beautiful panorama from there over the sea...and there is nothing of interest except for some trellises with grapes, sweetly-perfumed flowerbeds, orange trees and lemon trees'.*[6]

Just like the bishops, whose authority depended on Rome, the financial situation of the Dukes of Braganza, who aspired to the royal throne, was much better than that of the country as a whole, which was beset by economic problems. Although they had retired to their Palace of Vila Viçosa, they maintained a court there which thrived due to the drive and initiative of Duchess Dona Catarina, grand-daughter of King Dom Manuel.

A widow (Dom João, her husband, had died in 1583), King Filipe II himself proposed marriage to her but she turned his offer down with all the haughtiness of a great duchess, stating that she would not exchange the memories of her husband for the throne of Spain, nor prejudice the right of her son to the crown.[7]

Its *'extremely cool gardens'*, in the words of the secretary of Cardinal Alexandrino, *'one of which is very spacious ...set out in the Italian fashion',*[2] must have maintained this quality and work was carried out on them at the time.

A document in the archives of the house of Braganza mentions a payment made to Manuel Ribeiro *'for accompanying P. Bautista in the measuring out and laying out of the orchard which His Excellency had ordered be carried out once more'.*[8] The work was, without doubt, in the Reguengo gardens, which were spacious and well laid out in the Italian fashion (as referred to by the secretary of Cardinal Alexandrino), since the others were too small to be described in that way, especially by someone accustomed to the huge gardens of the European courts.

However, there were no significant alterations of an aesthetic nature in the gardens. Despite a certain grandeur which some authors (such as Father Manuel Calado, Diogo Ferreira Figueira, Moraes Sardinha and António Cadornega) who wrote about the palace mentioned, the descriptions seem to generate an atmosphere of rural sixteenth century. The absence of glazed tiles, significant statuary, shell-work and marble balustrades, sets these gardens apart from the sophistication of the large gardens of the second half of the seventeenth century.

As regards this garden, which has now disappeared, Father Manuel Calado writes in 1648: *'In one of the angles of this façade is an arch which opens on to a spacious path to the Reguengo, which is a garden planted with many tall trees, watered by many fountains and water machinery, with many wide and long avenues, the walls of which are of small myrtles shaped into many and different figures, this work being undertaken by a gardener of the Duke's who is very skilled in this art: there is there a lake of natural water with many fish, and wells, from which one extracts water with machines of various types, and which is used to water parts which running water cannot reach'.*[9] The twelve windows of the garden of the Bosque are also considered to be part of the work which Dona Catarina and her son[10] ordered be carried out, as are the alterations to the summer house at the bottom of the same garden.

The works undertaken in this wing of the palace,[11] which were called *'new houses'*, indicate a need for buildings.

According to Father Manuel Calado: *'All the walls in this garden are full of windows, in which one sees the Ladies seated on the days that there are feasts in the Courtyard...and at the bottom of this garden are three windows, two ordinary ones and a very large one with a balcony through which light enters into a leisure house, in which her highness Dona Catarina comes and sits with her ladies on some summer afternoons, where she can enjoy watching the many people passing by who ordinarily enter that street when they come from Borba, Estremoz...'.*[12]

* * *

In the same leisure house at the bottom of the Duchess Garden, the new Duchess, Dona Luisa de Gusmão, waited for news of the revolution which would finally place the Dukes of Braganza on the throne of Portugal.

Later on, Dom João IV amply recompensed the nobility which placed him in power. With the end of the War of Restoration, these nobles comprised the ruling class and received titles and administrative positions in accordance with their services in battles fought with the Spanish.

The second half of the seventeenth century was marked by the construction of a large group of palaces and country retreats concentrated mainly in the region of Lisbon.

The type of building and characteristics of style were, without doubt, influenced by the climate of nationalism that was felt after Spanish domination. The encouraging of the arts and the recourse to Portuguese artists by the church in the first half of the seventeenth century made it possible for the nobility to undertake a series of experiments in various areas of art and architecture in their palaces and gardens.

Constructed from new, or else the result of significant alterations, palaces appear everywhere, among them those of Azambuja, later known as the Meninos de Palhavã (Children of Palhavã), of the Count of Obidos at Belém, of the Counts of Calheta (the Cows Courtyard), of the Távoras, at Campo Pequeno, of the Counts of Alvor in Janelas Verdes, of the Dukes of Aveiro in Azeitão, and of the Marquises of Fronteira, in São Domingos de Benfica.

Although in the majority of cases we know that their gardens were of great quality and beauty, they have, for the most part been lost due to the vicissitudes of history. One of them was the earthquake of 1755; another was the persecution by the Marquis of Pombal of the nobles and their almost total annihilation after the assassination attempt on Dom José I.

So it is in the almost original layout and splendour of the gardens of the Fronteira Palace, in São Domingos de Benfica, that we find proof of the aesthetic qualities and spatial characteristics of the Portuguese garden of the time.

Travellers who were in Portugal in the seventeenth century, and whose comments for the most part were not very favourable to the country, did not fail to point out in their diaries the beauty of certain gardens.

Richard Flecknoe, who was in Portugal between 1648 and 1650, and who was under the protection of Dom João IV because of his musical talents, was made a guest upon the king's command in the house of a wealthy English merchant called John Muley. It was there that he wrote:

Famous throughout the world
There is a country retreat
Where all the rural graces have their home
(and the rural graces are much more beautiful in the summer
than those of the cities in winter).
With the most beautiful gardens full
Of delightful fruit-bearing trees
Such as the orange, the lemon, the damson and the peach
Mulberries with wide-spreading branches which give us silk
Fig trees and hundreds of others.[13]

Destroyed by the earthquake, the Palace of Annunciada was described by father António Carvalho da Costa, in his *Chorografia Portuguesa* of 1712.

This neighbourhood has many noble houses, such as those of the Counts of Ericeira, which was founded by Fernando Alvares de Andrade, illustrious descendant of the Counts of Andrade of Galiza, and also founder of the Monastery of Annunciada: these houses were built in the year 1530, and following some modern work on them, they are among the best in Lisbon. They have a magnificent entrance, which leads to a cloister of columns with a fountain in the middle, and on to a room at a lower level where there are grottoes and fountains which provide comfort in the summer, and a library considered to be the best in Portugal due to the large number of books of quality it contains, and which is adorned with globes and mathematical instruments, medals and other antique items. From here, one descends to a spacious garden with a fountain made by Beruino, which is one of the best to have come out of Spain. Outside the garden is a large pathway covered with netting, being full of birds, while another part is composed of trees and delicious vegetable-gardens. On the top floor, which one reaches by means of a sumptuous staircase, one

Retiring to their estates in the Alentejo, the Dukes of Braganza maintained a court at their palace between 1580-1640. The gardens retained, however, a sixteenth century and indigenous character, with high walls, orange and lemon trees and a large number of lakes.

Jardim do Bosque (formerly Jardim da Duqueza).
Ducal Palace of Vila Viçosa.

'Penha Verde, due to its location, is the best situated for diversity and beauty of any villa in the kingdom and the country on every side presents a wild assemblage of striking scenes: mountains and valleys interspersed with rocks, woods and water, and small temples and grottoes are constructed in diverse parts of the gardens...'
James Murphy. 1789. (I)

Terrace and belvedere of the circular chapel of Our Lady of the Mount, in the gardens of the Quinta da Penha Verde. Sintra.

sees four different rooms adorned with precious furniture and excellent paintings, and all open on to a courtyard with a mosaic floor and various fountains and statues'.[14]

Also lost to us are the gardens of the house of the Count of Castelo. Better ones were visited by Cosimo de Medici on his journey to Portugal, but Corsini noted: [the garden] is between the Count's house and that of the Countess of Odemira, which are very good, and which permits communication between both residences. The garden which is uneven, being very steep in one part, has some steps decorated with majolica, which are given the name 'talavera' in Spain, but glazed tiles here. There are various fountains with statues, among which is one made in Holland and offered by King Dom João: a very interesting grotto of shells and mother-of-pearl. The whole is elegant and well laid out; however, one is unable to see on what they can have spent those large amounts of money they are said to have spent there'.[15]

The fact that 'the garden is not very large' and 'one is unable to see on what they can have spent those large amounts of money' has to be seen in the context of European taste and the preference of European princes for very extensive gardens, which would have been incompatible with the Portuguese tradition of privacy and spatial containment. In comparative terms, Corsini is much more full of praise as regards this garden than he is about that of the Count of Torre (later the Marquis of Fronteira).

EVOLUTION OF THE STRUCTURE
of mannerist space

Despite a somewhat doubtful Italian influence, especially in decorative elements, the gardens of the seventeenth century maintain spatial characteristics which, in general terms, have little to do with the Italian garden, but which, instead, are connected to a more naturalist and organic indigenous tradition.

In architecture, we see large houses adapting themselves to the landscape, rather than imposing an orderly rationalist structure on both the site of the house itself and the land around it.[16]

The longitudinal axis along which the whole of the landscaping plan is laid out in the Torres estate — the approach lane to the house, the crescent-shaped entrance courtyard, the central courtyard, the main entrance, the great hall, the garden lake and small temple[17] — is a unique case of importation that had no influence whatsoever on the landscaping art of the seventeenth century.

The gardens of the time also reveal a certain absence of this rationalisation, which had previously been a self-contained element in both the house and its relationship with the exterior spaces.

Each garden seemed to acquire its spatial characteristics in

Dated 1651, the Birds' Fountain and the group of landscape works undertaken by Bishop Dom Francisco de Castro mark the beginning of the group of gardens constructed after the Restoration of Independence.

Quinta da Penha Verde. Sintra.

79

Above and to the right. *Details of the Birds' Fountain and the inscription 1651. Tile-work, which was almost solely restricted to religious architecture in the first half of the seventeenth century, makes its appearance here in the gardens. Used on frames, flowerbeds and pilasters, the tile-work of the period reveals qualities that are more architectural than pictorial.*

Quinta da Penha Verde. Sintra.

accordance with the conditions of the terrain and the views, adapting itself to the fact of life that Portugal was cut off from Europe.

This naturalist tendency shows itself in the words of Corsini when he writes about the gardens of the Counts of Castelo Melhor: *'The garden is not very large, but it has been marvellously adapted to the location, which is uneven, being very steep in one part'.*[18]

The same can be still be observed today in the gardens of the Fronteira Palace. The lack of grandeur that Corsini complained of in Portuguese gardens was passed over in favour of a quality that reflected a certain enjoyment of life and which was said to have more affinity with architecture than landscape.

Besides the discontinuous character of the different exterior spaces, especially in the south and centre of the country, one can see a clear spatial containment in gardens. Spaces return to the inside, protected by high walls, or are developed into terraces which have no connection with the landscape, except for taking advantage of the views afforded by them.

Alexis de Jantillet, when describing the main garden of the Fronteira Palace in *Horoe Subsecivoe*, wrote: *'Surrounding the garden, there is, besides an outer and higher wall, another inner*

Above. *The Tiled Fountain. Dating to the 1640s and 1650s the tile design continued the ancient influence of the Italian majolica tradition of the sixteenth century and the first half of the seventeenth century. On both the spout and benches, restoration work, carried out in 1940 by Eduardo Leite, is visible. Missing tiles have been replaced with Viuva Lamego tiles.*

Quinta da Penha Verde. Sintra.

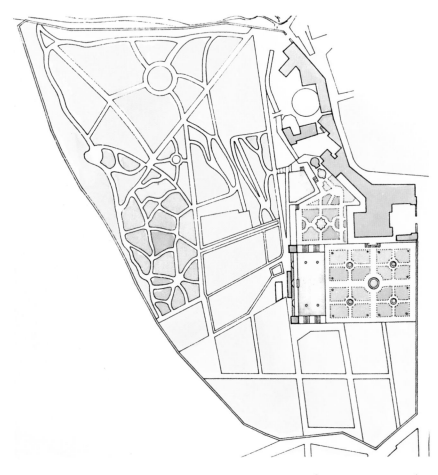

A unique case, the gardens of the Fronteira Palace were part of a group of gardens (most of which have disappeared today), which included the gardens of the Palace of the Counts of Castelo Melhor, the gardens of the Palhavã Palace and the gardens of the Counts of Ericeira (the Anunciada Palace).

Plan of the group of gardens of the Fronteira Palace. São Domingos de Benfica. Lisbon.

wall which is lower, the two being separated by alternating flowerboxes and benches'.[19] These walls, which in many cases were destroyed in the nineteenth and twentieth centuries, gave the gardens an atmosphere of spatial containment which was closely connected to their architectural concept.

Corsini also refers to the same spatial characteristics when he describes the gardens of the Palace of Alcântara *'...formed by various small gardens'.*[20] The archives of this palace, which was created between 1636 and 1643, describe it with a little more precision: *'and the whole of this garden is surrounded by walls of stone and limestone'.*[21]

These walls were decorated in keeping with the individual garden and the importance of its location, following the rigorous hierarchy of each exterior space.

Also of great importance was the place which women occupied in the house and social life. The need for absolute privacy on the part of a woman in relation to people from outside the house meant that certain gardens were more private, both in terms of not being seen and in terms of access to other gardens which were more social in nature.

We must not forget that in the seventeenth century the life of women, especially if they belonged to the nobility, hardly differed at all from that of women in an Islamic culture, which led to Duarte Nunes writing at the time: *'When the ladies go out, it is only to the church and they never leave their homes to go to any other place; the noblest of all go to church very rarely and when they do so, they take shawls to cover their faces'.*[22]

Monconys also referred to this practice when he wrote: *'The men here are very jealous and do not permit their wives to leave the home except to go to Mass, on feast days, and no one would dare to greet a woman without running the risk of being killed; maidens never leave the home and do not attend mass but three or four times a year'.*[23]

These customs are clearly reflected in both the structure of gardens and in their names. The exterior spaces of the Palace of Vila Viçosa today still bear names like the Duchess Garden and the Ladies' Garden (Jardim das Damas). The Palace of Belém also has its Ladies' Courtyard.

The gardens of the Fronteira Palace, despite their Italianate elements, also reveal a discontinuous spatial concept. From the Great Garden, privacy is progressive to the Chapel Terrace, the ancient Oratory Walk. The Garden of Venus, on a higher level than the Great Garden, has no direct relationship with this, the connection between them being made by means of a passage in one of the small towers of the Kings' Gallery. Raised up above the Garden of Venus, and laid out in an almost hidden part of the garden, is the Chapel Walk, which appears as a veiled jewel. It is connected to the Venus Garden in what might be termed a discontinuous way, namely by means of some small stairs that are part of the pavilion at the top of the terrace. The richness and splendour of the decoration emphasise the cryptic character and dignity of the place in relation to the other spaces.

These concepts have their roots in a Mediterranean-Islamic tradition, with a strong sense of contrast between sacred and secular, interior and exterior, which was, however, progressively diluted the closer Portugal moved towards the Franco-Germanic cultures, which were the originators of the main aesthetic currents of the eighteenth and nineteenth centuries.

'This (villa) which is small, is being constructed with taste, and has a garden with various flowerbeds, statues and embossed work... There are also five large fountains as well as other smaller ones distributed at various heights due to the irregularity of the land...' Corsini. 1669. (II)

View of the box garden with the house in the background and, left, a detail of the fountain.

Fronteira Palace. São Domingos de Benfica. Lisbon.

'Encircling the garden is, besides a higher, exterior wall, an interior and lower one, and these are alternately separated by flowerbeds and benches.' Alexis de Jantillet. 1678. (III)

The Lake House imposes on the box garden a character that is both monumental and intimate at the same time. This characteristic spatial containment of Portuguese gardens was to be seen in the seventeenth century in the form of a high wall encircling the garden.

View of the Large Garden.
Fronteira Palace. São Domingos de Benfica. Lisbon.

DECORATIVE SHELL-WORK
and Indo-Portuguese art

The great innovation of the period was decorative shell-work. This was closely linked to the taste for Oriental artefacts and can be seen in Indo-Portuguese furniture inlaid with various materials and bright colours, in hand-printed cloths and quilts which completely covered the interiors of the rooms, in religious statuary and items worked in gold, in the themes of the so-called 'carpet' glazed tiles and, in general terms, in the architecture of interiors.

The tendency towards 'magic', the refusal to give a structure any value, covering it instead with a shining film and reflected lights, and negating shape in favour of the value given to the space, separates Portugal from the rationalist tendency of Renaissance and European mannerism.

Decorative shell-work is also the result of the Portuguese link with India. It is interesting to observe that for Corsini this was the most typical aspect of the Portuguese gardens he visited. In his ill-humoured notes, he takes the trouble to mention the different materials: *'Grottoes adorned with mother-of-pearl, pieces of porcelain, glass of various colours, marble splinters of various types',*[(24)] when referring to the gardens of the Count da Torre, (later Marquis of Fronteira). Corsini also refers to the gardens of the Counts of Castelo Melhor: *'...a very interesting grotto of shells and mother-of-pearl'.*

The shell-work was not the only thing which encircled the grottoes, for they provided the right atmosphere for the expression of an art connected with the taste for magic and mystery.

The archives of 1673 relating to the possessions of the Marquises of Fronteira and, a little later, the description of the same palace by Alexis de Jantillet, provide us with a report and a detailed list of works in which shell-work was used.

Next to the present Garden of Venus and the summer house was a maze with a summer house (which no longer exists) in the centre. It was covered with laurel and supported by four marble columns and in the centre was *'a pyramid made of fragments of glass and Chinese ceramics, a kind of ornate covering of small shells and pearls, among other things, which spouts out water in the shape of an open crown, thereby creating a lake which is decorated in various colours; near to this is a couch on which one can lie down if one feels like it and sleep a siesta on summer days, with the sound of slowly falling water in the background'.*[(25)]

The archive of 1673 is, however, more precise when referring to the wall, which is smooth today, and which descends from the chapel terrace to the maze (the present Garden of Venus): *'...and the veranda decorated with shells on the garden side of the maze...',*[(26)] or when referring to the perfect and smooth arches which surround the statues on the chapel terrace, also formerly decorated with shells: *'...and above them in some niches containing eleven plaster half-busts encircled with laurel and with the niches partly decorated with shells'.*[(27)]

Also next to the present Garden of Venus, where the original summer house stood and which the archive of 1673 refers to as *'the house of mirrors'*, there existed other shell-work decorations: *'There is a walk that is flanked by stone flowerboxes next to the thorn bush maze, while on the same walk, where it passes along the side of the wall, there are seven large bronze figures placed in alcoves decorated with shells. Further on, next to the water tank, there are some stone seats decorated with crude glazed tiles which have shell-work both above and at the ends, where there are also plaster bosses, and there is a stonework staircase which leads on to the same walk and another which descends to the thorn bush maze, while in the water tank there are two large figures, also cast in lead, and six of the seven bronze figures spout water to different parts and they are all placed in their shell-work decorated niches'.*[(28)]

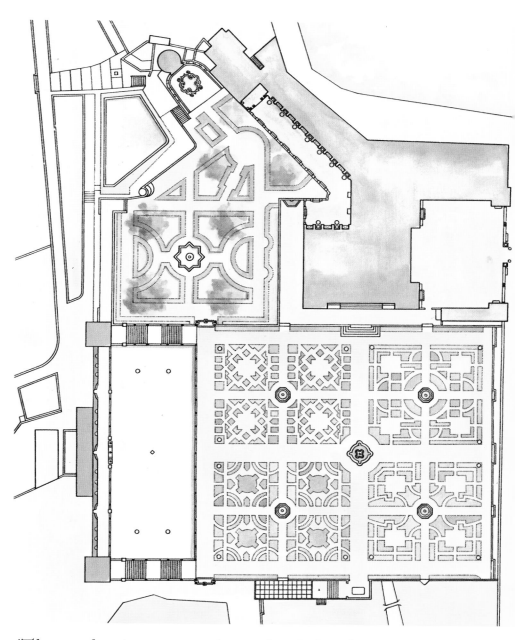

'The garden is not very large, but it has been marvellously adapted to the site, which is not level, being very steep in one part'. Corsini. 1669.[(IV)]

This capacity of adapting to the land which Corsini referred to in the gardens of the Count of Castelo Melhor, reveals an attitude in the conception of the gardens that is more empirical than rationalist, and this is also to be seen in the gardens of the Fronteira Palace.

Plan of the gardens of the Fronteira Palace. São Domingos de Benfica. Lisbon.

The shell-work (which has disappeared in some parts), was the most interesting aspect Corsini noted, both in this garden and in that of the Counts of Castelo Melhor.

The Lake House. Façade decorated with shell-work and tiles. Fronteira Palace. São Domingos de Benfica. Lisbon.

Shell-work decoration in grottoes, summer houses, walls, niches and arches, became one of the most typical elements of Portuguese gardens, and created an art form with a naturalist tendency, somewhat naive at times, but with a strong inventive and poetic value.

The use of diverse types of materials, bits of Chinese porcelain, glass, shells and small stones, made shell-work decoration an art form that was infinitely varied, and which introduced into the outside space a magical element which had a close affinity with the Portuguese liking for glazed tiles.

THE WALK
and the Roman tradition of the deambulatory

A careful reading of the archive of 1673 of the gardens of the Marquises of Fronteira mentions three walks that are referred to as being private places. The terrace of the chapel is called the 'formoso passeio' (the beautiful walk); created by Alexis de Jantillet,[29] its name suggests a different meaning from that which we give it today. The floor paving is 'notable for stones of various colours',[30] which emphasise the ceremonial character of the place.

These walks constitute autonomous spaces, spaces independent of the structure of the whole, and which tend towards the ancient concept of the Roman deambulatory. The deambulatory is a place for strolling and for leisure, and the benches and facing pairs of seats are always connected with its space. The deambulatory is radically different from the axial pathways and secondary lanes which allow European gardens to be crossed as if they were a single space.

The large trellis of the Reguengo orchard at the Palace of Vila Viçosa, which is truly grandiose, or the old trellis of the Agua de Peixes Palace, are both integral parts of this tradition which goes back to much earlier times, as we have seen in the walks of the Bacalhoa estate.

The walk of the Casa do Lago, inspired by the gardens of the Fronteira Palace, comprises a private place with two doors in the small towers and no direct passage to the two wide staircases which flank the lake.

POLARISING ELEMENTS
of space

With a non-rationalist vision of both the universe and of space, with no logical relationship between the interior and exterior, between the whole and its parts, each garden acquired its own characteristics and individuality. This individuality tended, especially in more elaborate cases, such as the gardens of the Fronteira Palace, to manifest itself in the form of polarising elements in each space. These elements, besides focusing attention inwards rather than outwards, and giving the gardens a certain crypto-spatial containment, were also structural elements of the space as opposed to the main axis of the whole in the central

'There opens up a beautiful walk: the pavement of this is notable because of the stones of diverse colours...and on the opposite side, along the whole of the length of the walk, there is a gallery of very beautiful marble, containing vases with flowers and benches ready to receive those people who are tired out from walking...' Alexis de Jantillet.
Horœ Subsecivœ. 1678. (V)

Jantillet also used the word ambulato for the chapel and the Lake House walks of the Fronteira Gardens, emphasising their residential qualities. The chapel walk, which is reached via the chapel, is decorated with tiles and shell-work.

Garden of the Fronteira Palace. São Domingos de Benfica. Lisbon.

'An open-air veranda walk which overlooks the maze and which faces the Oratory...it is composed of tile-covered arches in the niches of which are nine figures carved from jasper'.
Inventory of 1673.[VI]

The terrace or gallery of the chapel, which is part of the tradition
of the deambulatory (a place for meeting and walking), explains
the ritualised character of this fundamental element of Portuguese
gardens. There is a similar connection in the gallery of the Quinta
da Bacalhoa, or in the gallery which encircles the Great Lake of
the gardens at Queluz.

Above and opposite. *Oratory walk and chapel entrance. Gardens
of the Palace of the Marquises of Fronteira.*
São Domingos de Benfica. Lisbon.

89

'At the site of the spring of the aforementioned terrace is a beautiful lake and it is by the sides of this lake that one goes up two excellent staircases to a beautiful veranda...where there are twelve niches, in which one finds life-size statues, made in Italy, and the niches are connected to each other by a band of rough tiles'.
Description of the gardens of the Count of Castelo Melhor
— Later Antas da Cunha.
Carvalho Costa. 1716. (VII)

European tradition.

The great lake, the splendid fountain, the summer house, the walk, the small, isolated church or chapel (found more in the north of the country), became typical elements of the space of Portuguese gardens, as has already been seen in the fifteenth and sixteenth centuries. The water-mirror, which we have already seen at Agua de Peixes, Bacalhoa and Torres, as a fundamental element, remained with all its symbolic value in the gardens of the Fronteira Palace. Its Moorish character is specifically mentioned by Geoffrey and Susan Jellicoe in their book *The Landscape of Man*.[31]

Because of its scale and decoration, the great lake of the Fron-

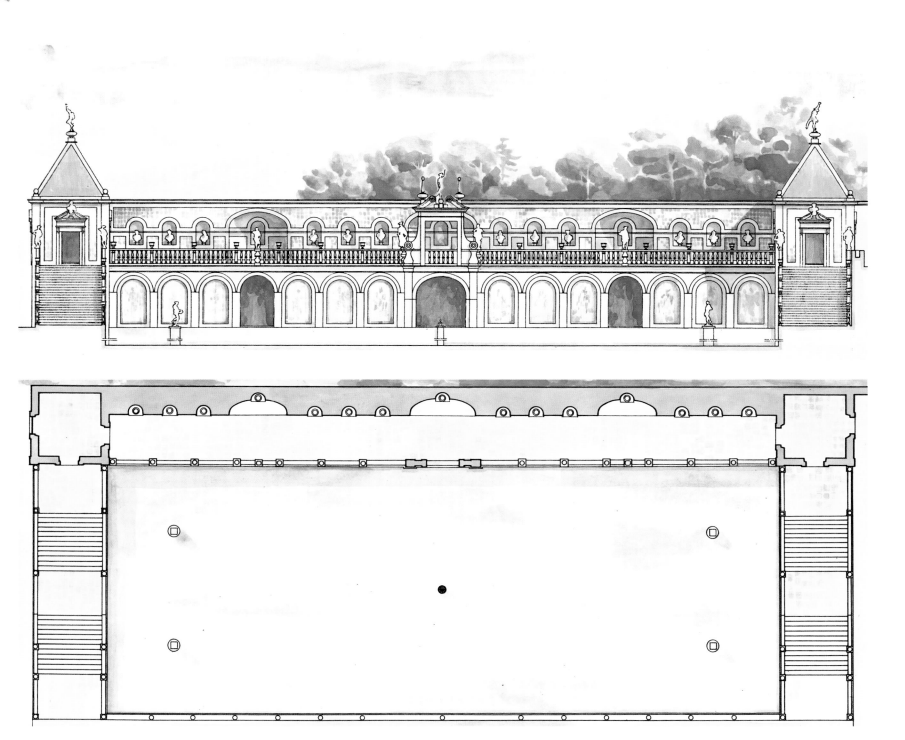

The affinity between the gardens of the Fronteira Palace and those of the Palace of the Counts of Castelo Melhor is clearly noticeable.

The lake, according to Carvalho e Costa, was 'constructed in the shape of an egg... it held over a thousand pipes of water... with a barrier formed of twelve pillars with balls and finials, and from pillar to pillar there ran architraves and balustrades which, with their bases, formed a beautiful railing, all in alabaster, which came from Estremoz...'. The group of gardens of the Palace of the Counts of Castelo Melhor is therefore of an earlier era — Corsini refers to it in 1669 — and would have been the inspiration for the Lake House of Dom João de Mascarenhas.

Left and above. *Elevation, plan and detail of the Lake House at the garden of the Fronteira Palace.*

Following pages

Global view of the Lake House. Garden of the Fronteira Palace. São Domingos de Benfica. Lisbon.

91

Camellias from the end of the sixteenth century brought directly from Japan. These old trees, internationally recognised as being the first camellias to have arrived in the West, are thus much earlier than the tree brought by Father Camélia to Italy and distributed in Europe in the eighteenth century.

Garden of the Palace of the Counts of Campo Belo. Gaia. Oporto.

teira Palace is, without a doubt, the most brilliant example of a water-mirror lake in Portugal. But a great lake also appears as a polarising element at the Calheta Palace, in the garden of the General Estate at Borba, and in the former lake of the Queluz Palace in front of the Throne Room.

THE NORTH OF THE COUNTRY
and the arrival of the Baroque garden

The rise to power of the Braganzas did not bring any significant alterations to the domestic architecture of the nobility in the north of the country. The austere tower was the essential element from which the noblemen's houses originated, although little by little a small residential element was added. In some cases, a veranda of Tuscan columns opened on to the exterior, which suggests a change in taste and a greater interest in the dwelling. The manor house was an important symbol of power and domination over the region.

Ilídio Araújo, in *Landscaping Art and the Art of Gardening in Portugal*, refers to this: *'From the middle of the sixteenth century to the end of the seventeenth century, it is still mainly in the southern part of the country that landscaping art is to be found both in greater splendour and a larger number of creations'.*[16]

During this period, however, the development in the gardens of the north can be seen much more clearly and was already noticeable in the country retreats of the bishops in the centre and north of the country.

The choice of granite as the material *par excellence* in the garden for walls, benches, flowerboxes and different decorative elements, gave an austere and robust atmosphere. The durability of granite does not allow for the detail found in stonework or marble, nor is it compatible with the glazed tile which, as we have seen, is more or less limited to the south and centre of the country.

In contrast to a certain sophistication in the south, the north developed a tendency towards magnificence and size as regards fountains (as is the case at the Quinta de Fiães in Avintes or the Quinta de Simães near Felgueiras), and also in topiary, in both the shaping of boxwood and, much more specifically, in the typical northern cherry trees.

The few examples of seventeenth century gardens in the northern part of the country clearly reflect the austerity of life there. The tendency of the north towards a more formal vision of art gave rise in the eighteenth century to the flourishing growth of northern Baroque, and this was also expressed in the seventeenth century in the development of topiary. This art allowed for a dynamic and spontaneous expression, which has always had little attraction for the more Mediterranean and Islamic south.

Topiary seems to have developed mainly from the time of the introduction of the camellia from Japan to Oporto at the end of the sixteenth century. The tradition is that on the estate of the lords of Campo Belo, at Gaia, the camellia planted in the garden had come directly from Japan in the sixteenth century. The truth of this tradition was proved a few years ago by international spe -cialists who, besides classifying the camellias as being from the sixteenth century, confirmed that they were the oldest in Europe.

The camellia adapted well to the climate and became a characteristic element of the gardens in the north and centre of the country, and were sculpted into various shapes.

The most interesting example is perhaps that at the country residence of Celorico de Basto. Here the the camellias have been trimmed into various shapes of small houses, in which windows have been cut. At one end of the garden, which is raised above the access road to the house, there is a granite balustrade of very simple design, characteristic of the late seventeenth century.

Also typically northern is the opening up of the garden to the outside and the countryside. At a higher level than the house, the garden is laid out over a wide terrace with a passageway leading directly to the first floor rooms. In relation to the house, the garden is a totally independent space, indicating none of the anxieties about a lack of privacy which existed in the south and centre of the country.

Identical in size to the garden of Celorico de Basto, and managed in the same way, are the gardens of the Palace of São Cipriano. Instead of camellias, we see box cut into different sizes and shaped into high walls with pine cones on top. Along a central axis, a narrow avenue connects the terrace at the front of the house to a lake which is next to the wall surrounding the garden. Superb Tuscan columns, of seventeenth century design and identical to those on the veranda overlooking the entrance, provide a framework for this lake, giving the whole a seventeenth century appearance.

The large size of this lake, which is not in keeping with the northern tendency of achieving dynamic effects from large fountains, indicates a cultural cross influence between the north and the south. The lake at the Palace of São Cipriano has some simi-

Radically separating itself from the South, the North developed a garden art with a strong formal and monumental appeal. The wall fountain here appears as a characteristic of this aesthetic trend.

Seventeenth century wall fountain and principal façade facing the entrance courtyard of the Quinta de Fiães. Avintes. Oporto.

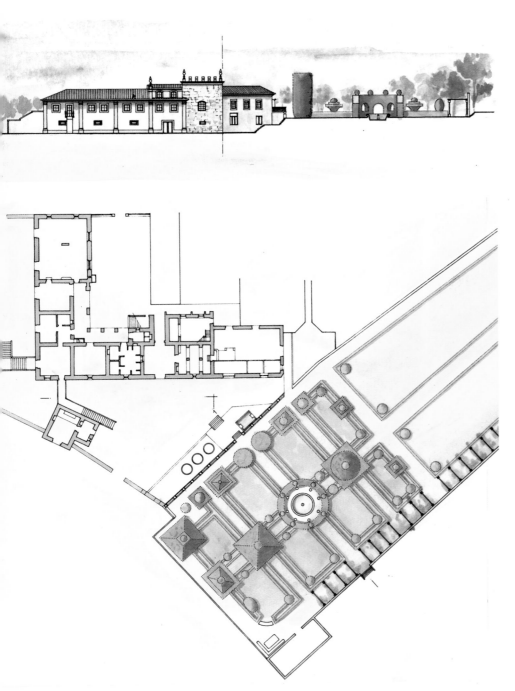

Elevation and plan of the house and gardens of the Casa de Campo. Celorico de Basto.

larities with the great lakes of Bacalhoa, Torres and Fronteira.

In this garden there is a summer house, now in ruins, but with two windows and a main door framed in stone-work of Manueline design. This design is the same as that on the entrance door of the palace, proving that the house underwent large-scale works at this time, and that they extended to the garden, a fact which is somewhat rare in the north of the country.

Also of interest, not only because of their monumental nature, but also due to the form in which they have reached us, are the gardens of the Quinta do Alão, on the outskirts of Oporto. Except for the last terrace, which seems to bear signs of renovation work carried out in the middle of the eighteenth century, the whole is perhaps the best preserved seventeenth century garden. The ancient camellias, and the watering system, walls, flowerboxes, benches and octagonal lake, which have been shaped out of granite, make the Quinta do Alão a typical example of a seventeenth century garden which, in the majority of cases, we only find in dispersed fragments or in descriptions.

Besides the development of the art of topiary, the gardens of the north were more influenced by religious art than those in the south. The bishops' palaces and their country retreats and, in particular, the staircases of the sanctuaries, came to influence the planning of outside space, for example in cases involving decorative elements.

In the Casa de Simães, near Felgueiras, an enormous walled terrace is marked by the presence of five enormous mannerist fountains. The ends of the wall are joined to the coping of the fountains, in an extremely effective entwined SS sequence. These fountains are, without a doubt, connected with the seven fountains at the Quinta de Santa Cruz of the Bishops of Oporto, which are described by Cadaval Gracio Calidónio,[17] as well as with the fountains of the staircase of the chapel of São Bento in the Tibães Convent.

This tendency to a formal monumentality is another reason why the gardens of the Palace of São Cipriano are held up as being atypical in the north of the country where great fountains have been substituted by a water-mirror lake instead.

THE GARDENS OF THE ROYAL PALACE
of Alcantara in 1636-1643

Though both house and gardens have been lost, documents of the estate, made between 1636-43, give a great amount of detail on the character, structure and decorative elements of a garden in the first half of the seventeenth century.

Although it is a royal garden, its recreational character is nea-rer to a typical garden of the numerous farms and palaces on the outskirts of Lisbon during the seventeenth century.

«A quinta d'Elrei sita em Alcantara que foj tomada a j.º Baut.ª Reuelasques pello q ficou deuendo no contrato da Mina, a qual tem casas sobradas com súas logeas per baixo e tres tercenas e per cima saõ des casas com dois antresolhos e huã escada de pedraria e são todas forradas e ladrilhadas com casa de adega cozinha e forno

It is from the camellias that were taken to the gardens of the Counts of Campo Belo that camellias spread, during the seventeenth century, throughout the north of the country, as can be seen in the gardens of the Fiães, Alão and Casa de Campo estates.

The latter estate is, without doubt, the most interesting monumental element in the North being expressed in topiary as well as in large wall fountains and free-standing granite fountains. Perspective of a group of summer houses shaped from camellias, and left, a corner of the garden with a view over the entrance courtyard.

Casa de Campo. Celorico de Basto.

The exceptional character of these gardens is seen mainly in the architecture which, in the eighteenth century, took on a more sculptural aspect.
Centre of the garden.

Casa de Campo. Celorico de Basto.

estrebaria e palh.º e casa de moços com hu corredor e pegado cõ as ditas casas. No Prom.ᵗᵒ coadro ha tres ruas de parreiras com quatro a atravessaõ e todas cõ seus pilares de aluenaria e madeiram.ᵗᵒˢ estão cheos de arvores despinho e outras fruitas e no dito prim.ᵗᵒ coadro ha tres tanques e dous delles tem figuras que lação agoa e tudo este coadro he cercado de parede de pedra e cal a roda e o 2º coadro he todo de vinha e as ruas delle são todas de aruores despinho e outras aruores e tem hu alpendre de madeiram.ᵗᵒ com hu nicho e assentos de pedra e azulejo e tem huã fonte de m.ᵗᵒ boa agoa em q estaõ tres figuras cubertas cõ seu alpendre e junto ao dito tanque esta hu aposento de casas que serue de hospedes cõ sua varanda e logeas por baixo e no 3º coadro ha does aposentos de casas piquenas com repartim.ᵗᵒˢ por baixo dellas q seruiraõ pa. auens ¹ e junto a estas casas está hu portal grande propianho que sae p.ª as terras do Casal da dita quinta tem ruas de paredes de muro com seus pilares per cima que bem maõ ⁿᵒ nas Parr.ᵃˢ que vaõ por cima, e no dito 3º coadro está huã arca de agoa que vaj a huã fonte que está pegada com o pombal e coelh.ᵃ e per baixo della tem vinhas tabolr.ᵒˢ desta. E o 4.º coadro he o q se chama do laberinto que he todo de aruores despinho e tem m.ᵗᵃˢ aruores de diuersas fruitas com hu muro q tem sete nichos com figuras de Releuo, e da outra banda do Pombal plo. Poente fica outra parede que tem dês nichos E oito figuras de Releuo e tre capelas.

Toda a dita quinta Redondam.ᵗᵉ assij e da man.ʳᵃ que está confrontada e com os muros que a cercaõ a roda e com m.ᵗᵃ contidade de canos cubertos e descubertos pellos quaes vem agoa aos tanques e esguichoˢ foj aualiada em i2 contos de r.ª tendose resp.ᵗᵒ aos tres mil E duz.ᵗᵒˢ rs. que se diz se pagão de foro das casas da dita quinta.

Transcribed by Júlio de Castilho, *A Ribeira de Lisboa,* 3rd edition. Volume III. Note 3.

(The description of the palace and gardens provides us with a Mediterra-nean ambience of exterior spaces divided into small walled-in gardens which have a magnificent view overlooking the mouth of the river Tagus. Also refer-red to is the presence of tiles and brick masonry decoration which we still find in eighteenth century Portuguese gardens in the centre and south of the country.)

DESCRIPTION OF THE GARDENS
of the Counts of Castelo Melhor

When Carvalho Costa described these gardens, they were no longer owned by the Counts of Castelo Melhor, but by the Antas da Cunha family.
The similarity of the description of Carvalho Costa to that of Corsini during the travels of Cosimo de Medici is clear.

A quinta occupa a distancia, que vay do bayrro de S. Joseph ao de Santa Anna, & da Annunciada ao Campo do Curral: tem doze passeyos largos, & compridos, alguns delles lageados, & azulejados de brutesco, com fermosos, & bem lavrados pilares de pedraria, grandes parreyras, & muytas paredes vestidas de varias, & vistosas flores. Nos taboleyros que dividem as ruas, se achaõ grandes, & frondosos arvoredos silvestres, & fructiferos, que formaõ amenos bosques, aonde continuamente se ouve a armonia dos passaros, que os habitaõ. Tem dous taboleyros de jardim, o primeyro fica debayxo das janellas da galaria, que olham para dentro da quinta, o segundo em huma elevaçaõ, a que se sobe do primeyro passeyo por huma escada de cantaria, que tem vinte degráos, & outros tantos palmos de largo. Ao Nascente do dito taboleyro está plantado hum fermoso lago, todo de bem lavrada cantaria, feyto em forma de ovado, que leva mil, & tantas pipas de agua, & nelle andaõ muytois & grandes peyxes de diversas castas: pelos lados deste lado se sobe por duas bem lançadas escadas a huma fermosa varanda, que em fórma de meya Lua cerca ametade do lago com huma grade, que se compoem de doze pilares de cantaria, com bolas, & remates, & de pilar a pilar correm alquitravas, & balaústres com seu guarda chapim, que fórmam huma

The interior gallery of summer houses shaped from camellias.

Following pages
Garden above the entrance courtyard.
Casa de Campo. Celorico de Basto.

the arched dome and the stone benches, the tiles are carefully applied in long bands and in corners, and are defined more as a structural element of the space than as a simple decorative element. Framed by the long bands and the corner tiles, the interior panels are subject to architectural lines, and are the fruit of the achievements and experiments carried out in the first half of the seventeenth century.

The date 1651 is inscribed in Roman numerals in the centre of one of the interior arches, and because the tile-work here looks later than that in the chapel of São João Baptista and the Fontes chapel, which date to between 1640 and 1650, it may be the inscription marks the end of Dom Francisco's work and his desire to set down this date in the gardens.

GARDENS AND PALACE
of the Marquises of Fronteira

In February 1669, Cosimo de Médici, Grand Duke of Tuscany, visited this palace which, although not completely finished, was worthy of receiving such a distinguished prince. His chronicler refers to the tiles in the gardens and other areas, omitting, however, the great lake which had not yet been constructed.[1]

According to the treatise of Dr. José Cassiano Neves, *The Gardens and Palace of the Marquises of Fronteira* (Lisbon, 1941), the palace (at the time a hunting pavilion, since the family's usual residence in Lisbon was at Camões) was built on the orders of the 1st Marquis of Fronteira, the 2nd Count of Torre, Dom João de Mascarenhas, general of the War of Restoration, who enjoyed the confidence of Dom João IV, and who, after the campaigns, was appointed Inspector of Finances and Counsellor of State and War.

The construction of the palace absorbed a large part of the Mascarenhas income, which caused the 2nd Marquis to consider selling it in order to pay inheritance taxes.[2]

After the earthquake of 1755, the destruction of the family's Lisbon palace by fire and the tendency of the great families to withdraw to the outskirts of Lisbon led to the 5th Marquis ordering improvements and extension work to be carried out, following which he set up permanent residence there. While the interior underwent significant changes, the sophistication and magnificence of the gardens ensured they were safe from the Rocaille fashion of the mid-eighteenth century.

The Great Garden, extending longitudinally to the north façade, is framed by the Great Lake whose size dominates the whole garden. The layout of the box maze, with its two octagonal axes, forming four parterres, in the corner of which is a lead statue, closely reflects the plan of Joseph Futtenbach, in 1628, for a palace and garden. In the Fronteira Palace, however, the lake takes on a size and quality which makes it a polarising element of the whole. Integrated in the box maze design are five octagonal tanks, the one in the middle being larger and topped with the coat-of-arms of the Mascarenhas family above an armillary sphere. Along one side of the Great Lake runs the Gallery of the Kings and a long arcade with Mediterranean-looking vases. Two pavilions at the ends of the gallery, with pointed four-sided roofs, give it a more Oriental and exotic air than that already given it by glazed tiles which are used in panels, borders, pilasters and fra

At the top of the flight of stairs; a lake and Baroque fountain date from the middle of the eighteenth century.

Gardens of the Quinta do Alão. Oporto.

-mes. All of the tile-work dates from the period between 1650 and 1680. In the first series polychrome tiles are used on the two benches in the summer house and next to the terrace; these are identical to those of the Fonte dos Passarinhos and bear the date 1651. The tiles from the years 1660-1670 see the colour blue being introduced.

The description of Alexis Jantillet, written in 1678, emphasises, however, that the works were not totally completed at this time: '...and finally a private chapel, magnificently begun but not yet completed, has a vestibule covered with a mosaic floor depicting various figures'.[19]

Both this description and the archive records made a few years before, in 1673, point out an extremely important aspect of the gardens which has long disappeared: that is a series of orchards and kitchen-gardens which surrounded the present gardens and which gave it a more grandiose and Mediterranean character.

The scenic grandeur of the terrace and the five fountains at the Casa de Simães are connected by tradition to the seven monumental fountains in the gardens of the Bishops of Oporto, in Maia — today almost completely disappeared. At the same time, they herald the great landscape staircases in the north of the country.

Plan and entrance courtyard of the Casa de Simães. Moure. Felgueiras.

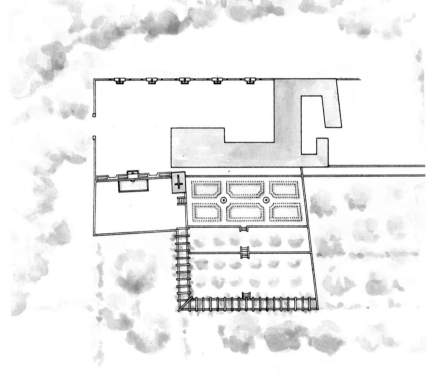

DESCRIPTION OF THE GARDENS

*and the Fronteira palace
in the archive of 1673*

Inventory and Division of the Possessions of Dona Magdalena de Castro Marquesa de Fronteira following her death, September 10, 1673.

(The most important Portuguese garden of the seventeenth century which has remained has, in this inventory of goods, all its architectural and decorative elements described in detail: many of them have now, of course, disappeared. Through this description we can obtain a much more accurate idea of the garden's characteristics in 1673.)

fólio 92 verso.

Cazinhas pequenas e a frontaria / do patejo a mão dereita digo do / patejo tem na frontaria colunas / de pedra debajxo da baranda tem / duas Cazas com duas janellas cada / huma e no mejo della huma fon / te de Agoa com sua Carranqua e a porta principal que uay pera / sima tem duas escadas de pedra / ria e cada huma por sua parte / e debajxo hum Arco com sua fonte / de duas serpentes de pedraria e Ca / rranqua e pia e ensima das duas / escadas ha pilares e bancada / de pedra com suas bolas e remates / de pedra vermemelha e tudo he ha / zulejado e fas outra baranda / mais adiane que vem a ser / vir de sala e na entrada ha sin / co portas huma delas que fica / a mão direita também huma Caza que serue de Ante Camara / de Azulejo athe o mejo da parede / com azulejo de figuras e tem Mais / huma Caza que tem huma Al / coba com o mesmo Azulejo ____ / ____ por cima de brutesco com tres jane / las que ficão sobre o patejo Com / portais de pedraria de jaspe / negro e azulejos e huma Caza / de Retrete e hum Corredor que tem / seruentia pera a Cozinha e huma //

fólio 93.

Huma baranda de pasejo descuberta / que fica sobre o Labarinto que uaj / entestar na caza do oratorio e toda / azulejada em Arcos e nichos com / noue feguras de jaspe de noue / palmos de comprido e por sima / delas huns nichos ouuados Con on / ze mejos Corpos de estuque Rode / ados de laurelles e os nichos enbrecha / dos em partes e as figuras todas lan / cão Agoa Com Canos de·dezaguar / todos pello mejo da patejo Con suas / pias de concha de·pedraria de Corte / gasa mais as lagens sobre que estão / as figuras lauradas e bornidas Con / fasse de Cortegasa e no fim da mesma / baranda Antes da porta do oratorio / esta huma baranda Cuberta de azo / lejada athe o mejo de Azulejo / de figuras e do mejo pera sima todo / embrexado Com huma fonte de / bajxo de hum Arco em Comrespon / dencia e no fronteespicio quatro / Colunas de jaspe e dois mejos Cor / pos de estuque e huma Imagem de / nosa senhora sobre a porta do ora / torio de Jaspe e os tres Arcos da ba / ranca (sic) de laurelles o oratorio / para perfeiçoar e huma Caza por / detras do oratorio Com escada que / dese pera a Carranquinha e Com ou / tra por detras do oratorio que saje / pera o Campo e toda a baranda //

fólio 93 verso.

e toda a baranda lageada de Pedras / de Cores Coadradas destremos he / seus acentos con sete Arcos na grosu / ra das paredes todos azulejados / de figuras Com seus alegretes e fages / de pedraria e a baranda enbrexada / pella parte do Jardim do Labarinto / tem mais a dita quinta a Carran / quinha huma Caza de Agoa em que / ha tres fontes Com seus Arcos ajolexa / dos de brutesco Com dezaseis nichos / e pera sima toda embrexada Com o teto / de meja laranja e suas pias de pe / draria e figuras nos nichos que bo / tão Agoa e lageada de pedra negra / e Vermelha e branca e na frontaria / da porta ha hum tanque de cara / col azulejado por fora e dentro de / Azulejo branco Con duas figuras / de dois Meninos Pedra de Jaspe / sobre dois pexes

'In this parish is the noble *Quinta de Simães*, home of the Lords of *Filgueiras*, which is enriched by many fountains, great houses, and gardens providing beautiful views, copses of many trees, and is wide in its circumference.' Serra Craesbeck. 1723. (VIII)

Lacoonte Fountain. Gardens of the Casa de Simães. Moure. Felgueiras.

Com asentos a Ro / da azulejados por bajxo de bru / tesco e por sima dos asentos Com pe / draria nelles e por sima nos Rema / tes e no mesmo jardim huma / fonte octavada Com a fegura / de A Venus e sua pia tudo de jaspe / e no coarto bajxo entrando na ba / randa do patejo ha des Cazas / humas majores que outras en·/ que ha huma abobada lageada / Com seus acentos de pedraria a Roda //

fólio 94.

que uaj pera a fonte de Venus e jun / to a Caza dos espelhos hum patejo / descuberto e todo lageado de pedra / ria de oceyras com quatro nichos / grandes azulejados the mejo / de brutesco e tudo o mais enbrexa / do e tres nichos pequenos enbrexa / dos e huma fonte com huma pia / e duas das ditas Cazas Com hu / ma Alcoba cada huma tem / mais esta quinta no coarto bajxo / hum pesejo da baranda / /lageada Com suas Colunas de pe / dra bornida de Cores Com tres degraos / que desem pera o jardim grande / Com huma ponte sobre o tamque / que tem grades de pedraria tor / neada e Com seu encosto da mes / ma pedra Com huma escada de / /pedraria que tem sete degraos / e hum pasejo pera a parte esquer / da donde esta huma nugejra / e o jardim grande Com doze Co / adros de murta e no mejo deles / ha sinco fontes de pedraria / de estremos toda laurada Com / quatro figuras de meninos Con / tronbetas na boca doiradas tem / mais doze figuras de negros Com / as Cabesas doiradas e algus Cor / pos em partes postos em seus pa //

fólio 94 verso.

em seus padrestais grandes de pe / draria branca e lavrada de des / palmos de Altura e no fim do / jardim a huma parte huma pa / rrejra Com quatro Colunas de pe / /draria Com seus acentos e hum / bofete de pedra uermelha grande / de treze palmos de Comprido e sete / de largo Com pes da mesma pedra / e todo o jardim pella parte esquerda / que fica pera a banda da estrada / he azulejada de brutesco he / Com acentos entremejos de pe / draria e por bajxo e sima na mesma / forma e a frontaria de diante / e da banda da escada a lomgo / dos tanques azolejada do mes / /mo Modo Com azulejo e pedra / ria e a parte direita do jardim / ha hum lago grande Com gra / des de pedraria redonda Com sete / figuras de jaspe grandes Con / treze Vasos de pedra estremos / branca para crauejros e tem Mais / este lago tres arcos abertos Ca / da hum Com sua caza e nichos he / quatorze arcos a face da ponte / azulejados Com seus laureis / e simalhas de enbrexado e sifras he / no mejo figuras de Corpo a Cauallo / Con os titolos dos mascarenhas //

fólio 95.

e no Arco do mejo hum Monte pamaso / Com figuras de jaspe que são noue / de quatro palmos cada huma e hum / Caualo en sima de jaspe com huma / fonte e as outras Cazas de dentro Com / sua pia e fonte Cada huma e tam / bem enbrexados dos nichos pera sima / e de cada jlharga do lago ha huma / escada de pedraria muito larga

/ e Com grades de pedraria redonda / encostos de huma e outra parte que / uaj pera hum pasejo e no remate / de cada escada ha huma Caza de / torre Coadrada e huma dellas Con / duas portas e duas janellas e a outra / Com quatro portas e o pasejo he to / do de grades de pedraria branca re / dondas com seus encostos Cõ huma ja / nela no mejo sobre o lago tudo / Com capitel e Remates de pedraria / e figura de Bronze Com doze figuras / grandes de jaspe sobre as grandes / e trinta e dois Vasos de pedra la / vrada destremos pera Crauejros / em que entrão os das escadas Com / uinte huma figuras de jaspe / de mejos Corpos dos Reis de portugal / metidas nos nichos das paredes Con li / treyros mais huã figura pera o tamque / dos lourejros também de jaspe e por / remates das duas torres ha duas fi / guras grandes de bronze e na ultima / Caza do pasejo que esta sobre o lago / pera o tamque dos lourejros pera //

fólio 95 verso.

pera a parte do sul ha hum pasejo / lagiado Com alegretes de pedra / ria ao labarinto de Aruoredo / de espinho e no mesmo paseo da / banda da parede ha sete figuras de / bronze grandes metidas en nichos / embrexados e mais pera diante jun / to ao tanque dos lourejros ha huns / acentos de pedraria bornida Com azu / lejo de brutesco embrexado por sima / Com Remates do mesmo Com figuras / de estuque e huma escada de pedra / ria que uem pera o mesmo pasejo / e outra que dese pera o labarinto / de Aruores de espinho e no tanque / dos lourejros ha des figuras gran / des também de chumbo vazado e seis / dellas botão agoa por deferentes / partes e todas estão metidas en / seus nichos enbrexados e no mejo / do labarinto de espinho ha huma / Caza Armada en quatro Colunas / de pedra Cuberta do mesmo Aruore / do e huã fonte pequena Com seu tan / que tudo enbrexado e tem muitas / aruores de lourejros e outras que / não dão fruito e pello mejo de toda / esta quinta uaj hum Rio en que ha suas / pontes que atrauesa os Jardins e he / murada e detras da caza do embrexado / há hum tanque que chamão o da fonte / de Venus e per detras do lago ha outro tan / que que serue pera regar as larangeiras / e huma fonte no mejo do laranjal //

Do laranjal de jaspe que fica de fora / do Jardim grande Com seu tamque do / mesmo jaspe ẹ botando hus Gol / finhos e a agoa tem mais a dita quinta / huma Vinha que leuara Cento / e sincoenta homes de Caua e toda / he murada a Roda e se declara / Render hum Ano por outro du / zentos mil Rs liures da despe / za não emtrando nesta Contia os jar / dins cazas fontes e Regado parte esta / quinta de huma banda com estrada / publica que uaj pera o mosteiro de / Sam Domingos de bemfica e pella / outra Con terras deste Cazal e por / outra parte com terras de Manoel / da Cunha e da outra Con terras de João / de Barreyra e humas Cazas terreas que / estão por detras do muro da quinta / a banda do Mar que são tres Cazas / em que viue o jardineiro as quais / são forras liures e izentas e huma / tera que chamão dos galegos que / leua de sameadura quinze alquej / res de trigo o que tudo declarou ho / jnuentariante ter nela gastado / asim no principal siza e escritura / e bemfeitorias the

If the interior design of the two terraces is characteristic of the eighteenth century, the surrounding box, topped by large balls and pyramids, is a seventeenth century aesthetic.

Plan of the Gardens of the Palace of São Cipriano. Tabuadelo. Guimarães.

In the foreground, the lake water-mirror with, in the background, the sixteenth century tower. The greater importance of the water-mirror to the detriment of the large fountain, sets this example as a case apart in the aesthetic of the gardens of the North, and reflects cultural interinfluences between the North and the South.

Above and left. Gardens of the Palace of São Cipriano. Tabuadelo. Guimarães.

DESCRIPTION OF THE GARDENS

and the Fronteira palace

in 1678 by

Alexis Collotes de Jantillet in Horoe Subsecivoe

"Em segundo lugar esta casa de campo está situada a uma milha da cidade, naquele caminho que chamam Benfica, donde lhe vem o nome; entrando pelo norte encontra-se o átrio, depois dois pórticos, um dos quais está construído em tríplice arcada, com seis colunas de pedra côr de ouro em cada arco, sustentando a abóbada; o outro, que está a seguir, tem os mesmos arcos e igual número de colunas de pedra transtagana azulada. Depois dos pórticos encontram-se duas alas do edifício, formando um átrio de elegante projecto; no começo destas, duas pequenas fontes abertas nas paredes servem de suporte e duas cabeças de silvanos de mármore de tamanho médio que deitam água corrente. Mais adiante um pórtico dá acesso a várias entradas; atravessando o arco médio uma fonte pura e cristalina se depara aos visitantes e nela uma cabeça de silvano, aberta num rictos, expele água para uma concha de puríssima pedra branca; ornam a fonte dois delfins iguais, de caudas erguidas para a figura do silvano e as suas bôcas, ávidas do líquido tão próximo, inclinam-se para a concha.

"Pela direita e esquerda da fonte se sobe ao andar superior, por duas escadas de mármore opostas uma à outra, as quais apresentam uma série de degraus direitos que depois se encurvam ligeiramente ao chegar ao pavimento superior, onde pequenas estátuas quadradas de mármore se defrontam.

"Igualmente nas grades, em tôda a extensão das escadas, estão dispostas colunas que susteem globos de pórfiro, tanto para uso dos moradores como para protecção dos que sobem. Estas escadas dão ingresso a uma câmara alegre e espaçosa, à esquerda da qual fica uma porta que dá entrada aos visitantes e conduz a um pórtico construído com três arcos e seis colunas a que se segue outro, igualmente em arcarias e colunas, sendo a construção de ambos sobranceira ao átrio.

"Poderei, sem despropósito, chamar a êste pórtico superior que tem uma vista ameníssima para jardins e campos, uma estufa, abrigo contra a fria tempestade do inverno, pois evita os golpes do vento norte e conserva diariamente o sol quási desde o seu nascimento; no final dêle existem dois gabinetes, luxuosamente arranjados, debaixo de cujas janelas, na mesma parede estão duas estátuas de pedra, alimentando com muita fôrça de água um lago que fica a todo o comprimento do edifício e dela é muito abundante.

"A seguir ao último dos gabinetes está uma sala adornada de estátuas e cimalhas sabiamente construídas, com as paredes revestidas de painéis pintados por mãos conhecedoras; na parte inferior dêstes estão incrustados azulejos de fundo branco, pintados de côr azulada que historiam os combates dos portugueses contra os espanhóis.

"A vista de três janelas dá para um passeio fechado cheio de jasmins perfumados e ternos nichos adelgaçados na parte superior e com lavor tecido, e do meio dos quais mana uma fonte que nasce da bôca hiante duma serpente.

"Na sala abre-se uma entrada de dois batentes para o formoso passeio; o pavimento dêste torna-se notável por pedras de diversas côres. Do lado direito fica um muro e neste, armários construídos em arco exibem imagens das artes liberais pintadas primorosamente em tijolos unidos; compartimentos cavados no intervalo dos armários, em hemiciclo, compreendem sete figuras de alabastro de planetas referentes a deuses entre os quais Apolo; próximo estão estátuas excelentes de Marsyas, êste despojado da pele que arrancou ao adversário; aos pés dêles várias figuras expelem água de canos, que recai em suave murmúrio sobre conchas fingidas e sobrepostas a um pequeno pavimento onde é absorvida por buracos de chumbo.

"Muros circulares cheios de flores e frutos variados adornam as partes mais altas e os intervalos dêles estão cheios de bustos de homens. Na parte contrária, a todo o comprimento do passeio, estende-se uma galeria de mármore de grande formosura, contendo vasos com flores e bancos dispostos para auxiliar as pessoas fatigadas do passeio.

"Ao fim uma capela particular, magnificamente começada, não tem ainda completo o vestíbulo que é revestido de ladrilho de mosaicos representando várias figuras; um menino alado oferece um gomil de bronze aos que chegam e uma pedra escavada em conchinhas recebe a água que dêle corre.

"Saindo dêste passeio existem três entradas com outras tantas portas, de dois batentes para um refeitório forrado de madeira, de pintura branquíssima, com espelhos grandes e trabalho de madeira e pedra trazida de itália, embelezada com flores de madeira; a êste, outro igual se segue com abundância e riqueza de móveis ornamentados com embutidos de tartaruga e ouro; as partes mais baixas das paredes são cercadas dos lados com pinturas importadas da Holanda, imitando o género variado de pintura de caça, montes e bosques. Existe neste refeitório uma cela mais retirada, decorada com uma mistura de pintura de ouro e onde em estrados e leitos pequenos se pode muito oportunamente dormir; seguem-se outros cubículos e alcôvas que servem de habitação às servas quando acontece ir a família morar no campo.

"Desce-se para a parte inferior do palácio por escadas de mármore; essa parte inferior é destinada ao serviço rural e uso dos trabalhadores e dos criados e contudo poucos aposentos podem competir com êles em ornato e elegância, principalmente o refeitório oblongo e contíguo ao passeio que é ornamentado de florinhas de subtil pintura semeadas pelo teto ao acaso, em alegre disposição; em redor das paredes pendem espelhos de diversos géneros com as molduras de lâminas de tartaruga e ébano e outras matérias preciosas, decorados de ouro e prata cinzelada.

"Daqui passa-se através de um pórtico baixo para a estufa, como já disse, e, depois duma pequena ponte colocada sôbre o lago, oferecem-se aos transeuntes, em direcção à parte superior do jardim; dezasseis talhões grandes, cada um dos quais está recortado em canteiros recortados de mil formas e bordados de mirto aparado, apresentando todo o género de flores em grandes variedades de côres, aos olhos desprevenidos em tôda a parte que eles incidam; estátuas de homens e mulheres, de pé, colocadas em pedestais, ornamentam, magnificamente o jardim, irrigado por cinco fontes construídas com arte notável e dispostas em xadrez: aqui numa espécie de açucena desabrocham as suas águas, ali brotam de um vaso do mais puro cristal donde repuxam no ar por múltiplos tubos.

"O espaço intermédio do primeiro passeio e das fontes é digno de ser visto pela sua magnífica estrutura: quatro meninos coroados e voltados uns para os outros, colocados pela base no cimo de colunas de mármores, expelem água por trombetas, numa grande taça de pórfiro; encosta-se a eles um vaso grande, circular cujo dentro é sustentado por um globo e este apoiado num vaso de jaspe cingido de cabeças douradas de sátiros que deitam água; no globo estão apostas as insígnias de família do dono da casa e em redor daqueles muitos tubos ressonantes.

"Acaba o jardim cheio de sombra. Desvia-te alegremente e dirige-te para um abóbada sustentada por quatro colunas e sombreada por expressas latadas; por debaixo está uma mesa de sólida pedra de pórfiro, de enorme tamanho com pequenos bancos em volta; grandes árvores que no inverno afastam e quebram os ventos mais fortes e no verão oferecem sombra aos que passam com a espessura das suas ramagens.

"Ao lado estende-se outro lago; o ponto do jardim em que ele se encontra é longo, fechado e bastante largo; ali verás patinhos nadando em bandos e um barquinho dourado. Nos quatro cantos do lago outras tantas estátuas apoiam-se em balaústres de mármore e lançam para o ar com grande ímpeto água que cai no lago com estrépito não desagradável. Marginam este, dum e doutro lado, grades de mármore sobre as quais vasos cheios e flores e figuras de ninfas estão colocados em intervalos iguais.

"Do outro lado, delineando em arcos e colunas, fica um muro mais alto com o corpo pintado, no qual são representados os antepassados da família Mascarenhas e os personagens mais ilustres, a cavalo, armados de couraças, ocupando os espaços entre colunas; na parte inferior do muro existem três grutas: a do meio mostra Helicão com Apolo e as musas e Pégaso ferindo o cume do monte com o casco; das outras correm duas fontes transparentes.

"Junto de cada extremidade do lago erguem-se escadas fronteiras e semelhantes com corrimãos e estátuas de mármore resplandecentes e na parte superior delas levantam-se duas tôrres com seu corpo hàbilmente construído; dum e de outro lado, nas frontarias, Mercúrio provido de chapéu, asas talares e caduceu, apoia-se na ponta do pé esquerdo e estende o outro como que prestes a voar.

"Entre as tôrres estende-se um passeio sôbre o lago, marginando o muro, munido de gradres decoradas com uma longa fila de estátuas; uma abertura colocada nas grades médias ostenta a figura de Mercúrio calcando um globo dourado; nas restantes grades compartimentos variados de elegante trabalho de mosaico conteem bustos dos reis lusitanos construídos de ónix.

"Uma das tôrres dá ingresso a um pequeno pórtico adornado de muitas estátuas e a êste veem dar os últimos degraus pelos quais se sobe para um pequeno mas alegre terraço.

"Êste terraço, calçado de pedras quadradas, é sombreado por árvores; ali surge um pequeno muro no qual um hábil artista criou, à semelhana da verdade, no escudo, símbolo da famílias Mascarenhas, o pelicano com os filhos e outras aves, marchetados de várias côres e formas.

"A piscina é pegada com o terraço e nela se observa um formoso bando de cisnes nadando; as margens são cercadas por estátuas que deitam água por tubos multiformes.

"Por aqui se desce para um bosque com veredas sinuosas, enrolando-se sôbre si mesmo, à maneira complicada de um labirinto; nela há um lugar umbroso tecido de frondosos e sempre verdes raminhos e abobadado sôbre quatro agradáveis colunas de elegante fabrico; uma pirâmide feita de fragmentos de vidro e de louça chinesa, espécie de ornato coberto de conchas, conchinhas e pérolas entre outras cousas, expele água em forma de coroa aberta, dando origem a um lago que é ornamentado de várias côre s; perto está um leito preparado onde te deitarás se te apetecer dormir a sesta em dias de verão, conciliando o sono com o som da água caindo lentamente.

"Um pequeno horto está junto ao labirinto e no cimo dêle um refeitòriozinho contém três compartimentos distintos, esplêndidamente calçados de mosaico com três estátuas e outras tantas fontes.

"Diante do refeitório está um pequeno lago com o pavimento e o cais de ladrilhos brancos; nêle estão quatro globos de cobre e de cada um sai água para o ar por quatro buracos estreitos; e dois delfins com as suas fontes, nas costas das quais estão sentados, soprando, meninos nus de mármore. Em volta dois canteiros cercados de buxo verdejante e denso oferecem aos espectadores narcisos, margaridas, jacintos, túlipas, escovinhas, anémonas, rainúnculos e outras delícias dos jardins; uma fonte chamada de Vénus ocupa o espaço entre os canteiros, porque a deusa, feita de mármnore polidíssimo, apertando a base do seio, esprime água numa concha redonda que lhe fica inferior; sustentam esta três delfins, reünindo as caudas num nó, com as cabeças colocadas sôbre três tartarugas, as quais derramam água em uma taça amplíssima. Do horto torna-se às casas inferiores do palácio por uma porta curvada em redondo.

"Pega-se ao palácio uma horta e no cimo dela fica a estrada militar que conduz a Lisboa. A meio há um terreno discreto no qual um monte cheio de árvores novas recebe os que entram. Alimenta-as a umidade de um tanque onde vão ter três fontes; a primeira dimana da cabeça de uma águia e o aspecto desta água assemelha-se a uma águia e o aspecto desta água assemelha-se a uma toalha.

"E do cimo do monte há descidas para uma única grande planície abundante de todo o género de produtos hortícolas tanto indígenas como estrangeiros; no plano médio está um vasto recipiente octogonal, tendo em cada canto um delfim acoco-rado que deita água pela bôca; no centro dêsse recipiente está um tronco de mármore rodeado por quatro fontes que saltam doutras tantas cabeças de faunos; colocado sôbre o tronco está outro recipiente de menores dimensões e debaixo dêste uma concha pequena sôbre um fulcro de jaspe que uma donzela esprime pelo meio com os pés, trazendo na mão um tubo do qual muitos canos pequenos lançam água que se mistura com um mumúrio muito agradável.

"Circundam o jardim, além dum muro exterior e mais elevado, outro interior e mais baixo separados alternadamente por canteiros de flores e bancos. Segue-se uma planície vasta e aberta semeada de macieiras dispostas em linha recta.

"E existem ainda no âmbito da casa de campo vários pomares e vinhas e entre estas um outeiro revestido de rosas que ninguém, pode imaginar mais belo.

"Perto, nas partes circundantes da região fica um lugar alegríssimo e campos e outeiros férteis; o conjunto dos edifícios é visível aos que os contemplam, quer em parte, quer na totalidade, notando-se em primeiro lugar o Mosteiro da Ordem de S. Domingos.

"Estas coisas que te narro vê-las-ás porventura mais pormenorizadamente, quando as tuas múltiplas ocupações to permitam, para o que te convidará não só o formoso aspecto do lugar como também a vizinhança, a não ser que tu, demasiada-mente amigo da cidade (como diz Plínio), desejes deixar de as ver.

"Adeus, Lisboa II dos Idos de Abril (11 de Abril) de 1678."

Translated by José Cassiano Neves in *Jardins e Palácio dos Marqueses de Fronteira*, 2nd edition. Pages 18-23.

(The historical importance of this garden is emphasised here by a foreigner, Alexis Jantillet, whose description was originally in Latin. He gives us details not only of the spatial characteristics but also of each of the plants and flowers which were planted in the original garden).

NOTES

1 Cited in Túlio Espanca — *Palácios Reai de Évora. Cadernos de história e arte Eborense*. 1946. Volume III, page 50.
2 Cited in Sousa Viterbo — *A Jardinagem em Portugal*. Coimbra, 1909. 2nd part, page 50.
3 Cited in Ilídio Araújo — *Arte paisagística e Arte dos jardins em Portugal*, Lis-bon, 1954, II Part, page 107.
4 M. de Monconys — *Journal des Voyages*, Lyon, 1666. III Part, page 17.
5 Transcribed by Júlio de Castilho — *A Ribeira de Lisboa*. 3rd ed., Volume III, Note 3.
6 Translated by A. G. Madahill — *Voyage of Cosimo de Medici in 1669*. In R. M., n.º 11-12, page 62.
7 José Teixeira — *O Paço Ducal de Vila Viçosa*, F. C. B. 1983, page 65.
8 Translated by Alexandre Herculano. Opúsculos. Volume VI. Lisbon 1884, page 85.
9 Transcribed by José Teixeira, ibid. Page 120.
10 Father Manuel Calado — *O Valeroso Lucideno*, 1648, page 96.
11 Túlio Espanca — *Inventário Artístico de Portugal*. Distrito de Évora. Volume I, page 630.
12 José Teixeira, ibid., page 67.
13 Father Manuel Calado, ibid. page 97.
14 Richard Flecknoe. Cited in Rose Macaulay — *Ingleses em Portugal*. Liv. Civiliza-ção. 1950.
15 António Carvalho da Costa — *Chorografia Portuguesa*. 1712 page. 306.
16 Voyage of Cosimo de Medici, ibid., page 65.
17 Idem, page 65.
18 Alexis de Jantillet — *Horoe Subsecivoe*. 1679. Translated by José Cassiano Neves in Jardins e Palácios dos Marqueses da Fronteira. 2nd ed., pages 18-23.
19 Document transcribed by Júlio Castilho, ibid., pages 246-247.
20 Idem, pages 246-247.
21 Duarte Nunes de Leão — *Descrição do reino de Portugal*. Chapter 88, folio 138.
22 M. de Monconys, ibid., 3rd part, page 14.
23 Voyage of Cosimo de Medici, ibid., page 65.
24 Alexis de Jantillet, ibid., page 22.
25 Document transcribed by José Moser, ibid., folio 93.
26 Idem, folio 93 verso.
27 Idem, folio 95 verso.
28 Alexis de Jantillet, ibid., page 20.
29 Idem. Page 20.
30 Geoffrey and Susan Jellicoe — *The Landscape of Man*. London.

Notes on Illustrations

I. James Murphy - Travels in Portugal...in the years 1789-1790.
II. Corsini - in Viagem de Cosme de Médecis por Espana y Portugal (1668-1669) Ed. and notes by Angel S. Rivero. Madrid. Page 278. Translated by A.S. Madahill. Ibid. Page 46.
III. Alexis Colletes de Jantillet - Horoe Subsecivoe. Lisbon 1679. B.N.L. Translated by José Cassiano Neves, ibid., page 23.
IV. Corsini, ibid., pg. 257. Translated by A.G. Madahill, ibid., page 65.
V. Alexis C. de Jantillet. — ibid. Translated by José Cassiano Neves ibid., page 20.
VI. Inventário de Partilhas... de 1673 ibid., folio 93.
VII. A. Carvalho Costa, ibid., page 306:
VIII. Serra Craesbeck. Memórias Ressuscitadas de Entre Douro e Minho. 1723, page 362. Manuscrypt 218-219. B. N. L.

THE CLAY CULTURE
and the tradition of the leisure-garden in the Alentejo

CHAPTER V

The fifteenth century saw a resurgence of interest in gardens and secular architecture, this movement having its origins in the Tagus basin and the Alentejo.

Only in the city of Evora '...*one of the most important in Portugal'*,[1] did Baron Léo de Rosmital, who crossed Portugal from the north to the south between 1465 and 1466, refer to a garden, one next to the Episcopal Palace, '*which contains a pleasant orchard of trees and bushes'.*

Some years later, in 1495, also in Evora, Dr. Jerónimo Müncher wrote in his itinerary about the lunch he had with King Dom João II: '*One day the king lunched in the garden lined with orange trees at the foot of the castle...this garden where he lun -ched was new, it having been planted four years previously and was surrounded by a cane hedge'.*[2]

This garden dates from a time prior to the work carried out by a new gardener whom Dom João II had had sent from Valença, in 1494, to his Palaces of Evora because '*we desire that the kitchen-garden of our palaces in the city of Evora be planted with beautiful trees and grasses of the finest quality so that the said kitchen-gardens retain a noble air'.*[3]

The few references or documents in the fifteenth century which mention gardens relate to examples in the Alentejo, and Evora in particular.

The Alentejo in the fifteenth century saw its capital become the seat of the court and the king, and it rivalled Lisbon in terms of political and cultural importance.

The almost regional character of the resurgence of Portuguese gardens, as well as all the so-called Manueline art, extends from the Lisbon area to the Alentejo, and its significance is mainly cultural in nature: it was there that one still found a Mediterranean-Islamic liking for luxury and outdoor life.

A comparison of the plans of the houses of the alcaides in the castles surveyed by Duarte D'armas at the beginning of the sixteenth century reveals a complexity in house layout of the alcaides of the south compared with the medieval Catholic simplicity found in the north.

While Serpa and Estremoz have dwellings with various rooms on two or more floors, and Moura has nineteen rooms with an orange grove carefully walled around and with an entrance door, the houses of the alcaides of the north are reduced to a tower with one or two rooms.

The cultural dividing line between the north and the south also reveals itself in the large country retreats which appear at this time in the Tagus basin and the Alentejo.

Proving that Mediterranean-Islamic cultural values had not been completely lost, the majority of these large estates displayed a soil use and spatial structure that suggests an earlier origin: Romano-Islamic.

The tower, which is integrated in some of these farms, was not the origin of the house, as has sometimes been stated, but was more a fashion and the symbol of an aristocracy which reoccupied the estates and undertook restoration work on them. As we can see in the case of the Ribafria Tower (Chapter III), the tower of the time of Dom João III which gave its name to the estate is of a later date than the houses and water tank of what was then called the Orange Grove of the Tank Estate given by King Dom Manuel.[4]

Particularly interesting is the analysis of the geographical framework in which it is to be found. The property extends into low-lying areas with no worries as to defence or dominance over the surrounding countryside. Its origin is clearly due not to defensive reasons, the medieval Catholic tradition, but to the existence

Opposite page. *Detail of the Great Lake.*
The Mitra Palace. Valverde. Evora.

of abundant water. The location of the estates in low-lying areas so that use can be made of the coolness offered by streams and springs, together with their geographical situation, namely that of being a few kilometres from a city or important town, suggests that they were at one time summer residences of the Moorish alcaides.

The Torre de Ribafria estate is located on the outskirts of Sintra, in a cool place, facing the north, on the banks of the stream at Colares. The palace of Agua de Peixes, with one of the largest springs in the south of the Alentejo, is situated on the outskirts of Viana do Alentejo. To the Palace of Sempre Noiva on the outskirts of Arraiolos, next to the Divôr river, one can add the Estate of Torre da Amoreira on the outskirts of Montemor-o-Novo, the Quinta do General on the outskirts of Borba, the Palace of Mitra on the outskirts of Evora and also the Palace of Vila Viçosa, the ancient Reguengo estate which, in the fifteenth century, was still outside the walls of the town.

Besides displaying a similarity as regards geographical characteristics, these estates almost always had a large tank — a water-mirror which combined pleasure with watering functions.

Very similar to the tank of the Estate of the Orange Groves of the Tank (later on the Torre da Ribafria estate), is the tank of the estate of Torre da Amoreira, near Montemor-o-Novo. In both cases the water-mirror runs next to and along the whole length of the façade which looks out over the gardens. To these two examples should be added that of the Palace of Aguas de Peixe and the Palace of Vila Viçosa, the latter possessing a tank which was much reduced in size in the eighteenth or nineteenth century, and referred to by different authors who describe the palace in the seventeenth century. Father Manuel Calado in the *Valeroso Luciderno* calls it: *'The lake of spring water with many fish'*,[5] and Cadornega: *'The Large Tank, which gets its name from the large amount of water it contains'*.[6] Moraes Sardinha in his *Parnassus of Vila Viçosa* (also seventeenth century), describes the Reguengo garden of the palace: *'On the right-hand side are two tanks, one of them being so wide and deep that a boat had to be used to go from one end to the other, swimming being the only other way'*.[7]

In the absence of archaeological investigation, this group of estates illustrates a particular way of dealing with outdoor spaces which shows the durability of ancient tradition prior to the fifteenth and sixteenth centuries, and which explains certain spatial characteristics and peculiarities of Portuguese gardens.

While there are few documents relating to the majority of the estates which prove their existence prior to the medieval Catholic period, we know, for example, that the Moorish alcazars of Evora and Lisbon passed from Islamic domination to Christian rule, being transformed into palaces yet never completely losing the splendour of great Moorish residences. Dom Fernando lived with Dona Leonor Teles in the old Moorish alcazar of Evora,[8] the Palace being the scene of the illicit love affair of the Queen with Count Andeiro.

According to local tradition, the south of Spain, due to the presence up to the end of the fifteenth century of the sophisticated Caliph of Granada, exercised a strong cultural influence over Portugal.

And while Dom João II had Gomes Fernandez sent from Valencia, Spanish gardeners were still to be found at the Palace of

Vila Viçosa at the end of the sixteenth century. Lorés was the gardener at the palace between 1594 and 1596,[9] and Miguel de Alcalá[10] between 1596 and 1615. The latter is also remembered by Cadornega: *'In these Royal gardens, the head-gardener was Afonso de Alcalá, who had many men under him who did what he ordered concerning the conservation and beautifying of that most attractive, delightful and sweet smelling magnificence'*.[11]

* * *

THE IMPORTANCE OF FRAGRANCE
as a feature of the garden

Cardonega, when defining the grandeur of the gardens of the Palace of Vila Viçosa, compares the olfactory aspect with that of the visual, and this reminds us of the descriptions of the Islamic poets when, in Chapter III, we analysed the characteristics of the gardens of this period.

The spatial containment of the Portuguese garden of the fifteenth and sixteenth centuries, which was created by high surrounding walls and by its small size, continued in the Alentejo almost to the present day and appears to be closely connected with the enhancement of the garden through the emphasis on fragrances.

In Chapter II we saw that the importance of the sense of smell varies from culture to culture. In the case of Portugal, it was most important up to the eighteenth century, after which it progressively lost its importance in favour of the visual sense, as can be seen in the nineteenth century with the creation of the romantic garden, a style which came about to take advantage of the available views.

The value that is placed on the olfactory sense explains the systematic use of the orange tree. As regards the Bosque Garden of the Palace of Vila Viçosa, Moraes Sardinha says: *'The flowers of the orange trees, the lemon trees and the cypresses which exist here, are the most sweet and strong smelling of all plants'*.[12]

Thus we see that the orange tree, which is the most typical element of Portuguese gardens up to the seventeenth century, and which continued to be found in the gardens of the south of the country until the twentieth, is present in the garden because it enhances the sense of smell rather than because it improves the visual quality of the garden. The Palace of the Castros (an ancient Moorish alcazar) today still has its garden of orange trees surrounded by high walls. Despite the magnificent view that the whole of the house has over the Alentejan countryside, the garden faces inwards on to itself as if to ensure that the fragrances are retained there.

Almost miraculously preserved is the Great Cloister of the Convent of Cartuxa. Its size (the largest cloister on the Iberian peninsula), and the fact that it comprises only an ample arcade without a second storey, gives it an air of being more Mediterranean-Islamic courtyard than medieval cloister, and one can clearly see that it is related to the Naranjos Courtyard in Cordoba. The orange trees are distributed regularly throughout the cloister, and a group of enormous cypresses rises up in the centre to surround a tank made of local stone.

Besides its specific architectural concept, the ambience created by the orange trees at Cartuxa reminds us of Father Jerónimo Roman's description of 1589 following his visit to the cloister of the garden of Manga where there was a fountain in the centre *'isolated among four orchards, separated by channels which fill everything with their coolness'*.[13]

The association of orange trees with cypresses takes us back from the sixteenth century to the fifteenth century and to one of the first documents about gardens: the orchard of the Palace of the Archbishops in the Fortress of Lisbon. In the contract the archbishop ordered the strict protection *'of the orange trees and the trees of the aforesaid orchards'* as well as the planting of a further *'twenty cypresses, six orange trees and three lemon trees'*.[14]

THE STUCTURE OF SPACE
and the quality of life

B esides the olfactory and visual quality of the Palace of Vila Viçosa gardens, Cadornega used the term *'delightful'*. To this quality one can add other adjectives such as *'cool'* of the gardens and *'shady enchantments'*,[15] this latter description being used in the sixteenth century at the time of the wedding reception of the Infante Dom Duarte and Dona Isabel in 1537.

Opening out from large verandas and loggias — areas which themselves are semi-exterior — the gardens of the Alentejo principally constitute spaces which are an extension of the house, and as such are treated architecturally as being areas of comfort and well-being.

Above and left. *Sixteenth century loggia and detail of the garden of the Palace of the Mascarenhas family. Vila Viçosa.*

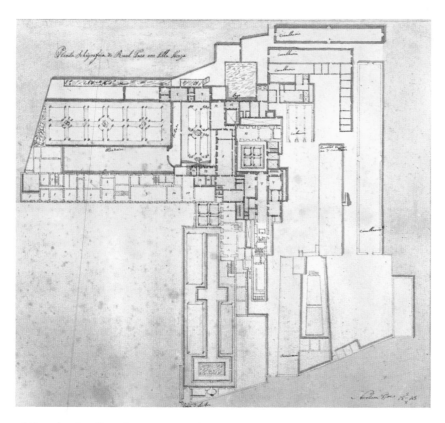

Like the Jardim do Bosque, the other gardens of the Palace of Vila Viçosa were also encircled by high walls until the nineteenth century, a feature which confers on these spaces a special character, today lost.

Plan of the Palace of Vila Viçosa. *Survey by Nicolau de Freitas in 1845. House of Braganza Foundation.*

The South Garden will always be associated with the garden concept of well-being and conviviality which is architecturally structured and closed in on itself. Communication with the exterior is established either by openings in the surrounding walls or by belvederes and porches.

Already constructed in the first half of the eighteenth century, the Quinta do Carmo, near Estremoz, is structured like a large walled-in space. From the lane which gives access to the estate, an entrance door and four windows open on to the large walled-in courtyard, which is itself walled in, there being a door and windows in the walls surrounding the garden.

These high walls give the garden a certain spatial containment and at the same time determine a strict hierarchy of privacy. We see in the Quinta do Carmo a gradual increase in privacy as we move from the access lane to the house itself, still completely open to the outside world, passing on through the entrance courtyard already reserved for the private life of the house to the walled garden, and, finally, to the summer house in the most intimate and secret part of the garden. The relationship between the summer house of the gardens of the Quinta do Carmo and that of the gardens of the Bosque at Vila Viçosa, is evident despite their being separated by almost two centuries. Both are situated at the end of the garden and are framed by a water-mirror tank, around which are distributed benches and flowerboxes. The summer house at the Quinta do Carmo may correspond to the description of Father Manuel Calado when, in the seventeenth century, he wrote about the garden of the Bosque: *'The inside of which is terraced and in it are planted many trees and beds of various flowers and the walls are full of windows... and at the end of the garden are three windows, two of which are ordinary and one, which has a balcony, is very wide and through them light enters into a pleasure house where His Highness and Lady Dona Catarina come and sit with their ladies on some summer afternoons'.*[16]

Although they possess a strict hierarchy of privacy, the gardens of the Quinta do General in Borba have a special enclosed space for open-air masses.

These masses, which were attended by people outside the close family circle, made it necessary to separate this enclosed space from the other more private gardens of the house. Separating the first garden from the second is a high wall forming a long avenue with the altar at one end and an entrance gate at the other which permitted direct entry from the exterior. Along the length of this high wall extends a long series of benches, flowerboxes and vases made from local marble. This garden has a particular refinement in the form of a narrow lake which runs between the wall and the backs of the benches. There is a row of ceramic gargoyle water spouts set into the wall which pour water out on to the lake. While the two great springs of this estate are almost completely dry today, due to the numerous water holes bored around the outskirts of Borba, one can imagine the cool atmosphere created by the numerous spouts gushing out water behind the benches.

In general terms, the gardens of the Alentejo may be seen as the representatives of the original Portuguese garden, their characteristics being eminently Mediterranean in style. The economic and social depression which took hold of the Alentejo from the eighteenth century onwards ensured that some of the most

'...and in it are planted many trees and flowerbeds of various flowers, both large and small; and the walls are all full of windows in which one can see the ladies sit on the days that feasts are held on the terrace...' Father Manuel Calado. 1648 (I)

View of the terrace and detail of a window in the Jardim do Bosque, formerly the Jardim da Duqueza.

Palace of Vila Viçosa.

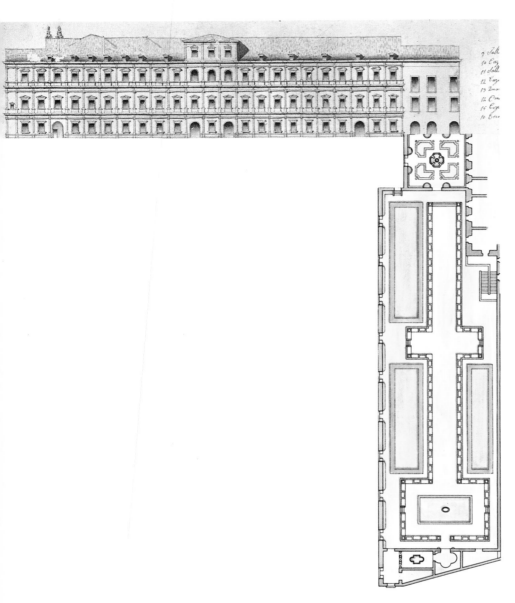

Plan of the Jardim do Bosque and elevation of the Palace of Vila Viçosa, by Nicolau de Freitas. 1845. Foundation of the House of Braganza.

interesting examples which have contributed to the history and understanding of the individuality of Portuguese gardens have been preserved up to the present day.

INDEPENDENT AND POLARISING
elements of space

I t is also in the Alentejo that we see, in the eighteenth and nineteenth centuries, the most significant elements of the Portuguese garden.

The Great Lake of the Quinta da Mitra, with its late eighteenth century design, continued a tradition that dates back to the beginning of Portuguese garden design. The great lake-tanks of the Palaces of Agua de Peixe, Torre de Amoreira, Vila Viçosa and the Quinta do General, reappear once more as a fundamental element of the garden. Set out around them are stone benches and chairs which face each other, as is the case at the Palace of Vila Viçosa or the Quinta do Carmo.

It is frequent to find the high walls which encircle the gardens framed by avenues of leafy trellises set in solid stone pillars, and with benches and flowerboxes. These places, which at the time were called 'walks', were specially conceived for the purpose of socialising and passing the time. The same function and spatial structure is to be seen in the walk of the Quinta do General which was used for open-air masses. On a day-to-day basis, this avenue, formed by a long series of benches, would be a sought-after place on hot summer afternoons.

A large lake with benches all around, 'walks' formed by lattice-work or an avenue with benches and flowerboxes, and a summer house all appear in the gardens of the south as polarising elements of space. The location and significance of each item is determined by a hierarchy of privacy and a life-style which are independent of the layout of the whole.

THE GRANDEUR OF THE GARDENS
at the Palace of Vila Viçosa

O n a level with the landscaping of the Palacio de Fronteira, in São Domingos de Benfica, are the gardens of the Palace of Vila Viçosa, about which more descriptions exist than any other. Unfortunately, their state of preservation does not correspond to the excellent quality of the documentation, especially in relation to the largest garden of all, commonly called the Reguengo orchard or kitchen-garden, as this was almost completely lost in the nineteenth century when leased out for agricultural purposes.

'...there is the garden of the Lady Duchess with
windows with wide railings that look out over a
large tank full of fish among the green shadows
of the lemon trees that encircle it...'
Diogo Figueiroa. 1633 (II)

Jardim do Bosque.
Palace of Vila Viçosa.

'...from this tank there stretches...a path which is lined with flowerboxes, myrtle and orange trees, and which ends at another tank...' Diogo Figueiroa. 1633. (III)

Central walk and detail of the entrance to the Pleasure House.

Jardim do Bosque. Palace of Vila Viçosa.

We find the first report of the palace gardens in the description in 1537 of the reception that followed the wedding of Dona Isabel to the Infante Dom Duarte, the son of Dom João III, which refers to *'orchards and gardens that are very cool, and tanks with fish and fountains of good water'.*[17] At that time, the Palace underwent great changes which altered both the architecture and the exterior spaces of the Manueline palace built by Duke Dom Jaime. In order to construct the great entrance courtyard, Duke Dom Teodósio ordered that *'a great stretch of the orchard that is to be found around it be dug up, and that a large square courtyard be constructed there'.*[18]

These orchards had, without doubt, a recreational character if we recall the Orange Groves of the Queen and of the Sun, in the Palace of Sintra (also from the time of King Dom Manuel) with their surrounding walls, stone-carved windows, benches and summer houses.

The reference in the description of 1537 to the *'orchards'* and the gardens should be understood as referring to the Bosque garden constructed by Duke Dom Jaime, since at this time the trees were already sufficiently large enough to provide pleasant shade: *'There are many fruit trees of diverse types, as well as others, which were only planted for purposes of simple pleasure, and covered with a canopy of creepers which provide a lot of much-wanted and delightful shade'.*[19]

The wall of this garden overlooking the courtyard still did not have the wide windows which were put in much later in the time of the Duchess Dona Catarina.

In 1571, during the travels of Cardinal Alexandrino, his secretary refers to the existence in the palace of very cool gardens, one of which is extremely spacious *'being laid out in the Italian style'.*[20] Venturino was no doubt referring to the Reguengo kitchen-garden or orchard, since the others would be small and the Bosque Garden never lost its Arab and indigenous character.

The Italian-style works in the Reguengo orchard coincided with the changes made to the palace during the period when an approximation to the Italian model was being undertaken.

We speak of an *'approximation'* to the Italian model since the different descriptions of the palace reveal an atmosphere of rural grandeur and true Mediterranean coolness without the sophisticated Renaissance decorative elements which we see, for example, in the gardens at the Quinta da Bacalhoa.

The departure of the Dukes of Braganza for the royal palace meant these gardens never had the aesthetic novelties of Portuguese mannerism found in the second half of the seventeenth century. This mannerism, imbued with a certain Oriental taste which can be detected in the gardens of the Counts of Castelo Melhor, the Marquises of Fronteira, the Counts of Sarzedas (Azambuja) and the Counts of Ericeira (Anunciada), and with a preference for shell-work, grotesque tiles, balustrades, colonnades and statuary, was never seen at Vila Viçosa.

The Italian-style layout of the Reguengo orchard was limited to a right-angled pathway pattern, *'the walls of which are of young myrtle'*,[21] and, especially, to refined topiary effects — an art that is Roman in tradition but which was revived in the Italian Renaissance — that were to be found in abundance in the Reguengo garden, *'many artificial figures being created out of the myrtles'*.[22]

The orange trees and lemon trees, the lattice-work covered walks, *'the tall pines and thick clumps of trees...the multitude of trees of so many different types'*, allied to the omnipresence of the lakes, tanks and water spouts, gave to the Reguengo garden a markedly Mediterranean and pastoral atmosphere.

The 1537 description also refers to another garden, about which there is little documentation, which Father Joaquim Espanca and Agostinho Augusto Cabral referred to as the Jardim das Damas (Ladies' Garden): *'From this dressing-room, there is a bal-*

'...and at the bottom of this garden are three windows...through which light enters into a pleasure house, where His Highness and Lady Dona Catarina came and sat with their ladies on some summer afternoons...' Father Manuel Calado. 1648 [IV]

View of the outer courtyard of the Pleasure House.

Jardim do Bosque. Palace of Vila Viçosa.

121

'...entering by the door of these crown lands, there is a long lane...with a trellis that is so beautiful and cool that for this reason alone...everyone feels obliged to stay there for a long time...' Moraes Sardinha. 1618. (V)

The great trellises are part of the tradition of the deambulatory, of which those at Bacalhoa and Fronteira are other examples.

Palace of Vila Viçosa. Trellis in the Reguengo Garden.

cony with iron railings which looks out over a cool garden, and which also leads to the quarters of the other Infantes'.[23] This name results in some confusion with the Jardim do Bosque which was also known in the seventeenth century as the garden 'Da Senhora Duqueza' (of the lady Duchess) and 'Das Damas' (of the Ladies). Without its ancient wall, this garden is today connected to the Jardim do Buxo and has consequently lost the character of a private space, as has also occurred in the Jardim do Bosque and the Jardim dos Príncipes (formerly the Orange Grove of the Queen) in the Palace of Sintra.

Due to its spatial characteristics and decorative elements, the Jardim do Bosque is the most interesting of this group of gardens. Surrounded by high walls, it has maintained the spatial structure of the sixteenth century, that is, of two poles of leisure separated by a promenade path, as is the case in the Jardim do Generalife or the Mirtos courtyard at the Palace of Alhambra in Cordoba. Each one of these two poles is structured around a lake-tank, only the Tritão lake remaining today. Diogo Figueiroa describes this for us in some detail: *'There is a large tank full of fish among the green shadows of the lemon trees which surround it...from this tank there extends an avenue which is surrounded by flowerboxes, myrtles and orange groves and which leads to another tank'.*[24]

THE QUINTA DO GENERAL
at Borba

S ituated on the outskirts of Borba, in a low-lying place with two large springs of water, this is one of a group of large estates in the Alentejo, all of which possess topographical features suggesting that they were the summer country retreats of Moorish alcaides in Islamic times.

Next to the kitchen, in the oldest area of the house, one can still find a wall with enormous cylindrical buttresses similar to

Above. *Two views of the ancient Jardim das Damas. The steps and surrounding walls (no longer there) give this garden an atmosphere of privacy.*

Left. *Detail of the box garden which was planted at the end of the eighteenth century.*

Ducal palace of Vila Viçosa.

those of the Palace of Agua de Peixes and the Mitra estate. These cylindrical buttresses, semi-hidden in a large storehouse, are the remains of a building whose construction seems to be much earlier than that of the present house which dates from the late sixteenth/early seventeenth centuries.

If, besides the cylindrical buttresses, the house possesses certain sixteenth century decorative elements, it was without doubt in the seventeenth century, with Dom Dinis de Melo e Castro, that the farm acquired the characteristics it has today, both in terms of the architectural design and the layout of the gardens.

The Quinta do General, it being called this in memory of Dom Dinis, hero of the Wars of Restoration,[25] is also integrated in the group of estates and palaces constructed by the nobility who supported Dom João IV on coming to the throne.

Despite the eminently Mediterranean characteristics, the gardens show the influence of the city and the court.

The Box Garden is closely connected to the style of the Reguengo garden at the Palace of Vila Viçosa, as well as to the art of topiary. At the centre stands a fountain with two bowls in the mannerist style which accentuates the erudite character of the place. A large water-mirror tank receives the waters from a summer house with an outer courtyard formed by lattice-work on Tuscan columns. In the interior, blue and white tiles in a detailed design have similarities to the panels of the second half of the seventeenth century at the Palace of Calheta and Fronteira. In front of the summer house, but on the other side of the lake, is a Baroque fountain which was brought from another part of the estate, and which in all probability replaced an earlier fountain. A high wall separates this first garden from a pleasure orchard where there is an extensive walk, laid out in such a way as to

From the entrance courtyard surrounded by high walls, passing by the fountains and the great lake, to the welcome shadows of the Chapel Walk, the gardens reveal affinities with the gardens of the ducal palace of Vila Viçosa. The great cylindrical buttresses in the oldest part of the house, identical to those of the Palace of Agua de Peixes and the Mitra Palace, Valverde, together with its topographical location, suggest that hundreds of years ago the house was the country retreat of the Moorish Alcaide of Borba.

Above and right. *Entrance courtyard with marble archway, sixteenth century; plan of the estate in the nineteenth century.*

Quinta do General. Borba. Alentejo.

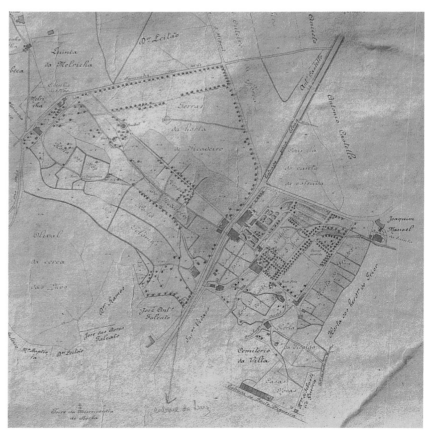

permit open-air masses. According to the tradition of the house, it was here that open-air masses were held for the troops before they left for the battles of the Elvas Line, Ameixal and Montes Claros, where Dom Dinis led the cavalry.

This walk was constructed in memory of these victories, with an altar at one end and an entrance gate at the other. The design dates from the second half of the seventeenth century, and both the altar and the entrance gate have stone benches at the sides, an interesting fact being that they are decorated with chequered green and white glazed tiles. Eighteenth century in design, and set against the wall which extends along the walk, is a series of benches carved out of local marble, and these are separated by small ledges for vases. The stone fountain in the centre is known as the Fonte do Dragão (Fountain of the Dragon), its design being very similar indeed to the gate of the summer house in the Bosque Garden at the Palace of Vila Viçosa. This garden is also noteworthy for the fact that behind the benches is a narrow lake which receives water from gutters in the shape of gargoyles set into the wall.

Other fountains are distributed among the old orchards attesting to the grandeur of the gardens in the seventeenth and eighteenth centuries.

In the twentieth century, the Box Garden and the fountain next to the great tank were covered with blue and white tiles dating from the first half of the eighteenth century: these tiles came from the Galveias Palace at Campo Pequeno (the former Tavora Palace), and reinforce the sophisticated character of this estate.

'...beautiful and appreciated gardens that are well cultivated and taken care of with many myrtles and small flowers, the myrtles being shaped into clever forms'. António Cadornega. Around 1630 (VI)

Cadornega was referring to topiary in the gardens of the Palace of Vila Viçosa. Connected to the House of Braganza, the Galveiras would, no doubt, have taken the gardens of Vila Viçosa as the model for their own.

Above and left. *Entrance courtyard and box garden.* Quinta do General. Borba. Alentejo.

Following pages. *Baroque fountain by the great tank, with tiles from the early eighteenth century.*

Quinta do General. Borba. Alentejo.

Seventeenth century chess-board tiles show the sophistication seen in the gardens in the second half of the century, after the War of Restoration.
Entrance gateway to the Chapel Walk.

Quinta do General. Borba. Alentejo.

THE GREAT CLOISTER
of the Cartuxa Convent in Evora

Despite the numerous troubles that have befallen this convent — occupation, fire, sale at public auction — the so-called Great Cloister is perhaps today one of the most interesting courtyard cloisters in the whole country.

What makes it exceptional is its size (one hundred metres wide), with an arcade of seventy-six semi-circular arches. The absence of an arcade or gallery at the first floor is common in cloisters, especially large ones, and makes for a feeling of openness which brings this space closer to a Mediterranean courtyard than a European cloister. The fact that it is planted with old orange trees reinforces the Mediterranean feeling, making it seem more like that of the Naranjos Courtyard of Cordoba and the Islamic courtyards of the north of Africa and the Middle East.

If today the Great Cloister of Cartuxa surprises us with its Mediterranean atmosphere, it is because it is related to the courtyard gardens of the south and the habit of planting orange trees in cloisters, as is the case with the Manga Cloister which Father Jerónimo Roman described in the following way at the end of the sixteenth century: *'The centre is occupied by a fountain of such rare good taste that I almost do not know how to describe it, it being isolated among four orchards'.*[26]

The Convent for the order of St. Bruno was founded by Dom Teodónio de Braganza, third son of Duque Dom Jaime. The grandeur and brilliance of the whole is due to his close relationship with the royal family and, later on, the Filipes of Spain. The refined Mediterranean taste of the Great Cloister seems to hold memories of Dom Teodónio, if we remember the descriptions of the Palace of Vila Viçosa at the time of the marriage of his sister Dona Isabel with the Infante Dom Duarte, son of Dom João III: *'There is another house which is very large and spacious with windows all over that look out over orchards and gardens, these being very cool due to tanks that contain fish and fountains with lots of water'.*[27]

The Great Cloister corresponds, therefore, to the beginning of the seventeenth century, and to a period of growth. Its classical mannerist layout reveals a certain economy of means in the stone work, this being in the form of semi-circular arches with austere pillars of soft brick.

The centre of the cloister is occupied by a large tank which is used to water the orange trees. The old irrigation system is still visible and continues to function perfectly. In the centre of the tank is a fountain carved from the granite of the region, with three bowls one above the other.

THE BISHOPS' GARDENS
Mitra Palace, Valverde

Accompanying this progressive interest in domestic dwellings and the refinement of open-air life in the fifteenth and sixteenth centuries, this estate was transformed into a country retreat for the bishops of Evora.[28] The characteristics of the place, which is situated just a few kilometres from Evora, suggests that the estate had already been a country retreat in earlier times (Romano-Islamic), as has been proved by archaeological remains.

The suppression of religious orders in May 1834, and the transformation of the estate to agricultural use in 1913, resulted in the deterioration of the gardens.[29] The interesting circular tank, in a late eighteenth century design, indicates that another earlier tank existed, since the aqueduct which feeds it bears the coat-of-arms of the archbishop Dom Domingos Gusmão, brother-in-law of Dom João IV.

Set around this lake are benches and stone work which forms oval windows and these give highly interesting visual effects.

Spread throughout the ancient gardens and orchards are various lakes, these being fed by the tank, and there is also an ancient 'water house' with cylindrical buttresses which is identical in type to that of the Peixinhos estate on the outskirtes of Vila Viçosa, both of these being possibly Islamic in origin.

SOME DESCRIPTIONS
of the gardens of the Palace of Vila Viçosa

With the entrance gate at one end and the altar at the other, the Chapel Walk included a large number of benches and flowerboxes behind which ran a narrow lake with numerous water channels. Chapel for open-air mass.

Quinta do General. Borba. Alentejo.

JARDIM DO BOSQUE

Festas e apercimentos que se fez em Villa Vicoza ... no mês de Abril do anno de 1537[30]

"... da parte de sima das cazas do Duque vai também cercando este terreiro, à parede de hum grande e fermoso jardim, que tem dentro tanque de muitos peixes de muito boa agoa nadável e corrente que se rega todo o jardim em que ha muitas arvores de diversos frutos e outras que somente para recreação humana forão postas, tecidas e cubertas de muitas edras que fazem muito aprazíveis e deleitosas sombras sobre que cae o aposentamento, que agora he da Sra. Infante com muitas janellas de grades de ferro sobre elle..."

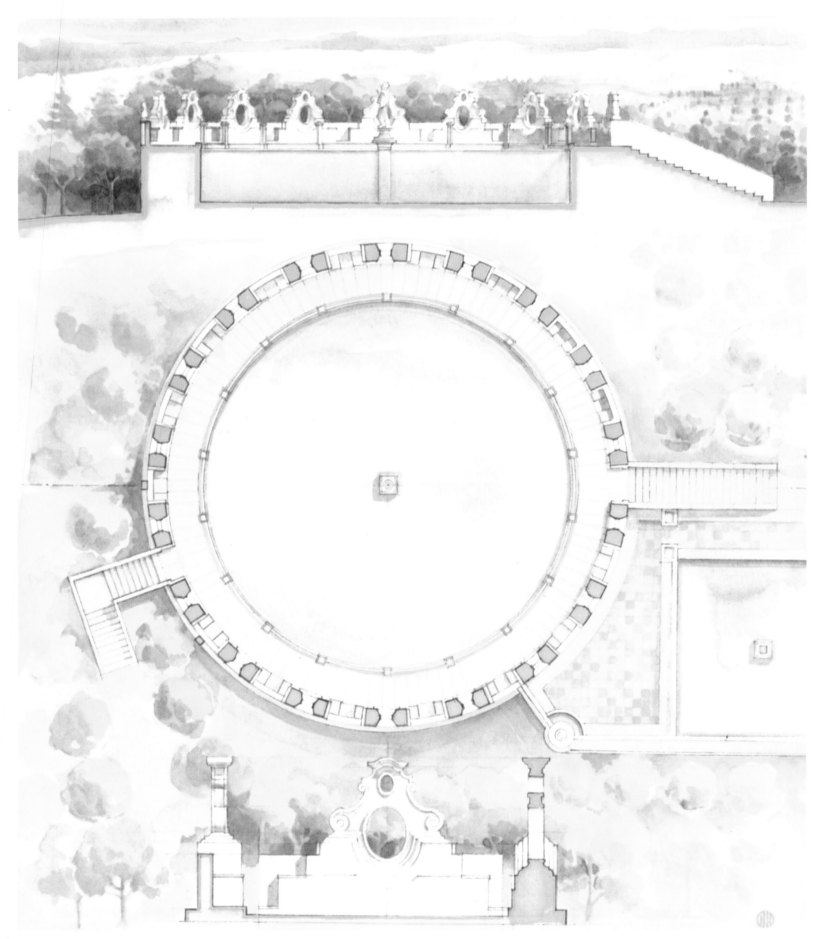

Francisco Moraes Sardinha in Parnaso de Villa Viçosa de 1618[31]

"daqui este adrom se vai continuando cõ o terreiro, o qual esta a mão dereita ornado cõ hu Jardim do Principe Apollo, que tem para o mesmo terreiro doze janelas e he elle plantado de infinitas arvores de espinho, que depois de deixarem ver sua frescura por sima das paredes, que o defende..."

Diogo Ferreira Figueiroa — Epitome de festas 1633[32]

"...a quem para o Norte fica o jardim da Senhora Duqueza com hum lanço de doze janellas sobre o mesmo campo".

"Realçase a famosa fabrica desta casa cõ duas janellas de grádes rasgadas sobre hu largó tanque cheio de peixes que entre as verdes sombras dos limoeiros que o cercão: para deleitação dos sentidos e ocupação ... Desde este tanque nace hua espaço a rua que cercada de alegretes, tozada murta e laranjeiras vai rematar-se em outro tanque, do meyo do qual para varias partes, pelos olhos boca e orelhas esta lançando copiozos canos de àgoa e feo trõbeta de Neptuno...".

Frei Manuel Calado. O Valeroso Luciderno... 1648[33]

"O outro quadro deste terreiro ocupa o jardim das Damas, o qual está por a parte de dentro terraplanado e nele plantadas muitas árvores e canteiros de várias flores e boninas (pequenas flores); e as paredes todas cheias de janelas nas quais se veem assentar as Damas no dia em que se fazem festas no terreiro, aonde os cavaleiros vão fazer suas continencias às Damas e abater suas lanças àquelas a que são afeiçoadas ou conjuntos em parentesco e obrigação, e no fim deste jardim estão três janelas, duas ordinárias e uma rasgada com seu balcão, por as quais entra luz a uma casa de prazer, aonde Sua Alteza e Senhora Dona Catarina se vinha sentar com suas damas algumas tardes de verão, para se entreter com ver passar a muita gente que ordinariamente entra por aquela rua, quando vem de Borba, Estremoz e outras vilas circunvizinhas e a muita também que sai da vila a tomar refresco ao contorno das igrejas de S. Bento e S. Jerónimo ... E tinha Súa Alteza grande alívio e regalo em perguntar aos que passavam e principalmente às mulheres que iam e vinham da romaria, quem eram e aonde moravam e outras cousas mais ..."

JARDIM DO REGUENGO

Festas e aparecimentos... de 1537[34]

"chegado a estas casas passando hum pequeno corredor esta logo outra caza grande e espacosa com janellas de todolas partes, que caem sobre pumares e jardins, mui frescos de Tanques com peixes, e fontes de muita agoa...".

F. Moraes Sardinha — Parnaso de Villa Viçosa ... 1618[35]

"Por este corredor se vai adar em hua grande porta porque se entra do terreiro, aqual amostra abobada da antecamara e deixa ver a porta do reguengo, que lhe he hua das mais frescas e airosas cousas, que na multidão dos que disse, e tenho de dizer se pode considerar ... Tem este reguengo em si tantas cousas coriosas que odiselas seria infinito, por é assi de algumas direi, ainda que poucas arespeito das muitas, que ha nele. Entrando pella porta deste reguengo, se va hua larga rua, que ao nível da porta amostra logo sua fermesura, cõ huma latada tão coriosa e fresca, que soo por esta razão se o interesse de suas funtes obriga a todos a se deixare ficár aqui por muito espaço, vendo o como agardece a terra a virtude, que lhe da em afazer tão copiosa e tão liberal de frutos e de ramas ... porque a sua mão direita achara dous Tanques hu delles tam largo e tão profundo, que tras hu bàrco em que se vai a seus extremos e corre todo, porque de outra sorte soo anado se pode chegar aelles ... entre a sombra de altos pinos e espesso arvoredo ... da multidão das arvores de tantas naturezas diferentes, ... ha neste famoso reguengo as mais excellentes frutas... é tem este reguengo duas novas cõ que se rega sua terra toda e fontes ... Todo este reguengo vai arruado de arvoredo, por entre o qual vão de muita e doutras hervas de sua natureza...".

Frei Manuel Calado — O Valeroso Luciderno — 1648[36]

"e em hum dos angulos deste frontispicio está um arco por onde se abre espaçoso caminho para o reguengo, que he hum jardim plantado de muitas e exquisitas arvores, regado cõ muitas fontes e engenhos de água e com muitas ruas largas e cõpridas, cujas paredes são de murta miúda cõ muitas e diferetes figuras, para cujo ministério tem alli o Duque Jardineiros mui primos na arte de suas curiosidades, tem alli hum lago de agua com engenhos para isso feitos..."

'...a large and beautiful round lake with very strong walls...and in the middle is a statue...on columns surrounded by four marble satyrs, which make a four spout fountain...'
Anonymous description of 1736 (VII)

Little remains of the famous gardens of the Archbishops of Evora. The large lake alone remains to attest to its former grandeur.

Above and opposite page. *Detail of the late Roman(?) statue in the centre of the tank; the large tank; plan of the large tank.*

Following pages. *A view of the large tank.*

Gardens of the Mitra Palace. Valverde. Evora.

'...the dormitory is also very large
and contains 72 rooms,
some having a view over the sea and
others over a large courtyard planted
with lemon and orange trees...'
Monconys. 1645 (VIII)

'Le dortoir est aussi fort long. & contient 72
chambres dont les unes ont la vue de la mer, & les
autres d'un grand clos, planté de citronniers &
orangers'.

According to different descriptions, the courtyards
and cloisters contained orange trees and lemon trees,
as is the case at the Jerónimos Convent.

Main Cloister. Convent of Cartuxa. Evora.

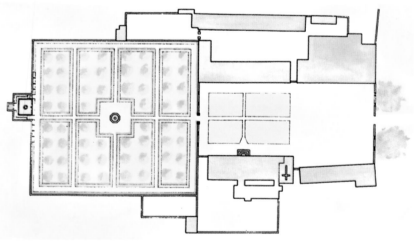

Entrance gate to the terrace and plan of the estate.
Quinta do Carmo. Estremoz. Alentejo.

JARDIM DO REGUENGO E BOSQUE

António de Oliveira Cadornega — Descrição Da Villa Viçosa 1640-1680[37]

"Em frente das gienelas das salas e galerias do Paço se viam dous vistosos e aprazíveis jardins muito bem cultivados e preparados de muitas murtas e boninas fazendo-se das murtas artificiosas figuras. Não flôr cheirosa que ali não achasse, com fontes de muitas bicas saídas pelas bocas de figuras de pedra jaspe, feitas com bizarra arte. Havendo em a curiosidade destes Jardins Reais, jardineiro-mor, que era Afonso de Alcalá, com outros muitos homens que faziam o que ele mandava à conservação e realeza daquela vistosa, aprasível e cheirosa grandeza, todos com bons salários e moradias. Estava logo o Tanque Grande, que lago se pudera chamar, pela muita água que em si encerra...". Ele, de muita altura, colmado de muitos peixes de toda a sorte, com grossos barbos, em que os Senhores se recreavam das ginelas que pera ali corriam, com a pesca de cana, e com verem nadar nele, no tempo de Verão, muitos moços do Paço e daquela Vila, dando de cima dos arcos que cingia grandes margulhos, tomados de todo o alto.

Socedia alguns anos ficar algum moço pelas custas afogado nele, por se embaraçarem, com os margulhos, nos limos, e não poderem tornar acima, e ter no meio um sorvidouro, ou caldeira. E com lhe defenderem não chegassem a ela, alguns mais ousados o faziam, e lá ficavam. E nem por isso deixava de concorrer muita gente a nadar nele, levando-os àquele desenfado também o interesse, porque os Senhores, aos que milhor margulhavam, lhe mandavam botar pelos criados seus tostões.

"Por esta razão não me parece que fico muito fora della em dizer que ainda os aindarão asustentar, pois as flores das laranjeiras, limoeiros e cidreiras, que neste lugar ha, são das mais odoriferas e esforçadas que tem todo o outro género de plantas. Neste jardim estão tantas galdrinas [28], tantos alegretes, quantos compade ofício de que os soubera desejar ..."

(Few Portuguese palaces have had so much written about them. In the descriptions of Moraes Sardinha, Diogo Figueiroa and Father Manuel Calado, we can follow the works as they were carried
out in the palace and the gardens of Vila Viçosa, and learn about the spatial characteristics which were lost during the nineteenth and twentieth centuries.)

DESCRIPTION OF THE GARDENS

of the Mitra Palace estate in the manuscript of the Manizola Library, 1736

"No distrito desta freguesia à parte do norte em distância de meia légua está a quinta de Valverde retiro dos Ex.^{mos} Arcebispos da cidade de Évora prantada junto à ribeira que chamam de Valverde. Fica-lhe ao poente a mata de Montemuro, ao sul uma tapada. É sítio ameno e delicioso ennobrecido com um nobre palácio formado de salas e galerias obra do Sereníssimo Senhor Cardial Rei como também as mais grandezas desta quinta e o convento de Religiosos Capuchos que está contíguo com a quinta e aumentado com outros edifícios dos Ill.^{mos} Arcebispos e Sedes Vacantes como direi. Forma um espaçoso páteo. Na entrada se patenteia por uma espaçosa porta que tem um nicho no frontespício e lhe fica ao sul dentro do qual lhe ficam as portas principais. Para a parte do poente fica o palácio que disse e nele se entra pelo pavimento do páteo. Fica a porta que é magestosa debaixo dum grande alpendre formado sobre fortes e altas colunas e coberto de abóbada. A primeira sala é larga e espaçosa com quatro janelas rasgadas que caem para a parte da ribeira e em bastante altura. Continuam para a parte do norte mais duas salas quadradas e cada uma tem duas janelas na mesma correspondência das da sala grande. Sobe-se por uma alta torre que no seu âmbito tem duas ordens de grandes salas. Tem a de baixo uma linda janela de sacada para o norte e em correspondência para o sul e para dentro do páteo uma varanda da qual desce uma linda escada para o páteo... continua o palácio para sul mais com três salas e com as janelas para a ribeira formando uma soberba galaria e na sala do meio fica uma tribuna para a igreja que tem a porta para o páteo. No fim destas salas se atravessa uma galaria que tem também uma janela para a ribeira e continua com seis janelas rasgadas para um jardim interior do palácio para donde tem porta e se desce para ele por uma bem feita escada e tem mais uma linda porta para o páteo. Continuam fazendo quadro ao jardim mais três salas com janelas para o jardim na mesma proporção e com portas para o páteo e detrás a última que fica no fim do palácio tem duas grandes alcovas e em cada uma sua janela contígua quase com o chão da parte de fora e com fortes e bem feitas grades de ferro e olham para o campo. E continua uma alta parede a fechar o jardim ficando no canto um pombal...

A igreja que disse tem tribuna para uma sala... com o corredor da galaria para a parte de dentro e é de abóbada com um bem... que lhe devide a capela-mor que tem retábulo de talha dourada antiga. Aos lados da parte do Evangelho está a imagem de Santa Rosa de Lima e da parte da Epístola S. Jacinto ambas de glória e estofadas de ouro e no meio uma bem feita cruz. Tem um cachão de pau fino e bem feito donde estão os paramentos para se dizer missa.

Faz correspondência a este palácio para a parte do nascente um novo e moderno quarto obra do Ill.mo Senhor Arcebispo D. Frei Domingos de Gusmão para o qual se sobe por uma espaçosa escada e compõe-se ele de quatro salas com janelas rasgadas para o páteo e com outras correspondentes para a porta do páteo que fica para o campo da parte do sul e para esta parte tem uma varanda para tomar o sol coberta sobre colunetas de mármore e cercada de alegretes de várias flores e no meio tinha uma fonte obra de mármore de repucho; discoartinada para o norte tem outra varanda da qual se serve como passadiço para se subir a um grande e fermoso lago de forma redonda e fortíssimas paredes que tem de circuito cento e vinte passos e de fundo catorze palmos e no meio fica uma como coluna cercada de quatro sátiros e de mármore e faz de fonte de quatro bicas e uma boa perspectiva. Toda esta obra é do sobredito Arcebispo e para este lago conduzem água de várias fontes de distância de mais de mil passos por aqueductos e sobre arcos e alguns de cantaria até ao lago e sobre o grosso da sua parede tem uma grande guarita onde se reparte para o dito lago e para um grande tanque que está perto dela e continua com cano para dentro do grosso da parede donde tinha repartimento para a fontinha que disse dá varanda e descendo para dentro do páteo e deste corre água para outro que está mais abaixo mas com pouca distância e está raso com a terra e era para nadarem gansos e patos; continua até ao fundo do páteo por uma fonte que está defronte da porta do Palácio em distância de vinte passos e é de mármore e de primorosa arquitectura. Tem sobre uma bela taça um escudo de armas do Ill.mo Arcebispo D. Frei Domingos de Gusmão. Sobre ele assenta um chapeu episcopal e da parte superior da copa sai a água que

caindo por toda a circunferência das obras forma um vistoso chuveiro que caindo sobre a taça por quatro bicas se recolhe em tanque da mesma e saindo desta por um cano subterrâneo vai fertilizar o jardim interior do palácio. Em distância de seis passos estão em correspondência de uma parte e da outra ficando a fonte no meio, duas pedras de mármore de figura quase quadrada e de altura de seis palmos e com notáveis molduras; tem as faces que olham para a fonte umas inscripções romanas em letra latina as quais não... porque sei as traz o M. Resende e que foram já tiradas a suas... de buchos. Fecham o páteo várias casas ainda que... que servem de morada a alguns moradores e para oficinas necessárias como são cavalharisses espaçosas e palheiros porque se não lastimem os animais de não terem parte nesta grande arquitectura.

Do lago continua o aqueduto por arcos e deixando sua porção em um tanque que está em um jardim fechado que fica atraz das casas térreas vai por arcos botar água em um tanque que está sobre um grande edifício sobre abóbada a que chamam por baixo casa de água pela ter em si nativa; em algum tempo teve engenho de nora que botava água no mesmo tanque que digo está sobre a casa. Hoje corre por um cano subterrâneo que vai ter a um tanque que está no laranjal que fica contíguo à ribeira. Do tanque disse está sobre a casa de água que tem suas altas paredes e portas de cantaria vestidas de verdes ervas que fazem uma agradável vista. Desce a água deste tanque para um repucho de uma fonte que está em um quadro de jardim que foi labirinto e formava um chuveiro de altura mais de um dique a que hoje se não dá uso. Junto da mesma casa de água está outro grandíssimo tanque todo de cantaria. A este lhe vem água duma nora que fica junto da porta da quinta que diz para a parte da cidade e por esta porta entram carruagens e rodam por uma espaçosa rua cercada de altíssimos freichos que unidos a povoam em correspondência sem outro desconcerto de desiguais e dista da porta até à casa da água quatrocentos passos e continuando mais duzentos passos com uma pequena volta vão sair pela porta da quinta para o páteo. Tem mais esta quinta um largo posso de cantaria junto à parede da cerca dos Religiosos, obra do Ill.mo Arcebispo D. Simão da Gama com um engenho de nora que bota água a uma grande altura da qual busca o arquido dos arcos para suprir da falta de água nos anos de seca. Todo o âmbito desta quinta que é muitas vezes grande cruzam várias ruas de arvoredos e latadas de parreiras que a dividem em quadras de laranjais e vinhatarias, e hortas e árvores de vários frutos.

Junto ao lago vai uma rua larga acompanhando de uma parte e outra duas bem feitas calhas de tijolo que servem de repartir a água do lago e do tanque que disse que está junto dele para regar um grande laranjal da china que fica em um quadro e chega à parede da cerca dos Religiosos estende-se até à rua dos freixos a que emparelha outro quadro povoado de excelentes peras e ameixas de todas as castas e masans e não só se regam estes dois quadros com esta auga mas também outros dois em que se semeiam as hortaliças de todas as castas. Cruza esta rua a dos freixos e se estende até uma capela que está no centro da quinta bem feita e airosa de abóbada em que em algum tempo foi venerada uma imagem de S. João do Deserto que com o tempo se

'...there is a path which...ends at a tank, in the middle of which there issue copious jets of water from... eyes, mouth and ears of Neptune...'.
Diogo Figueira, 1633 (X)

Neptune above a group of dolphins.
Quinta do Carmo. Estremoz.

The great-lake tank — fundamental to the life of a garden — occupies an important place in the Portuguese garden, especially in the south, where it is an essential element. Around it are to be found the pleasure or summer house, with benches and flowerboxes, as is the case at Vila Viçosa, the Quinta do General at Borba, the gardens of Bacalhoa, Fronteira and, later on, at Queluz.

Quinta do Carmo. Estremoz.

139

Surrounded by high walls with windows, the Alentejo preserved almost until the twentieth century a tradition of pleasure gardens which were more architectural than landscaped.

Top. *Detail of the courtyard of the Amoreira da Torre Estate. Montemor-o-Novo.*

Above. *Detail of the surrounding wall and windows of the garden at Vila Viçosa. Alentejo.*

fez velha e não tem hoje culto. Na distância de quarenta passos e em par desta está outra capelinha fundada sobre uma lagoa donde está a imagem de S. Teotónio nova por lha mandar fazer um devoto a quem o santo livrou umas impertinentes quartãs; foi esta ermida guarnecida por dentro de galantes embrechados; também hoje não tem culto.

Mais adiante na distância de quinze passos se mostram as ruínas de umas capelinhas formosas entre rochas com singular arquitectura; uma delas é pequena, em forma redonda; não tem sinal de ter tido altar e com porta. Tem à entrada dois nichos como que servir de ter neles algumas imagens; por cima é coberta de grandes penedos em forma de penhasco. A outra capela é subterrânea também redonda com uma singular abóbada na arquitectura pois é em forma de concha e com relevos tão fundos que hoje se aproveitam os pardais dos seus côncavos para fazerem os seus ninhos. Tem uma linda janela para o norte com grades de ferro e da parte de dentro duas paredes de mármore que servem de assento; tem altar mas já destruído. Para esta capela se entra por um trânsito entre rochas tão apertado que com trabalho cabe um homem. No fim deste trânsito à entrada dela está uma bem feita porta a qual serve de patim e um singular reduto de quatro arcos que fazendo debaixo deles côncavos fechados de abóbada com muitos buracos para cima na abóbada formavam uma admirável vista; voltando para fora da capela por entre outras penhas também apertadas se dá com a entrada que tem sobre a última penha um globo de pedra mármore que anda de roda e é o mundo que se deixa quando para o deserto se entra; também esta obra toda está coberta das mesmas pedras brutas e toda arruinada; a estas capelas fazem sombra vários e altos loureiros e murtas que tudo cobrem com suas ramas; aqui se chama o deserto.

Fronteira à porta do Palácio em distância de duzentos passos fica a porta duma grande tapada que há-de ter três quartos de légua em circuito, murada de muro alto; segue as margens da ribeira em bastante distância volta cercando uns altos montes ao mais alto deles que fica fazendo frontaria à cidade que lhe dista légua e meia ao nascente; está este coroado de altos arbustos, pinheiros, e o mais centro da tapada está povoado de altos matos silvestres por entre os quais cruzam várias ruas e comunicando-se com a porta rodam por elas carruagens.

Tem uma ladeira iminente à ribeira uma fonte que corre todo o ano por um cano subterrâneo e aparece dentro da quinta em bem feita guarita de abóbada e detendo-se pouco em uma pequena pia que está no meio passa a botar a sua água em um chafariz que está raso com a terra se deixa babar hoje dos coelhos e mais animais que na tapada se criam. Nesta tapada se criavam rebanhos de corças e viados que para ela tinha metido o Ill.ᵐᵒ Arcebispo D. Frei Domingos de Gusmão quando a fez e hoje porém não traz mais que uma corsinha.

Junto da guarita está uma barandinha com cadeiras e assentos feitos de alvenaria. Por coroa deste delicioso sítio e magestosa quinta se ostenta o religioso convento dos Capuchos da Província da Piedade que tem por orago o Bom Jesus de Valverde, obra hoje tão singular na arquitectura que ainda que pequena não tem a arte nas obras claustrais em que possa pôr nota na sua fábrica. Compõe-se esta dum claustro quadrado ainda que pequeno. Tem no meio uma linda fontinha de pedra mármore com uma só bica que cai em um como tanquinho feito de uma só pedra e deste se reparte para a cozinha e para a casa que serve aos religiosos de se lavarem os seus paninhos e a que sobeja vai por outro cano para a cisterna.

Nos dias de festa também lhe põem um chuveiro que espalha água por todo o claustro. Está este rodeado de oito grandes colunas de pedra parda e sobre elas fecha também em quadro uma abóbada que serve de solo à varanda que cai para o claustro que também se levanta sobre colunas mais pequenas e sobre elas fecha uma outra abóbada.

Esta varande se comunica com três corredores que é os de que se compõem os dormitórios por quatro portas e uma em cada canto. Os corredores correm dois do sul para o norte donde tem cada um sua janela rasgada; o terceiro cruza estes dois de poente para nascente com outras duas janelas. Estão povoados de catorze selinhas acomodadas aos habitadores; são todas quadradas e todas de abóbada. Dos dormitórios se desce por duas bem lançadas escadas uma para a ante sacristia outra para o de profundis que é uma airosa casa; tem um espaçoso refeitório e em correspondência uma grande casa de cozinha; tem o capítulo porta para o claustro que é uma bem feita casa e todas estas oficinas fechadas com fortes abóbadas.

Do de profundis se sai por uma varanda que rodeia a face do norte; do nascente e debaixo dela está uma grande cisterna de abóbada formada sobre vinte arcos e uma grande casa de água e enche-se esta não só com água da fonte do claustro mas também com água dos telhados que se colhe. Junto ao aqueduto dos arcos que atravessam pela horta do convento tem também um tanque que se enche quando é necessário da auga que vem pelos canos e com esta água regam a horta e o seu laranjal que tem dentro dela e estas são antigas que ainda conservam o nome de laranjeiras do Cardial.

Coroa enfim toda esta grandeza uma... singular igreja na arquitectura; compõe-se a sua fábrica de zincos zimbórios formados sobre trinta e duas colunas de pedra mármore e forma uma regular figura de cruzeiro que de tal sorte que de qualquer parte que se veja se acha no feitio a mesma correspondência. Tem o zimbório do meio mais levantado o seu ponto na sua cúpula e sobre ela uma claraboia com seis luzes rasgadas de vidraças de que a igreja toda recebe luz.

Fica a capela-mor à parte do poente ocupando o âmbito de um zimbório e as colaterais os dois das ilhargas e o do meio com o que fica ao nascente compõem o corpo da igreja; desta se dividem as capelas por umas bem feitas grades que fecham em oito colunas. Tem o altar-mor de finíssima pintura de Roma, uma devotíssima imagem de Cristo crucificado com a sagrada invocação do Bom Jesus de Valverde, de tão devoto aspecto que infunde devoção a quem o vê. É o orago deste religioso convento. Esta dita imagem é visitada de muitos romeiros em todos os tempos do ano, principalmente nas sextas-feiras da quaresma, em que, com mais frequência, da cidade de Évora, a pé e muitas pessoas descalças as traz a sua devoção a implorar a sua misericórdia. Neste mesmo altar está o tabernáculo do Santíssimo Sacramento e sobre a sua porta em uma peanha uma agradável imagem do Menino Jesus, de vestidos; da parte do Evangelho está o Patriarca S. Francisco e da epístola Santo António. Na colateral da parte do Evangelho está um retábulo de pintura de Roma, a Ascensão de Cristo Nosso Senhor e a imagem de Nossa Senhora da Conceição e na outra capela, no retábulo pintado, a Adoração dos Pastores e em vulto a imagem de N.ª Senhora da Esperança e outro do Menino Jesus. Entre esta capela e a do altar-mor fica a porta para a sacristia e em correspondência a porta que ia para a tribuna do Serreníssimo Cardeal-Rei.

Tem a porta da rua debaixo de um alpendre que também cobre a portaria do convento coberto de abóbada, que se firma sobre oito colunas de mármore, a que se segue um airoso átrio fica à parte do Lesnordeste; o corpo fica em correspondência do altar-mor, por fora do quinto zimbório.

É esta obra tão singular que nela mostrou o braço régio do Serreníssimo Senhor Cardeal-Rei que em área tão pequena podia acumular tanta grandeza; da parte de fora do átrio, contíguo com a igreja ficam as hospedarias do convento com escadas para o poente. Neste convento quis o seu fundador ter por companheiros aos religiosos capuchos da Província da Piedade e deixá-los na partição dos seus sucessores na mitra e nesta acumulou grossas rendas e lhe deixou a obrigação do sustento de doze religiosos de que hoje se compõe o seu número. E foi obra tanto do agrado de Deus como mostrou o mesmo Senhor no ano em que desocupando os religiosos o convento dizem que por causa da... se ouviu em sua ausência tocar o sino a matinas da meia... no coro e não entendendo os que isto ouviram o mistério... inar com a vista o que não alcançavam com o entendimento subindo escadas as janelas do coro donde ouviram o canto... deserto de toda a pessoa humana e entenderam que os anjos supriam os louvores de Deus no lugar que desamparavam os religiosos o que entendendo os Prelados povoaram de novo o convento e assim se conserva hoje, recebendo dos Prelados deste arcebispado não só o sustento mas também tudo quanto é necessário para a conservação da vida humana; o que tem feito todos os Ill.ᵐᵒˢ Arcebispos com mão liberal e não menos os Ill.ᵐᵒˢ Cabidos e Sedes Vacantes principalmente esta que mandou pôr o convento na perfeição em que hoje se acha... e pondo-o todo de abóbadas e o puseram no estado em que já o relatei em que se tem dispendido muitos mil cruzados.''

(Although they have practically completely disappeared today, these gardens of a country house in the south were described in the first half of the eighteenth century. From this description we can clearly see the spatial affinities they had with the gardens of the Palace of Vila Viçosa in the previous century.)

NOTES

1 Transcribed by C. Castelo Branco, *Um viajante em Portugal há 393 anos. O Mundo Elegante*, 1858 N. 6-9.
2 Translated by Basílio de Vasconcellos. *Itinerário de Jerónimo Müncher* (1494-1495). Coimbra 1931, page 60-61.
3 Transcribed by Sousa Viterbo. *A Jardinagem em Portugal*. Coimbra 1906, page 72.
4 Chancellery of Dom João III, book 45, sheet 136 - and Chancellery of Dom Manuel, book II, sheet 114 A.N.T.T. Transcribed by Alice Estominho.
5 Father Manuel Calado. *Valeroso Luciderno*. Évora 1648, page 97.
6 António de Oliveira Cadornega. *Descrição de Vila Viçosa*. Introduction by Heitor Texeira, 1983, page 88.
7 Francisco de Moraes Sardinha. *Parnaso de Vila Viçosa*. Manuscript work, page 64.
8 Túlio Espanca. *Inventário Artístico de Portugal*. Évora City Council. Lisbon. 1966, page 95.
9 Túlio Espanca. *Inventário Artístico de Portugal*. Évora City Council. District of Vila Viçosa. Lisbon 1978. I Vol., page 630.
10 Túlio Espanca. Ibid., page 630.
11 A. Oliveira Cadornega. Ibid., page 88.
12 F. Moraes Sardinha. Ibid. page 59.
13 Transcribed by Virgílio Moreira. A sixteeth century description of the Monastery of Santa Cruz de Coimbra. Coimbra, 1930, page 27.
14 Transcribed by Júlio de Castilho. *Lisboa Antiga* 3rd ed., vol. VII. Note III, page 342.
15 Transcribed by José Teixeira. *O Paço Ducal de Vila Viçosa*. Fundação da Casa de Bragança. 1983, page 115.
16 Father Manuel Calado. Ibid., page 97-A.
17 José Teixeira. Ibid., page 118.
18 Idem. Ibid., page 114.
19 Idem. Ibid., page 115.
20 Translated by Alexandre Herculano. *Opúsculos*. Volume VI. Lisbon 1884, page 85.
21 Father Manuel Calado. Ibid., page 97.
22 A. Cadornega. Ibid., page 88.
23 José Teixeira. Ibid., page 118.
24 Diogo F. Figueiroa. *Epítome de Festas*. Évora 1633, page 7.
25 Túlio Espanca. *Inventário Artístico de Portugal*. District of Évora. Council area of Borba. I vol. Lisbon 1978, page 109.
26 Virgílio Correia. Ibid., page 27.
27 José Teixeira. Ibid., page 118.
28 Túlio Espanca. Inventory.
29 Transcribed by Augusto Matos Rosa in *Lavoura Portuguesa*. April-August 1965 (V. chapter V, pages 138-140).
30 José Teixeira. Ibid., page 115.
31 F. Moraes Sardinha. Ibid., folio 58.
32 Diogo F. Figueiroa. Ibid., pages 3-7.
33 Father Manuel Calado. Ibid., page 97.
34 José Teixeira. Ibid., page 118.
35 F. Moraes Sardinha. Ibid., folio 63 verso and folio 64.
36 Father Manuel Calado. Ibid., page 97.
37 A. Cadornega. Ibid., page 88.

Notes on Illustrations

  I. Father Manuel Calado. Ibid., page 97.
 II. Diogo Ferreira Figueiroa. Ibid., page 7.
III. Idem. Ibid., page 7.
 IV. Father Manuel Calado. Ibid., page 97.
  V. Moraes Sardinha. Ibid., folio 63 verso.
 VI. António Cadornega. Ibid., page 88.
VII. Augusto Matos Rosa. Ibid., April-August 1945.
VIII. M. de Monconys. *Journal de Voyages*. III Part. Lyon, 1666. page 45.
 IX. Transcribed by Agusto Matos Rosa. Ibid., April-August 1965.
  X. Diogo Figueiroa. Ibid., page 7.

THE CONCEPT OF THE WALK IN A GARDEN

and the development of ecclesiastical art in the eighteenth century

CHAPTER VI

In countries with a south European culture — Spain, Italy and Portugal — where Protestant asceticism was inconceivable, the Counter-reformation, from the seventeenth century onwards, saw the development of an art form with a clear sensory appeal reflecting the culture.

While the origin of the Renaissance has its base in superiority of reason, the Baroque opts for the superiority of the senses, denying both physical limits and a rational perception of space.

The ritual of the mass will be one of the more complex and sophisticated elements of this aesthetic taste. The sound of the organ, the splendour of the carvings and glazed tiles, the gold of the ceilings and altars, the smell of incense, the rich vestments — all envelop the enraptured believer in an unreal atmosphere which exceeds all rational limits.

All of the statuary in the gardens of the Bishops of Castelo Branco seem to have been taken directly from an altar.

Their distribution along the walks, especially down the sides of the staircases, transfers outdoors the church's taste for ambiguity and a sensory envelopment. Apostles, kings, bishops, saints, all line up in a long and majestic procession of stone.

This ecclesiastical aesthetic taste has, however, different repercussions in the north and south of the country.

The north, due to its more Celtic and European tradition, took on the whole of the European Baroque movement and gave its gardens a vision of space that was both dynamic and expansive. In the Baroque of the south, due to the Islamic-Mediterranean tradition, a crypto-magic concept of space continued, though this took on new decorative forms.

It is in the north, however, that the concepts of the dynamic space of central-European Baroque found a cultural home that permitted their transfer from the mannerist garden — limited to

architectural values of great spatial containment — to the urban garden with more open landscaped layouts.

The north, with its connections to the Celtic and Druidic forest culture, where Roman and, especially, Islamic culture penetrated only very tenuously, never saw any difference between exterior, regarded as profane, and interior space, held to be sacred. The southern nature refused to accept this direct contact with the exterior and the gardens are therefore surrounded by high walls and face inwards on themselves.

Courtils, who visited Lisbon in June 1755, specifically mentions this absence of a relationship between the interior and the exterior — architecture and urban space — which is to be seen in the south when he writes about the Ribeira Palace: *'It is extremely large and appears immense...one could say with some exactitude that the palace has no avenues or courtyards [cours] that announce its presence. It is more an amalgam of stone than a royal palace'.*[1]

To achieve the continuity between exterior and interior space, which governs the approach paths to the structures — porches, courtyards, outside staircases, colonnades — the European Baroque in its vision of a continuous and expanding multiplicity of spaces, tended to base its structure on a single axis which dictated the whole of the architectural and urban layout.

At the end of the sixteenth century, the gardens of Maia — the country retreat of the Bishops of Oporto — which have now almost disappeared, were organised around a large avenue, a pathway dotted with monumental fountains and small chapels. A similar structure can still be seen in the gardens of the Quinta de São Martinho, belonging to the Bishops of Coimbra, on the outskirts of the city, despite being in a greatly ruined state.

Even without the dynamic elements of staircases, landings

Opposite Page. *View of the gardens of the Bishops of Castelo Branco.*
Episcopal Palace of Castelo Branco.

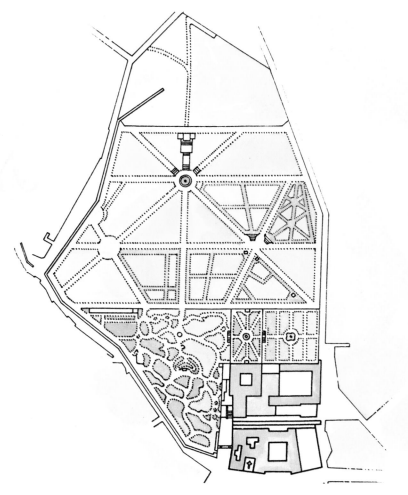

'Their garden is very beautiful despite being small...There is also a large walled-in garden full of orange and lemon trees which grow there freely...' Courtils. 1755. (I)

'Leur jardin est fort joli, quoique petit...il y a encore un grand clos plein d'orangers et citronniers qui y croissant sans presque de soin...'

Plan of the garden of the Necessidades Palace. Lisbon.

and porches, this axis revealed the resolute nature of the man of the north in relation to life and the universe, a characteristic that was not possessed by the man of the south.

As the centre of all that was happening and of the universe, the man of the north developed within himself a perception of directional space and an aspiration to an expanding universe, characteristics which were seen in all their splendour at the beginning of the European Baroque period.

For the man of the south, who was more fatalistic and contemplative, the magical *élan* of an expanding space-universe was something completely unknown.

In the south of Portugal, in particular in the so-called clay culture, from Manueline times to the mannerism of the seventeenth century, and continuing into the eighteenth century, gardens continued to reflect a concept of crypto-magic space that was incompatible with the development of the European Baroque. Surrounded by high walls with no contact with the exterior, except for enjoyment of views, these gardens tended to be laid out in accordance with the geographical conditions. Lakes, water tanks and benches were organised as elements of an architectural space with a reserved and domestic atmosphere about them.

Link, who was in Portugal at the end of the eighteenth century, refers to this aspect in his book *Voyage en Portugal: 'The outskirts of Lisbon, especially on the eastern and north-eastern sides, are, for a great distance, covered with gardens surrounded by high walls. It is most frustrating and annoying to ride around and face the risk of being lost for hours because of these high walls which do not permit anyone to enjoy the views. It is probably due to the austere and oriental character of the Moors, or else to envy or other identical passions that one owes the construction of these walls, which seem to be more the walls of fortresses than those of gardens'.*[2]

Link was mistaken about these gardens not taking advantage of the views. Miradors, porches, arbours and summer houses all had a strategic role to play in enhancing the beauty of the views or else overlooking the avenues of access to see who was passing by or arriving.

ECCLESIASTICAL ART
and liturgical ritual

Enjoying unlimited economic and political power, the church ruled over much of the destiny of the nation, and was therefore able to carry its ecclesiastical aesthetic taste into public and social life.

This aesthetic taste reached the height of splendour and excess in the reign of Dom João V. The gold which Portugal obtained from Brazil was badly distributed. England, which invaded Portuguese markets with its products, benefited as did the church, which the king, more pious than religious, covered with riches.

The church was the great patron of the arts and science at the time, making possible a vast range of experiments mainly centred

144

around the so-called decorative arts. Carving and glazed tiles — aesthetically original and characteristically Portuguese — reached unrivalled heights of true craftsmanship. It was the era of the great master-manufacturers of glazed tiles: the Oliveira Bernardes (father and son) and Gabriel del Barco; and of the master builders of innumerable churches and convents: André Soares and Marcelino de Araújo.

Glazed tiles and carving began to appear in gardens, the latter being done in stone, as it was more resistant to the climatic conditions, although it was always secondary to wood.

While the statuary of the gardens of the Bishop of Castelo Branco seems to have been ordered by a church, the balustrades, vases, fountains and niches which decorate the gardens also reveal an ecclesiastical aesthetic taste.

THE ART OF THE COURT IN THE SOUTH
and the garden of comfort and well-being

The city court and nobility were not in favour of the construction of new palaces and gardens. Since no great social transformations had taken place — as had been the case previously when the new aristocracy which had supported the Braganzas came to power — no garden construction was undertaken. In his *Chorografia Portuguesa* of 1712, Father Carvalho da Costa made special reference to five great gardens: Castelo Melhor, Fronteira, Sarzedas (later on Azambujal), Aveiro and Anunciada. All these were of an earlier period. Later on, Father João Baptista de Castro in his *Mappa de Portugal,* which he brought out after the reign of Dom João V, added only two gardens: Santo António do Tojal and the Necessidades Palace. The connection between these gardens and the hegemony of the church can be clearly seen. The first belongs to the country retreat of the Cardinal Patriarch Dom Tomás de Almeida, and the second to the Necessidades Convent.

From the descriptions and documents we find that structurally these gardens present nothing new in terms of spatial character. The absence of large staircases and an axis along which the gardens develop, together with a clear spatial containment, also link these gardens to a mannerist style.

Courtils, who visited the Necessidades gardens at various times in 1755, stated: *'Your garden is very beautiful despite being small. One can see seven marble statues representing the seven cardinal virtues in the flowerbeds. There is also a large walled-in garden [clos] full of orange trees and lemon trees which grow there at will. At the top of this garden [clos] there is a very beautiful grotto decorated with shells [rocaille] from which a cascade of water falls. This flows under the ground for 100 metres to create a beautiful water spout and then goes on to form another at the bottom of the natural slope of this garden [clos]'.*[(3)] The statues were of great quality as are the marble vases, balustrades and frames that are to be found in the garden today. Tollenare, who visited the garden in 1816, also refers to these statues in his

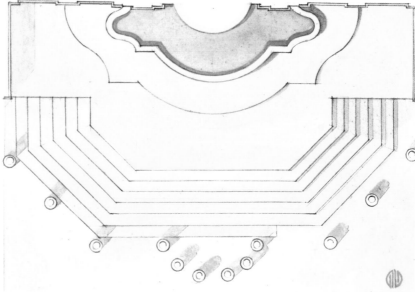

Elevation and plan of the fountain.
Quinta de Santo António do Tojal. Lisbon.

145

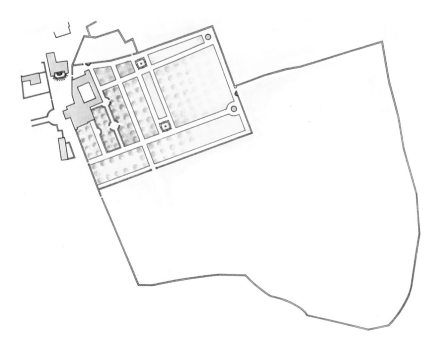

*'...One sees many types of fountains, flowers and
exquisite trees... two cylindrical-shaped dovecots
serve to mark the ends of the main square of the
garden...'* Baptista de Castro. 1762 (II)

Above: *Details of buildings and gardens.*
Above right: *Plan of the layout.*

Quinta de Santo Antonío do Tojal.

*Notes Docinicales: 'The terraces [parterre] composed of shaped
box are notable not only for the quantity but especially the
quality of the statues which decorate it. Larger than life-size, they
represent some of the Christian virtues'.*[4]

The exceptional quality of the statuary and of the decorative
elements which we see distributed around the gardens expresses
the tastes of a king and a court used to importing from Rome the
best that Italian art was capable of producing. Even today, the
silver plate of the Chapel of São João Baptista of the Church of
São Roque in Lisbon is considered to be the best set of eighteenth
century silver work outside Italy.

For his country retreat, Cardinal Dom Tomás de Almeida had
sent *'some statues of saints made in Italy from fine jasper'.*[5] The
large spouting fountain in the courtyard that provides access to
the estate combines a certain grandeur with an impeccable quality
in the finishing. In the interior, the gardens have, over the centuries,
lost the statues which Baptista de Castro describes: *'With this
same objective, the cardinal decided to have a delightful and large
garden constructed next to the palace which dominates it, it being
laid out in squares ennobled by beautiful porphyry stone statues.
There, among the ever-green shades of the plants, myrtles and
cypresses, the statues take on various shapes which an excess of
otherwise admirable culture has obliged them to adopt. One also
sees many types of fountains, flowers and exquisite, but sterile,
trees... Two cylindrical dovecots denote where the main part of
the garden ends and the doves of various colours which flutter
round and round through the air, and over the country-side
increase the pleasure of the eyes'.*[6] The two dovecots still exist
and are decorated with tiles set inside fine bosses[7] considered
to be the work of Bartolomeu Antunes. Of the many types of
fountain and statue, only two water tanks of delicate design
remain. Next to the palace there are still some paths lined with
low walls covered with glazed tiles which, together with stone
benches, form enclosed spaces. Although it is almost in ruins, one
can still make out the original structure and the intimate character
of the whole. The palace opens up directly on to the gardens

without terraces or staircases in between, and the garden extends over an area of flat land.

The topiary effects formed by the shaping of both box and myrtle continue a seventeenth century taste which was diluted by the so-called parterre with low box rocaille designs. At the end of the eighteenth century, Beckford complained about this on his visit to the Palhavã Palace: *'In the great courtyard in front of the garden of the residence one can see sad-looking mazes of shaped myrtle hedges, in the middle of which rise tall pyramids'.*[8] More elaborate was the box in the gardens of the fathers of Alcobaça which James Murphy visited in 1788: *'The monks of Alcobaça have a large garden, situated near to the church and it is planted with avenues of trees and camellias which form pleasant walks... from time to time one comes upon small enclosed spaces in which benches are set out...In the middle of the garden there is a beautiful oval tank 130 feet in diameter with an obelisk in the centre. The garden terminates in cypresses and box which the treasure of a gardener has caused to take the most ingenious shapes: people hunting, monks praying, heads with elaborate hair-dos and others with wigs'.*[9]

The few alterations that can be seen in the gardens of the south at the time were more or less restricted to Roman-style decorative elements, the main emphasis being on statuary.

In order to construct a great royal palace surrounded by extensive gardens, Dom João V bought various farms in Belém. Besides the two properties of the Counts of Aveiras, he also bought the Quinta da Calhete which borders the Quinta de Belém on the north and the Quinta dos Condes de Óbidos in the Alto da Ajuda (today the Botanical Garden). Although Dom João V conceived the idea of a great royal palace in Belém, it was in Mafra that he eventually built. The king never inhabited his Belém palace and the dimensions of the improvements to the house and gardens were reduced. The king limited himself to linking the ancient vegetable gardens of the Quinta da Calheta (today the Colonial Garden) and the Quinta de Belém, thereby forming a star-shaped series of paths identical to that at the Necessidades Palace which he called 'Regis Hortus Suburbanos'. As tradition dictated, the garden was planted with a wide variety of trees: oranges, lemons, tangerines and almonds, to which dwarf cherries, olives, cevadilla and asparagus were also added. Later Gorani wrote: *'The only items of singular note are two groups of sculptures which came from Rome'.*[10] These statues are still to be found in the garden and were part of the landscaping for the Portuguese World Exhibition (today the Colonial Garden).

Gorani continues: *'In cages in the annexes live an elephant, lions, tigers, leopards and zebras. There was also an aviary where one could see the rarest birds of America, Africa and Asia'.*[11] Like the aviary, they were the works of the third Count of Aveiras, Dom João da Silva Telo de Menezes. The scant attention that Gorani paid to the construction of the aviary suggests it was in poor condition and with none of the splendour it acquired later with the works undertaken in the reign of Dona Maria I. The large statues in the niches of the arcade, such as the statue of Hercules overcoming the seven-headed hydra, are from the reign of Dom João II and the era of the 3rd Count of Aveiras, which confirms that the works of Dona Maria did not alter the structure of the aviary and that at the beginning of the eighteenth century it already had a certain grandeur.

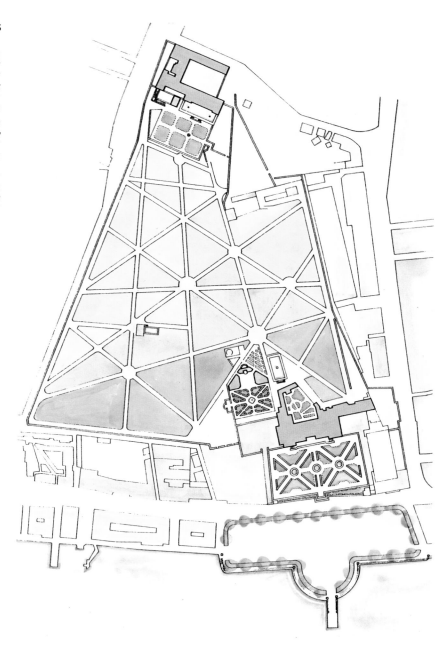

In 1726, Dom João V bought the Quinta of Belém from the Count of Aveiras and joined this estate to another, higher up, of the Counts of Calheta. With them he created a great garden: Regis Hortus Suburbanos.

Plan of the gardens of the National Palace of Belém.

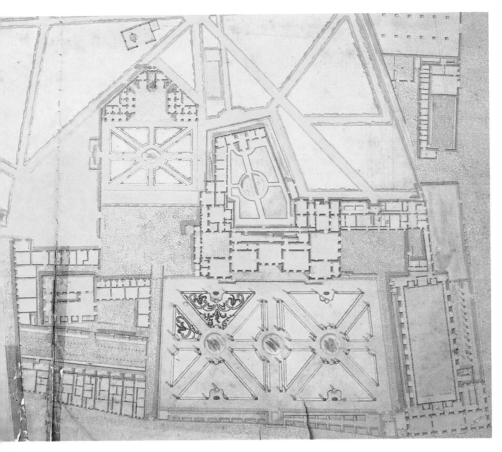

'...and after the year 1681...Count João da Silva
Telo (carried out) many works and
improvements on the aforementioned property.'
Carta Padrão. 1726 (III)

*In the time of Dom João, Count of Aveiras, the first quarter of
the eighteenth century, the gardens were composed of two spaces
closely connected to the palace: the Great Garden — at the front,
overlooking the Tagus, and the Upper Garden — in front of the
aviary.*

Detail of the plan in the *Historical Archive of the Ministry of
Finance.*
National Palace of Belém.

President of the Senate of the Lisbon City Council, Dom João
revealed himself to be a man of action and it is due to him and
not the king, Dom João V, that we have not only the aviary but
also the garden which faces the river Tagus, these works being
carried out throughout the eighteenth century until the sale of the
estate.

At the beginning of the seventeenth century, and following
the fashion of the day, Dom João abandoned the palace on the
Castle Slope (Vagos Palace) in order to spend the whole of the
year on his Belém farm.[12]

A vast veranda-walkway with a mannerist balustrade and
covered with glazed tiles from the beginning of the eighteenth
century[13] opens up on to the box garden decorated with statues
in the style of King Dom João. The structure is similar to that at
the gardens of the Marquises of Fronteira, whose layout must
have influenced the gardens of the capital for a long time: for
example, one can see certain similarities with the gardens of the
Bishops of Castelo Branco. The axis of the garden formed by the
centre of the veranda and lake terminates in both cases in a
prominent enclosed space which has a stone table. The large lake
house from the Fronteira Palace was transported here for the
aviary constructed in the form of an amphitheatre, thereby re-
viving a tradition of large autonomous elements which polarised
the space. The aviary is like a majestic backdrop that opens up
over a small garden. The same thing occurs, though on a different
scale, in the Fronteira gardens, but here it does not permit an
overall view of the layout.

To sum up, we can say that the gardens of the south during
the first half of the eighteenth century did no more than continue
earlier concepts of space under the guise of new decorative
elements.

The more architectural than landscapist sense of the spatial
containment and the refusal of an overall vision of the whole is
clearly expressed by Courtils when he writes about the gardens of
the Palace-Convent of Mafra: *'It is more of a room of greenery
than a garden'.*[14]

* * *

ECCLESIASTICAL TASTE
and the gardens of the
Bishops of Castelo Branco

Their original layout preserved, the gardens of the Bishops
of Castelo Branco, despite their affinities with the south,
are some of the finest and most interesting examples of the
development of northern Baroque art in the first half of the
eighteenth century.

The construction of the gardens is due to the Bishop of
Guarda, Dom João de Mendonça. An inscription on one of the
statues of the garden gives the date of the construction of the
garden and its founder: *'There was never born of woman a
greater man than São João Baptista* [St. John the Baptist], *and to*

'...the lower garden, at the same level as the entrance which leads to Belém, with three houses of recreation, the one in the middle decorated with embossed plaster shapes... a fountain with a figure made of jasper... a fountain with a marble statue from Italy...' Carta Padrão. 1726 (III)

While in the first half of the eighteenth century there were no significant transformations in the structure of the space of the gardens, in the gardens of St. Antonío do Tojal, Necessidades and Belém, there was a clear preference for statuary of great quality in the Baroque-Roman taste.

Above and left. *Detail of the statues and the box garden.* National Palace of Belém.

this preacher in the desert, João, the humblest of all, the Bishop of Guarda dedicates this retreat in the year of our Lord 1725, the thirteenth year of his episcopate'.[15] Another date, 1726, on the statue of Moses at the top of the cascades which descend on to the great tank, gives another clue to the date of the construction of the garden.

The two vast water-mirror tanks are clearly connected with a southern tradition which rejects the massive size of large granite fountains. Although there is a certain amount of privacy, the layout tends to be concentrated around an axis which begins at the main entrance door and extends to the staircase, to the main garden and the door to the old wood. The path which follows this axis gives way, however, to the gallery-walk which is in the form of an amphitheatre with steps leading from one level to the next, down to the lake with three stone crowns on pedestals.

The principal novelty presented by this garden is a concept of space which is based on pathways. The garden is not a space structured by walls or other elements of spatial containment, as is seen in the south, but has a structure based around pathways. The walks which we saw in the Fronteira gardens as autonomous elements of the layout are used here to define the layout. Statues, balustrades and vases, distributed in large numbers, accentuate this effect, and give to the space a religious and processional ambience.

Far from the court and Lisbon, where the most sophisticated centres of artistic production were to be found, the statuary of the garden is somewhat basic and provincial. However, this effect is to some extent weakened due to the profusion of the statues which are to be found flanking staircases and the box maze paths. The paths are clearly defined by a continuous series of shapes and sizes, and herald the great staircases that would later be built in the north of the country.

* * *

'...in cages in the outbuildings there lived an elephant, lions, tigers, leopards and zebras. There was also an aviary where one could see the rarest birds of America, Africa and Asia'.
Gorani. 1766 (IV)

In its spatial and scenic relationship, the aviary at the Palace of Belém reflects the tradition of the great polarising elements of the garden space, as is the case with the Lake House at Bacalhoa and Fronteira.

Above and right. *Plan and façade of the aviary. Historical Archives of the Ministry of Finance.* National Palace of Belém.

'...and at the end of the same garden, a dovecot in the form of a theatre, and in the centre of the dovecot a cascade with a Hercules overcoming the seven-headed hydra'. Carta Padrão. 1726 (V)

Despite much work being carried out on the aviary during the reign of Dona Maria I, the architectural structure was not altered, the work being limited more to the interior, and to the urns, statues and coat-of-arms with a delicacy that is incompatible with the scale of the building.

Above and left. *Two views of the aviary.*
National Palace of Belém.

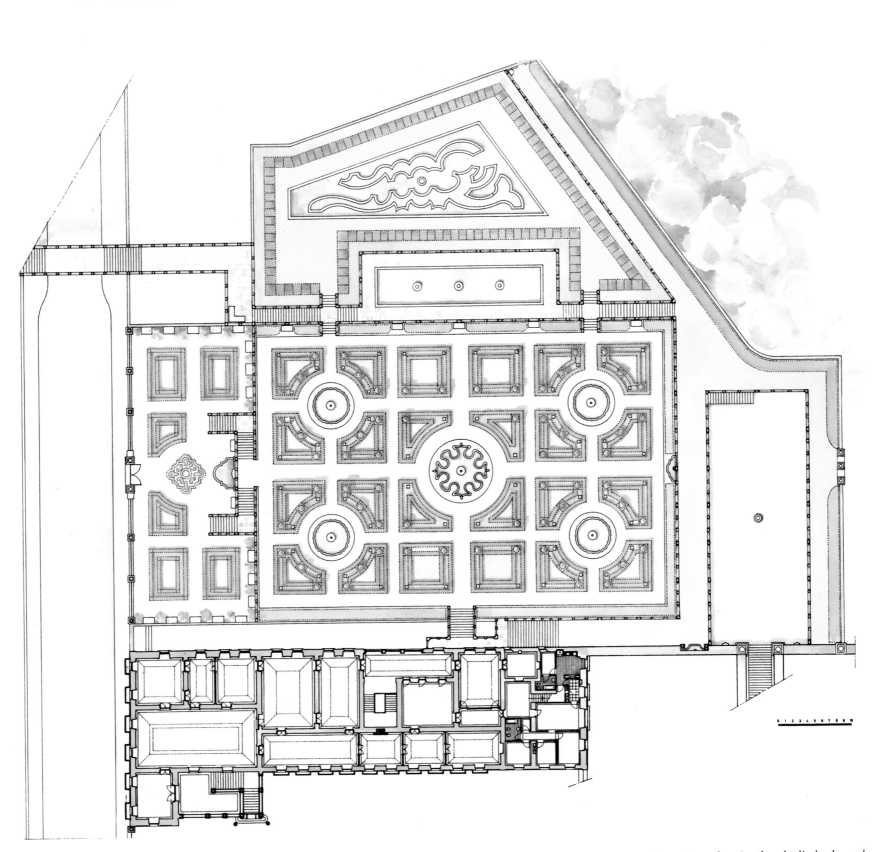

In terms of the plan, the bishops' garden is clearly linked to the gardens of the second half of the seventeenth century. The central section, with five fountains distributed around it, the central one being the biggest, repeats the design of the Fronteira Palace. The novelty of the plan is in the profusion of statuary accentuating the paths — an ecclesiastic aesthetic of ritual and processional taste.

Plan of the Bishops' Gardens. Castelo Branco.

THE BAROQUE STAIRCASE

and the concept of the 'walks' garden

The religious aesthetic which had an important effect on public and domestic life in the country created in the north a garden with specific characteristics which set it radically apart from that of the south.

The overflowing formal dynamism of the façades of the convents, churches and manor houses in the north reflected an urban expression directed towards courtyards, squares and driveways. Staircases, which were maintained in the interior of the house in the south, were transferred to the exterior in the north as elements of spatial linkage and continuity.

It was within the confines of church patronage that the landscaping layout which best expresses the Baroque vision of dynamic and directional space manifested itself.

Without the vast resources of the crown and the nobility connected to the royal family, the gardens of the northern manor houses never attained the grandeur of the large European landscaped layouts such as Vaux-le-Vicomte or Versailles in France, Stowe in England, or Drottningholm in Sweden.

Those who did not suffer from the economic limitations that affected the northern nobility were the monastic orders and the bishops who competed among themselves in terms of the grandeur of their monuments. Pilasters, columns, pediments, alcoves, saints, façades covered in shell-work, scrolls, cornices, gargoyles, heraldic and religious emblems all returned to the exterior in a secular style which extended to courtyards, atriums, avenues and balustrades. This is the case with the Grijó Convent and the monumental wall fountain which was ordered for the Pilgrims' Courtyard or the wall fountain of the Palace of the Archbishop of Braga ordered by Dom Rodrigo de Moura Teles in 1723.

But it is in the large staircases that one finds the antithesis of the south.

Unlike the Ribeira Palace which, according to Courtils, did not deserve admiration due to the lack of *'avenues and courtyards'* [16] which announce its presence, it is in the approaches to the staircases and the stations of the cross that we find so much excellence concentrated.

Until the seventeenth century the stations of the cross and the exterior layouts of pilgrims' chapels in both the north and the south were characterised by a certain adaptation to the terrain and geographic conditions.

Pathways snaked around hillsides in a simple layout, and recesses were cut into the side of a hill, either with benches around a fountain so that the walker could rest, or else in other places where one could appreciate the landscape that stretched out in all directions. The handsome flights of stairs of the north in the eighteenth century, of which Tibães is without doubt the best example, as well as in the seventeenth century, reflected a radically different attitude. The overall layout of the whole was based around an axis which organised each one of its parts hierarchically. The basic characteristic of this layout is that the axis is transformed into a pathway totally composed of flights of stairs.

'...there one sees among the multi-coloured plants, the ever-green box and myrtle in a variety of shapes that art with skill and admirable culture has obliged them to take...' Baptista de Castro. 1763 (VI)

The author was referring to the gardens of Cardinal Dom Tomás de Almeida at Santo António do Tojal which would have influenced the bishop who created the gardens at Castelo Branco.

Detail of the central pathway.
Bishops Gardens. Castelo Branco.

'Of women there was not born a greater man than St. John the Baptist, and to this preacher of the desert, John, the most humble of all, is dedicated this retreat in the year of the Lord 1725, the 13th of his episcopate.' (VII)

The humble John was the bishop Dom João de Mendonça who wanted to leave for posterity the name of the person who had had the gardens made and the date.
Tank surrounded with lions and view of the gardens.

Gardens of the Episcopal Palace. Castelo Branco.

The perception one has is that of space in movement and the visitor is led in a spatial sequence which continually unfolds as one either goes up or down the stairway. In a complicated arrangement of landings, steps and balustrades, staircases increased the number of views and spaces on an infinite succession of levels. Porches, arches, chapels, fountains, statues, stone ornaments and pinnacles, were forever in front of the visitor-believer's eyes, creating the sensation of a universe which opens up through expansion while at the same time denying any rational perception of space.

At the same time, in the painting done directly on to the construction itself, we see on the ceilings of churches colonnades pointing to the sky, where clouds and angels on different levels give the effect of the roof of heaven and of rising into infinity.

These projects did not, however, manifest themselves in the first of the staircases. It is not until the complex and subtle concepts of the staircase at Nossa Senhora do Monte in Braga that we can see the culmination of this aesthetic concept. In the staircase of the Monastery at Tibães, one can see an example of the type of landscaping work which took place around chapels and churches where, with more or less ingenuity, effects of dynamism and spatial continuity were explored, though such works were mainly concentrated in the north and centre of the country.

In the Convent of Santa Maria da Costa, although one cannot exactly speak of staircases as such, the visitor descended from the

'With this same vitality he was disposed to create a large and delightful garden which would dominate the palace, and divided the plan into beautiful pictures ennobled by porphyry statues'.
Baptista de Castro. 1763 (VIII).

church at the top of the hill by means of a sequence of three terraces linked by a complicated set of steps. Balustrades crowned with pinnacles in the shape of pyramids lined the path taken by believers who came up to the convent from Guimarães. Inside, the land around the convent was decorated with gardens. A description of 1748 mentions *'that those who live on the surrounding land have the pleasure of seeing a closed-in vegetable garden, which they call a small back yard'.*[17] It is interesting that the name vegetable-garden is still given to an enclosed space which is clearly a garden. This vegetable-garden was surrounded with walls *'around which are trellises of sweet black grapes, which are divided by box-lined avenues, and in the centre of the garden is a fountain which was already in existence behind the church. It is further decorated with two other fountains, a great variety of flowers and with stone benches placed around the central fountain, shade being provided by trellised vines'.*[18]

Today, this vegetable-garden has been completely transformed by time, sold in public auction, been used for a college and has, this century, been damaged by fire. From the garden one goes up to a round lake which has stone benches all around, spherical pinnacles and two small altars for saints, and continues up to a final enclosed garden surrounded by walls. Although now in ruins, one can still make out benches with carved backs and two niches containing mutilated statues.

Although they had a certain southern sophistication, the friars of the Convent of Santa Cruz in Coimbra, despite having always

All the statuary seems to have been taken directly from an altar. Its distribution along the pathways carries to the exterior the taste of the Baroque church of the eighteenth century, namely an ambiguous and sensual envelopment.

Details of the pathways beside the lake.
Gardens of the Episcopal Palace. Castelo Branco.

157

possessed one of the most luxurious convents in the country, did not attach any particular importance to staircases in their gardens. The grandeur of the wall around the gardens is based on elements of a more recreational character such as the playing field with a cascade at one end, and the vast lake with an island in the centre where *'the canons usually have some rowing boats'*.[19] Its proximity to a southern style of art that is more urban and sophisticated is seen in the glazed tiles which cover the different benches of the playing field and the steps, which rise not to a chapel but to a fountain, forming an enclosed space with benches which have backs lined with blue and white tiles dated 1749.

The great staircases were built further up, at Tibães for example and Senhora do Monte near Braga, the latter being the most complex and monumental example of this art.

THE STEPS OF THE CONVENT
of Tibães

S ituated in one of the greatest and richest Benedictine convents in the country, the steps of the convent are, on account of their mannerist features, dated to the second half of the eighteenth century. Father Leão de São Tomás, in his description of the convent in 1644, referred to the large-scale work that was being

'...and it ends in a delightful covered veranda, in the middle of which one sees a fountain topped by a pyramid, pouring water out of four spouts into four cups...' Francisco Camelo. 1748 (IX)

The church, and especially the religious orders, with their enormous economic resources, were great builders and patrons of the arts, and extended their architectural taste to exterior spaces and gardens.

Above and right. *Veranda with central fountain overlooking the wood and circular tank surrounded by benches.*

Convent of Santa Marinha da Costa. Guimarães.

carried out at the time: *'It has two perfect cloisters...one next to the new church which is being constructed'.*[20] This certainly corresponds to the final phase of the works and to the laying out of the exterior spaces.

Seven large fountains of mannerist design are to be found between the first and the last of the staircase terraces and, altogether, they form a series of nine small terraces interconnected by steps. The paving of the sloping terraces reduces the dynamic effect of the stairs which are transformed into a series of small steps between each platform. Each terrace is polarised by the presence of a large fountain, on either side of which are six small steps.

This gives each small terrace a greater importance than the continuity of the pathway itself, and places the stairs in a series of autonomous spaces. The distribution of the fountains in a straight line down the line of the slope, in the direction of the overall outline of the whole, reveals a clear dynamic sense of continuity and the opening up of a series of spaces. The layout of the stairs is therefore more architectural than landscapist in concept. Tibães was, therefore, the first great experiment to pave the way for one of the most powerful and successful landscapist layouts in Baroque history: Nossa Senhora do Monte, in Braga, just a few kilometres away from Tibães.

THE GREAT STAIRCASE
of Bom Jesus do Monte

B etween 1722 and 1725, the archbishop of Braga, Dom Rodrigo de Moura Teles, decided to restore and extend the stations of the cross and sanctuaries of Bom Jesus, and he prepared to mark becoming an archbishop with one of the most grandiose religious works constructed in the north of the country. On either side of the great door, over the centre of which is his coat-of-arms, he engraved for those who were to visit in the future: *'Holy Jerusalem Restored and Rebuilt in the Year 1723',* and *'By the Most Illustrious Senhor Dom Rodrigo de Moura Teles, Archbishop'.* It is to this period that we are indebted for the Staircase of the Five Directions as well as the stations of the cross which connect the main door at the foot of the hill to the first step of this staircase.

Unlike Tibães, the steps of the staircase widen out into a small staircase landing which permits a continuous and uninterrupted walk.

On the other hand, each terrace is reduced to a simple staircase landing without benches, again accentuating the continuity of the walk. The fountains at each landing lose the effect of focal points, which they are at Tibães, and have the same visual value as the different statues and pinnacles which are distributed along all the staircases.

The whole of the staircase thus takes on a visual unity in

Constructed in the second half of the seventeenth century, the Tibães staircase was the first landscape plan which had a central axis governing the whole layout. It heralded the great Baroque staircases.

Above. *View of the fountains on the staircase.*
Convent of Tibães. Braga.

159

'On what do these holy reformers spend the vast sums of money and gifts given to them...I would humbly reply...on columns, cascades, paths paved with stones, water tanks, jets of water, gardens, lawns as flat and smooth as a billiard table; on magnificent buildings and on great forms of entertainment that only princes indulge in...'
Francisco da Pina e Melo, circa 1740. (X)

Entrance gate, cascade and plan of the Jardim da Sereia. Cerca do Convento de Santa Cruz de Coimbra.

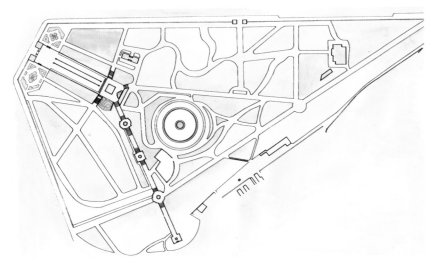

absolute sensory envelopment. The scale of the saints and pinnacles, together with their location, divided up in a sequence of visual plans on different levels, gives the sensation that it is the staircase which is moving.

Terrace gardens are to be found on each side of the staircase and these, following the rise of the staircase, reinforce the effect of an increased number of spaces and views. Decorated with box, the ends of the terraces culminate in flower arrangements and have a tall cypress in the centre. The layout of these gardens is a reproduction of each staircase landing. In them are statues at the sides and a central fountain topped by another statue.

160

Courtyards, chapels, fountains, statues, flamboyant stone ornaments and pinnacles are superimposed on the visitor's retina creating a spatial ambiguity of a universe which opens up and expands and denies any rational perception of space. Extension of the Staircase of the Five Directions of Neo-classic taste by Carlos Amarante.

Bom Jesus do Monte. Braga.

DESCRIPTION OF THE SANCTUARY
of Bom Jesus do Monte in 1788

"Sôbre todos aparece como obra imortal da piedade dos Bracarenses o ternís-
simo e devoto santuário do Bom Jesus do Monte, situado em um frondífero e copado
monte, distante meia légua ao nascente da sua cidade. Neste devotíssimo santuário,
vêem-se figurados os mistérios da redenção do mundo, desde a Ceia do Senhor até à
sua gloriosa ascensão, em multiplicadas capelas, e um templo no qual se representa
vivamente o Monte Calvário, com tudo quanto nele executou a execranda impie-
dade. Sôbre a porta principal dêste templo, que olha para o Ocidente e donde se vê o
mar costeando mais de cinco léguas de terra, está gravada em lâmina de pedra
mármore esta inscrição:

> CRUCIFIXO DOMINO SACRATUM HOC
> TEMPLUM POSTERITATI COMMENDAT, ET
> ANIMAM SUAM ILLUSTRISSIMUS DOMINUS
> DOMNUS RODERICUS A MOURA TELLES
> ARCHIEPISCOP. BRACHARENSIS,
> HISPANIARUM PRIMAS. AN. DM. NOSTRI
> JESU CHRISTI 1725.

"A pequenhês dêste templo, que verdadeiramente não corresponde à grandeza
de tôda a outra obra, excitou a devoção dos Bracarenses a edificar outro, cuja planta o
representa igual às maiores Catedrais do Reino. Há cinco anos que se lhe deu
princípio; mas tarde chegará a completar-se se a piedade dos fiéis não concorrer com
as esmolas necessárias. As quatro colunas aparelhadas para o seu frontispício não têm
outras semelhantes em tôda a província, tanto em altura como em grossura e
qualidade de pedra.

"Parece que a natureza e arte competiram mutuamente para formarem neste sítio
a residência do bom gôsto. A majestosa fábrica de catorze capelas que, cingidas de
outras tantas aceadas ruas campestres, se elevam em igual proporção pela suave
ladeira daquele monte; o viçoso e copado arvoredo de robustos carvalhos e pompo-
sos castanheiros que as rodeiam; as copiosas e perenes fontes de cristalinas águas; as
estátuas lapidares, os bustos, os obeliscos, as pirâmide, os jardins, os diferentes
registos de água que neles rebentam por todos os lados; os passeios públicos,
semeados de flores em tôdas as estações do ano, tudo isto faz com que, suspensos os
sentidos do homem e arrebatado êle mesmo docemente, contemple com íntima e
curiosa atenção tôdas estas belezas.

"No ano de 1718 deu princípio a esta imortal obra o Arcebispo Primaz D.
RODRIGO DE MOURA TELES, e a acabou no ano de 1725. Desde o ano de 1748 até o
de 1770 a aumentou e pôs na perfeição em que hoje está o devoto zelo de **Manuel
Rebelo da Costa**, falecido a 21 de Março de 1771 na mesma cidade de Braga, aonde
foi ilustre **cidadão** e casado com D. MARIA VIEIRA D'AZEVEDO, dos quais eu sou
filho. Êste benfeitor, além do que reformou em tôda a obra antiga ampliando a
extensão dos jardins, a das casas da hospedaria, a da grande cêrca, fez com despesa do
seu próprio cabedal tôda a obra moderna, que se vê desde o Templo Maior até o
terreiro último que se remata com as três capelas que contêm os Mistérios do Castelo
de Emaús, da Aparição à Madalena e da Ascensão, passando a total despesa de 50 000
cruzados. Da mesma sorte instituiu três Capelães, um dêles com obrigação de missa
quotidiana por sua tenção e de sua mulher e filhos. Tem êste santuário jubileu
perpétua, concedido por Clemente XIV, e promulgado em 12 de Setembro de 1779."

Description of the City of Oporto. *Agostinho Rebello da Costa* 1789.
Pages 28-29.

(Constructed in various phases which continued into the nineteenth century, this description focuses on the characteristics of the staircase of Bom Jesus
do Monte in the second half of the eighteenth century.)

*The grandeur of the construction, much superior to that of Bom
Jesus of Braga, has an excess of monuments and lacks authority
over the essential values which should be found in great Baroque
staircases: spatial continuity and sensual envelopment.*

Above and left. *Views of the Senhora dos Remédios Staircase.*
Lamego.

Constructed at the end of the eighteenth century and extended throughout the nineteenth century, the Senhora dos Remédios staircase is the expression of an out-of-date art form, the epilogue of a style which came to an end in the eighteenth century.

View of the staircase seen from the Adro dos Reis (King's Churchyard).
Staircase of Senhora dos Remédios. Lamego.

DESCRIPTION OF THE MAGNIFICENT GARDENS

at the Convent of Santa Cruz de Coimbra by Tollenare in 1816

La quinte ou le parc du couvent m'a paru contenir 20 à 25 arpents. Il est entouré de murs. Quoique des cyprès superbes garnissent ces murs, comme le parc entre dans la ville et qu'une grande partie est dans la vallée, on y est vu de presque tous les côtés. Son revenu principal consiste en vignes dont le produit est très estimé. Il est orné de bosquets d'orangers, de lauriers et de quelques arbres exotiques. Il y en a de disposés pour toutes les saisons. Des cabinets, des bancs ornés, des retraites auprès de fontaines || aussi ornées qu'on en trouve dans les jardins de nos princes, sont répandus de tous les côtés. Ces ornements sont tous tirés des sujets saints et font au moins autant d'effet que ceux que nous tirons de la mythologie. L'effet qui résulte de l'introduction des sujets mystiques dans les jardins est même si sûr que j'ai vu ailleurs des parcs où l'on n'avait pas craint de placer des Magdeleines, d'autres saints ou des emblèmes monastiques au lieu de sujets profanes. Saint Augustin est le héros de toutes les scènes du jardin et, comme c'est un saint un peu philosophe et sentimental, il offre des ressources à qui vient chercher des sensations vives.

Parmi les scènes qu'offre le parc de Santa Cruz, je citerai comme une des plus belles que j'aie vues dans aucun jardin royal celle du jeu de boule. Il faut, pour y parvenir, monter une colline d'environ 100 pieds de hauteur. La montée est ménagée par des escaliers doux et vastes, interrompus par des repos ornés de salles de verdure, de bancs magnifiques. Elle est toute protégée par des ombrages élevés et néanmoins si épais que le soleil n'y saurait pénétrer. Chaque repos est embelli par des jets d'eau abondants qui ne laissent accès à aucune chaleur. Le jeu de boule est placé sur une plateforme que j'estime avoir 300 pieds de longueur sur 200 de large. Un seul magnifique canapé en faience peinte l'entoure. Le dossier du canapé est garni de vases de fleurs et de statues. Son extrémité d'honneur reçoit une décoration plus élevée, d'un grand style, surmontée par une fort belle Assomption, du pied de laquelle tombe une masse d'eau imposante. La plateforme est divisée en quatre compartiments pour former quatre jeux de boule; elle est raffraîchie de tous côtés par des jets d'eau qui vont se perdre dans la verdure. || Il est difficile de mettre plus d'épicuréisme dans un jeu qui oblige à un exercice un peu violent pour le climat du Portugal.

Une autre scène représente un vaste lac; mais il est entouré par une haute charmille de cèdre roidement taillée et dont le vert est peu agréable. Un superbe oranger s'élève dans une petite île placée au milieu du lac; on s'y rend dans une barque élégante. Je lui préfère beaucoup la scène du jeu de boule, et aussi une longue allée couverte, raffraîchie par de petits canaux d'irrigation et que, je crois, on appelle l'allée de St Augustin.

Seize ou dix-huit chanoines vivent dans ce séjour délicieux, dans l'abondance de toutes choses, recevant leurs amis avec hospitalité et noblesse, pouvant se livrer sans inquiétude aux douceurs de l'étude, de la contemplation et de la promenade, ou, dit-on, quelquefois, à des distractions plus profanes. Ils ont, à quelque distance de la ville, des maisons de campagne qui, m'assuret-on, n'offrent pas moins d'agréments. Comme leur clôture n'est qu'à demisévère puisqu'ils peuvent sortir à deux et en voiture, je conçois qu'ils ne doivent point manquer de profès, et surtout qu'ils doivent fortement s'opposer à l'introduction des principes modernes qui leur sont peu favorables. Il m'eût fallu rester plus longtemps au milieu d'eux pour pouvoir leur faire traiter ces questions délicates. Une grande politesse et une chaude hospitalité, voilà ce que j'ai rencontré dans le monastère de Santa Cruz.

L.F.Tollenare. *Notes Dominicales Prises Pendant une Voyage en Portugal et au Brézil en 1816, 1817 e 1818*. Paris. F.C. Gulbenkian. 1972. Pages 105-106.

(Greatly altered in the nineteenth and twentieth centuries, these gardens were described by Tollenare during a period of great opulence.)

NOTES

1 Courtils. *Une Description de Lisbonne en Juin 1755*. Lisbon. 1965. Page 146.
2 Henry Frederic Link. *Voyage en Portugal depuis 1797-1799*. Paris, 1803. Page 231.
3 Courtils. Ibid. Page 155.
4 Tollenare. *Notes Dominicales. Prises pendant un Voyage au Portugal et au Brézil en 1816, 1817 et 1818*. Paris, 1972. Folio 67 V.
5 João Baptista de Castro. *Mappa de Portugal*. Volume III. Lisbon, 1762. Page 450.
6 Idem. Page 452.
7 José Meco. *Azulejaria Portuguesa*. Lisbon, 1985. Page 58.
8 William Beckford. *Diário de... em Portugal e Espanha*. Lisbon, 1983. Page 43.
9 James Murphy. *Travels in Portugal... in the years 1789-1790*. London, 1799. French translation. Paris, 1797. Page 106.
10 José Gorani. *Portugal, A Corte e o País nos anos de 1765 a 1767*. Translated by Castelo Branco de Chaves. Lisbon, 1945. Page 101.
11 Idem. Page 101.
12 Standard letter for the sale of the Palace... to King Dom João V, Historical Archives of the City of Lisbon. Rosa Palace.
13. Although José António Saraiva in his book "the Palace of Belém" says that in 1758, some 902 tiles had been substituted from the facade of the palace, either there tiles were never placed or place somewere else.
14 Courtils. Ibid. Page 150.
15 Sousa Viterbo. *A jardinagem em Portugal*. 2nd Series. Coimbra, 1909. Pages 57-58.
16 Courtils. Ibid. Page 146.
17 Cited by Ilídio Araújo. *Arte paisagística e arte dos jardins em Portugal*. Lisbon. 1962. Page 159.
18 Idem. Page 159.
19 Idem. Page 168.
20. Idem. Page 142.

Notes on Illustrations

I. Courtils. *Une Description de Lisbonne en Juin 1755*. Lisbon, 1965. Page 155.
II. João Baptista de Castro. *Mappa de Portugal*. Volume III, Lisbon, 1762. Page 452.
III. Standard letter for the sale of the Palace of Belém by the 3rd Count of Aveiras, Dom João da Silva Telo, to King Dom João V, in 1726. Historical Archives of the City of Lisbon. Rosa Palace.
IV. José Gorani. *Portugal, A Corte e o País nos anos de 1765 a 1767*. Translation Castelo Branco de Chaves. Lisbon, 1945. Page 101.
V. Ibid. Standard letter for the Sale of the Palace of Belém...
VI. João Baptista de Castro. Lisbon, 1762. Ibid. Page 452.
VII. Inscription at the bottom of the statue of St. John the Baptist which stands on a base in which the tank water-spouts are to be found.
VIII. João Baptista de Castro. Ibid. Page 452.
IX. Francisco Xavier Camelo. *Catálogo dos Priores do Real Mosteiro da Costa* in *Boletim de Trabalhos Históricos*. Guimarães, 1957, XIX. Page 103.
X. Francisco da Pina e Melo. *Memorial de... ácerca dos excessos e usurpações dos religiosos monachaes...* Transcribed by Luiz de Sousa Reis, Institute of Coimbra, 1865. Vol. XII. N.º 1. Page 20.
XI. William Dalrymple. *Travels through Spain and Portugal in 1774*. London, 1777. Page 131.
XII. Agostinho Rebello da Costa. *Descrição da Cidade do Porto*. Oporto, 1789. Page 28.
XIII. Idem. Page 29.

discontinuous structure, and perhaps it is here that we find one of the reasons for the rapid disappearance of the greater part of these gardens.

THE ROBILLION LAYOUT
the second phase of the gardens at Queluz

A round 1758, Dom Pedro decided to hand over the Queluz works to the French architect Jean Batiste Robillion who had recently arrived from Paris. The reasons were probably connected with the displeasure felt by Dom Pedro and his brother Dom José I at the pace of the works. Mateus Vicente could not resolve the relationship of the levels between the palace and the lower area of the estate, next to the Jamôr stream, and the palace appeared to fall almost vertically on to the gardens. It was to this particular area that the Frenchman directed his attention, and where he built the pavilion which took his name.

The Robillion pavilion connected the area of the palace

'...destined for an orchestra which was to be heard there on the occasion of parties given on summer nights, or when the royal family relaxed, sailing around on a small boat in the shape of a gondola...' Caldeira Pires. [1]

Cross-section and plan of the Lake or Music House.
Historical Archives of the Ministry of Finances.

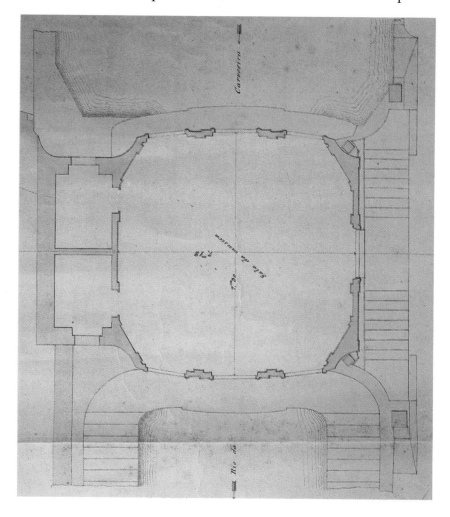

'...of the coloured tiles that are to be added to the two paths outside the lake...on the flowerboxes and the part of the Lake House facing the pathway...fifteen thousand nine hundred and thirty-nine tiles...Palace of Queluz, September 2nd 1756'.[II]

The Lake House, as can be seen in the document relating to the payment of the tiles, was part of the initial complex of the Great Lake, and was included during the time Mateus Vicente was involved with the gardens.

The front 'walk' of the Great Lake.

178

In the centre of the Great Lake was a type of summer house — a lake or music house, which has now disappeared and which gave a more balanced and monumental character to the complex.

Left. *Drawing of the former Music House. Great Lake.*
Historical Archives of the Ministry of Finances.

'...it begins in the garden at the foot of the shellwork next to the horse statues...' 'Harlequin — figure represented by a black man dressed in patchwork squares of various colours, such as white, blue, green, red, black and yellow, with a hat on his head, a dagger at the waist, and yellow shoes'. Inventory of 1761 (III)

From the inventory made by the Royal Treasurer, José Gomes, we find that the atmosphere of the eighteenth century gardens was very different, with statues and lead vases painted in various colours as well as gilded.

Pensil Garden and detail of the Horse Gateway attributed to Manuel Alves.

Following pages. The Neptune Lake.

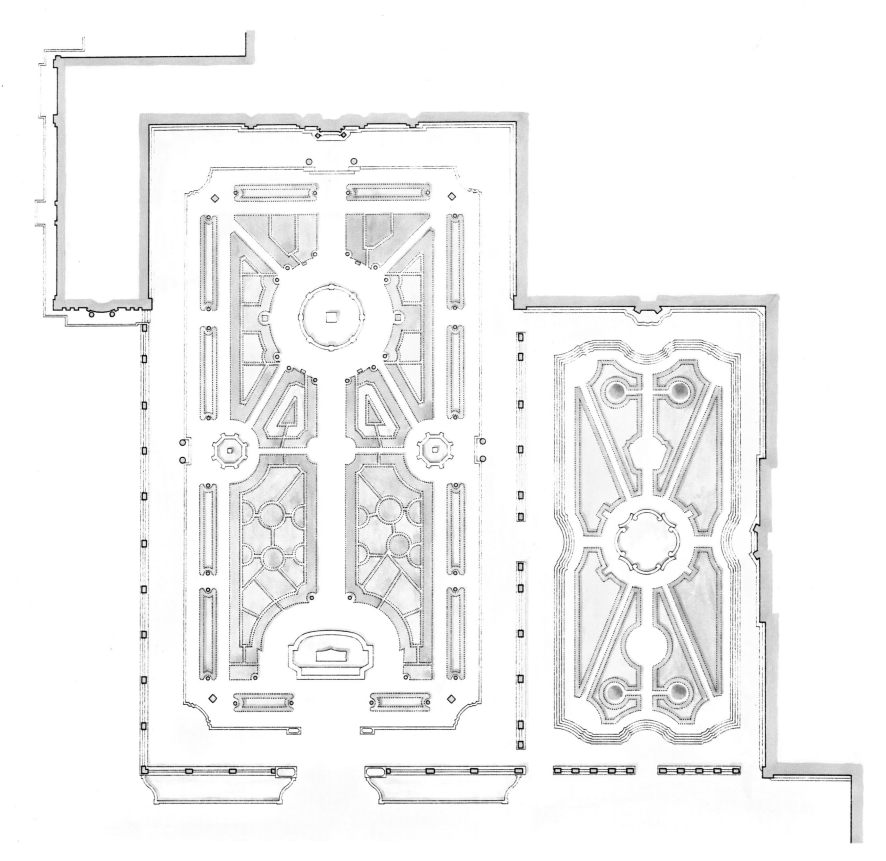

Plan of the Pensil and Malta Gardens.

184

facing west, where the ancient palace of the Marquises of Castelo Rodrigo was situated, with the lower area of the estate and the Great Lake. The succession of verandas and colonnades dissolves the effect of the mass of the façade overlooking the estate. The first veranda is at the level of the main storey of the building, connecting the Pensil Garden to the Pátio das Lontras (Otter's Terrace). On the lower storey is another veranda, which juts out more, from which a series of stairs originate, one of them being that of the Leões (Lions). Opening up into a half-orange shape, the Lion Steps connect the palace to the Lake House and to the Great Lake. The difference of scale and the proximity of these two elements has never been resolved, the Great Lake being tightly hemmed in by the proximity of the west wing of the palace.

Once the question of the relationship between the architectural mass and the exterior spaces had been resolved, the new layout of the gardens was concentrated mainly around the Pensil Garden and the Malta Garden, and its extension to the cascade.

Robillion certainly tried to create a grand axis, beginning at the façade used for ceremonies, the Cavalinhos entrance, the avenue and the cascade.

The works can be placed between 1758 and 1760, the year in which Dom Pedro married his niece Dona Maria. The inventory of the palace in 1761 gives these gardens as being completed, in contrast to the Robillion pavilion, above the Great Lake and the Lion Steps, where reference is made to finishing work.

More trees came from Amsterdam in 1758 and in the same year from Genoa '58 cases of marble'.[25] The great water-mirror in the Garden of Malta was broken up, the proximity of which to the Throne Room and extension had continued an ancient tradition which went back to the fifteenth and sixteenth centuries, as may be seen in numerous cases such as at the Palace of Agua de Peixe, Torre da Ribafria, in Sintra, Amoreira da Torre, near Montemor-o-Novo, the Palace of Mitra, near Evora and the Quinta das Torres. These great water-mirrors near the house were the most characteristic element of Portuguese gardens, and, with Robillion, the initial layout of Queluz lost the most significant of elements.

Payments were made to Diogo Ferreira, Filipe da Costa and André Claro for the balustrades of these gardens. The Fame statues, attributed to the sculptors Filipe Costa and Manuel Alves, were clearly inspired by the horses at the royal gardens at Marly.

Surrounded by balustrades, the Pensil Garden is raised on arches in order to create the effect of a greater surface area. The space is structured around two large lakes, one at each end; possibly there was a smaller one in the centre, although this has since disappeared.

It is here that all the architectural and decorative elements were is concentrated, thus subtly passing the centre of interest to this side of the gardens, to disadvantage to the area round the Great Lake and the Barraca Rica.

If Robillion wanted to give the Pensil Garden and the Malta Garden a more European look he did not succeed.

The 1761 inventory stated that these gardens had a large number of statues, lakes (besides the three lakes there were other smaller ones), and ceramic vases, and that the lead statues were painted and gilded — they therefore looked quite different from today's statues.

View of the central lake in the Malta Garden and view of the balustrade and tank which separated the Pensil Garden and the Malta Garden from the former shell-work garden.

Garden in front of the south of the old palace... Autumn — 'The standing figure, naked from the waist up, with a band of skins at the waist, grapes on his head, a bowl in his right hand and a rolled sheet of paper in his left'. Inventory 1761 (IV)

The same statues mentioned in the inventory still stand near the Neptune Lake.

View of Autumn and, in the background, The Successes of Endemião, also in the same place since 1761.

Next to the Cavalinhos entrance is an octagonal lake, around which are six leads statues identical in form to the present statues found next to the Neptune lake, the only lake that has retained the original lines designed by Jean Robillion.

The lake next to the Cavalinhos entrance was substituted by the present one at the time of the works carried out by the Infante Dom João.

Besides the six statues which act as a counterpoint to the present statues on the Neptune lake, this original lake was surrounded by four small lakes, each one of which has a lead statue wearing a tail-coat, painted in various colours.

The central lake which was hexagonal, had *'in the centre a gilded naked figure, standing up, which represented Triton, and at the sides figures with shells in their mouths, from which they spouted water'.*[26]

The lead statues in the other lakes would naturally be gilded, thus conferring an atmosphere of luxury. Besides these lead statues gilded and painted in various colours, there were also to be found in the Pensil Garden *'seventeen blue painted porcelain vases from the Rato factory, with four grim-looking countenances on the sides'* and *'eight lead vases painted in various colours with two handles, and gold-coloured snakes, which sat on top of small jasper shelves'.*[27]

* * *

According to the description of 1761 the Garden of Malta underwent fewer transformations; the central lake retained the *'dolphin being lifted up by three children'*[28] and there still existed in 1933, on two sides *'two large shells lying on the ground and between them ... a rock with figures of boys spouting water'* and on the other side *'two angular basins, with figures'.*[29] These groups were almost certainly removed to clear the space of an excess of statues, thereby giving the garden a more European look which did not correspond, as we have seen, to the Portuguese taste of the eighteenth century.

The Garden of Malta was closed off on the south side by a balustrade with six sets of statues of small boys and six marble vases. A payment note from the king's treasurer to Rodrigo de Lessert, in 1760, refers to these statues: *'2 statues of boys, set apart, 6 vases, 2 sets of two boys together and 2 bigger ones'.*[30]

The cascade, due to its close connection with the Pensil Garden and its development, was probably built at this time despite it only being in 1778 that we find a document referring to 'the painting of the statues'. A nineteenth century map of Queluz (in the Historical Archives of the Ministry of Finances) shows the cascade as being larger than it is at present. On each side a type of gallery is indicated and in front a large lake. The greater complexity of the cascade corresponds to the decoration in the eighteenth century with *'eighteen marble busts, on pedestals, sixteen columns and ten wooden figures painted in various colours'.*[31] On the balustrade which ran from the upper part, there existed a further *'four statues, two made of lead and two of stone'.*[32]

The works at the bottom of the gardens at Queluz were

'...in the centre a naked standing figure, all gold, which represents Triton, and on the sides figures with shells in their mouths from which water spouts out.' Caldeira Pires.[V]

The statues of the lakes were gilded, giving a feeling of luxury and exoticism which is difficult to imagine today.

Lake of Tritons with the ceremonial façade in the background.

Following pages. Malta Garden with statues and vases, which came from Genoa, 1758.

Spring — 'standing figure, naked, with flowers on her arms and head'. Inventory 1761 (VI)

Lead statue near the Neptune Lake.

190

finished around the year 1760, the date of the marriage of the Infante with his niece Dona Maria.

THE FINAL PERIOD
the third phase of the gardens at Queluz

I n the following years, until the time of the departure of the royal family for Brazil in 1807, the work carried out on the gardens was limited to small improvements which were mainly concentrated in the Grande Garden which connected the other gardens to the Bull Ring.

At the end of the life of Dom Pedro, significant work was carried out in the Grande Garden and, in the form of improvement work in the Pensil Garden, this continued until the time of Dom João.

An important point can be seen in the documentation of this period: foreign artistic labour ceased to be important in the work being carried out. The last order of statues from Genoa was in around 1760 (although it was only completely paid for in 1769). Silvestre de Faria Lobo, master wood carver, carved models out of wood which were then cast in lead, for both the Grande Garden and the Pensil Garden.

After Faria Lobo's death, he was followed by Francisco Leal Garcia as master sculptor, although it is likely that the latter had previously worked with Lobo at Queluz.

The Lake of the Tritons was constructed in the Pensil Garden at this time as were two other small lakes in the middle of the same garden, all three altering the initial structure of the whole. The lead vases were substituted by marble ones and ceramic vases from the Rato factory were used to decorate the Grande Garden. Great lakes were also constructed in the garden, and it is possible that these were the old ones which existed in the Pensil Garden.

Besides large bird cages, the gardens were also likely to have had cages for exotic animals from the very beginning. The existence of these animals was not a rare occurrence. Ever since the fifteenth century, the kings and the court delighted in the animals which came from Africa. The cages in the gardens at the Belém palace can still be seen in the Animal's Courtyard (Páteo dos Bichos), which Gorani described: *'there was an elephant, lions, tigers, leopards and zebras which lived in cages'.*[33] When the royal family returned from Brazil, new cages were put up and in 1833 there were *'lions, buffaloes, tigers, deer, monkeys, cats, hunting dogs and greyhounds'.*[34]

The elegant cages, *'built of stone and plaster',*[35] were constructed in 1759 and painted by José dos Santos, who also worked on the Barraca Rica and on the Lake House, and were probably in ruins at the time of the royal family's return. There existed, however, in 1833 *'different birds from India, Angolan fowl, royal ducks, peacocks, cockatoos, eagles, falcons, canaries, pigeons... and swans'.*[36] This last, of which there was only one pair in 1833, had been the best loved in the palace until the royal family left for Brazil. There was a special guard for the swans, Manuel de Boi, and *'he had 183 in his care, including black, white and young'*.[37] These swans were distributed throughout the different lakes and gardens: *'In the Pensil garden there were three black swans and a white one; in the Malta or Shell-work garden there were two white ones; in the Maze gardem, three white ones; in the Ribeira garden (this refers to the Great Lake) four black and five white; in the garden of the Greenhouses, five white; and in the swans breeding area at the water deposit lake, at the far end of the farm, 17 white and 8 black with their young'*.[38]

THE YEARS OF LONELINESS
the abandoned palace

The departure of the royal family for Brazil marked the end of Queluz as a royal residence. During the nineteenth century, palace and gardens were abandoned as if a curse had fallen on the place, where everything was *'sad, desolate, deserted'*,[39] dominated by *'an evil genius, which holds sway over that land'*.[40]

But even though abandoned, the gardens were, during the nineteenth century, a source of materials for other royal palaces: *'King Dom Fernando transferred various lakes from Queluz to the palaces of Alfeite, Belém and Necessidades'*.[41]

The pavilions fell into ruin and were demolished; the statues were scattered and ultimately lost; and the original layout of the majority of the gardens — with the exception of the Pensil and Malta Gardens — became unrecognisable. The remains and the vast amount of documents existing are enough, however, to throw light on the so-called transformation that Queluz underwent. Extending over a vast area and with no parallel in any other royal garden, Queluz ended up between two worlds. While importing everything from Europe, the general layout and atmosphere remove it completely from the great European garden tradition of the eighteenth century.

The daily life and the standards of taste of the court filtered everything that came from Europe, imposing an atmosphere of intimacy and privacy which was closer to that of Oriental than European courts. These Oriental customs, of which books and diaries of foreigners in Portugal made detailed mention, corresponded in essence to another concept of space and of the world which extended to the concept of the house itself. The habit of the ladies *'sitting down in the oriental fashion, with legs crossed'*,[42] the *'inviolable Portuguese custom'* of the ladies never being able to approach strangers or men known to them without special authorisation, and the existence of *'close relationships between male servants and ladies'*,[43] transformed the house into a closed community that faced inwards on to its gardens and which possessed no significant exterior. Queluz was the most perfect example of this.

Summer — 'standing figure, naked' with ears of corn on his head and a scythe in his left hand'. Inventory 1761 (VII)

Lead statue near the Neptune Lake.

191

SOME DOCUMENTS ON THE GARDENS AT QUELUZ
from the time of
Mateus Vicente, 1754-1757

Em 1755, pelo navio Snr.ª Maria, do Capitão Fede Mellis, vieram as seguintes árvores:

400 Arvores chamadas *Lindes* em

100 pacas	a	$945 rs.	378$000
20 *Castanheiros bravos* em 70 pacas	a	$733 rs.	14$660
28 Piramides piquenas de buxo	a	$365 rs.	10$220
172 Dittas grandes	a	$915 rs.	157$380
100 Piramides de Taxis, velguive	a	809 rs.	80$000
100 Dittas xatas	a	$365 rs.	36$500

No mesmo ano, no navio Adrianna, do Capitão Gieuveris Segenbergh, vieram as seguintes:

200 Arvores chamadas Lindes	a	1$060 rs.	212$000
200 Olmos	a	$390 rs.	78$000
50 Arvores de uvas de tordos	a	$208 rs.	10$400
20 Figuras de buxo	a 1$630 rs.	32$600	
8 Piramides de buxo grandes	a	1$008 rs.	8$064
172 Ditas piquenas	a	$380 rs.	65$360
6 Arbore Vita	a	1$000 rs.	6$000
100 Feixes de buxo solto	a	$260 rs.	26$000
50 Trepadeyras	a	$106 rs.	5$300

Juntamente com estas árvores vieram mais:

2 Tizoiras de jardim	a	2$880 rs.
2 Ditas mais piquenas	a	$789 rs.
2 Fouces e seus cabos	a	1$332 rs.
1 Rede com diversos papeis de sementes de ortalice e legumes	a	3$500 rs.

According to the inventory of 1761, the Pensil Garden was decorated with seventeen ceramic vases from the Rato factory, painted blue, of which only a few remain, and eight lead vases with two handles in the shape of golden snakes and painted in various colours. These gave an exotic atmosphere, now lost.

Above. *Vase on plinth in the Pensil Garden.*

THE WELL ORDERED GARDENS OF THE SOUTH

during the eighteenth and early nineteenth centuries

CHAPTER VIII

The 1755 earthquake and the social transformations brought about by the reforms of the Marquis of Pombal created a new wave of interest in country retreats and their gardens in the second half of the eighteenth century.

For several decades, the earthquake remained in the memory of the population of Lisbon as a terrible curse that had fallen on the city. The great families who had withdrawn to their country retreats mostly chose to abandon the ruins of their palaces in Lisbon and to set up permanent homes on the outskirts of the city. Loures, Benfica, Carnide, Lumiar, Algés, Pedroços, Caxias, Belas and Sintra were the places chosen by the aristocracy and rich middle class. The Cadavals set up residence in Pedroços, abandoning the ruins of their palace in São Sebastião de Pedreira; the Marquises of Angêja moved to Lumiar (Quinta de Monteiro-Môr); the Marquises of Marialva to Belém; the Counts of Mesquitela to Carnide; the Correios-Mor to Loures together with the Marquises of Valadares — to name a few. With the exception of the Quinta de São Domingos de Benfica, belonging to the Marquises of Fronteira, the magnificence of which dispensed with the need for significant alterations, many of these estates required large-scale restoration work and their gardens were transformed in accordance with the changes in taste and customs.

At the same time that the consequences of the earthquake were still being felt, the Marquis of Pombal, using the support of a new middle class imbued with European influences, introduced reforms in an attempt to modernise the country and alter the traditional way of social life.

As these reforms were only half introduced, in part due to the compulsive and haphazard way in which they were applied, only a slow change was apparent. The middle class, protected by the Marquis, and in particular by the very rich foreign merchants Devisme, Gildemeester, Ratton and Horne, had customs that were entirely different from those of the old Portuguese aristocracy. The house and its gardens had a place in social life, being constantly used for dinners, receptions and musical soirées. For this middle class the house was the principal symbol of sophistication and wealth, and one in which the woman had a role to play alongside the man, which was not the case among the old aristocracy.

Around this old aristocracy, which Pombal violently attacked, was concentrated an ancient tradition and radically different concept of the house which extended to the gardens. The standing of a family was a direct consequence of the close ties between its relations (grandparents, uncles, brothers, cousins, nephews) and the servants and members of their families. The more powerful a family, the greater the number of people associated with it, and they set themselves apart inside a closed community in which the intimacy between the master and servant always disturbed foreigners.

Carrère in his *Tableau de Lisbonne en 1786*, refers in an extensive chapter to *'armies of servants'*.[1] In his memoirs, the 6th Marquis of Fronteira considers his family as a group of relatives and servants: *'My family, as has already been said, is composed of my mother and my aunts, João Evangelista Machado, who exercises the functions of butler of the house, Dona Mariana, my sister's chambermaid, and, all in all, including both masters and servants, more than eighty persons'*.[2] Ruders and Beckford were surprised at the intimacy between servants and masters, the former writing: *'The nobles rarely maintain relationships with persons who do not belong to their caste, but with the servants they are usually very condescending. It is not rare to see the countess and her maid at the same window in a very familiar attitude'*.[3]

These customs were reflected in architecture and gardens and

Opposite page. *Detail of the Cascade of the Poets.*
Gardens of the Marquis of Pombal. Oeiras.

contributed to the scant attention the nobility paid to the outer façades of their palaces or the relationship of the house with its surroundings. In the eighteenth century, house and gardens were still enclosed in a world of privacy limited to a small social circle, and these gardens did not acquire that urban theatricality which one sees throughout Europe and which the new middle class of the Marquis of Pombal tried to introduce.

Although small alterations in customs did occur, it was only very slowly, and we find that later on some of the palaces and gardens built by the rich foreign traders were bought by the old aristocracy. This was the case of the Palace of Seteais, sold by the widow of Daniel Gildemeester to the Marquises of Marialva, and the Palace of Devisme in São Domingos de Benfica bought by the Marquis of Abrantes.

The gardens of the second half of the eighteenth century reveal, however, a pseudo-metamorphosis which can be seen quite clearly at Queluz. Queluz, which imported everything from Europe, including the gardener and the architect, has the most beautiful and imposing of façades and these face on to and enclose the gardens. The community there was also closed in on itself and, as happened to other members of the aristocracy, Dona Maria I was criticised for her friendship with Dona Rosa, a 'black maid with a squashed nose',[4] who accompanied her everywhere. The pseudo-metamorphosis of Queluz, which is to be seen in other Portuguese gardens of the time, reveals an apparent adoption of European spatial and aesthetic values which were basically limited to a simple alteration of the decorative elements.

* * *

THE PERMANENCY OF THE CONCEPT
of the crypto-magic garden

An analysis of the different diaries and books written by foreigners regularly reveals a certain surprise as regards Portuguese customs in both architecture and garden design. Normally written from an egocentric and superficial point of view, these texts ridiculed everything the writers saw, without distinguishing between what constituted real backwardness in an economically ruined country dominated by foreign interests and what constituted a true aesthetic and cultural tradition.

In 1791 Link described the permanence of the concept of spatial containment of Portuguese gardens when he wrote: 'Almost all the outskirts of Lisbon, especially to the east and north-east, to a great distance away, are covered in gardens surrounded by high walls. It is unbearable that we run the risk of losing our way for hours between these high walls, from which one can obtain no view. It is to the shadowy and oriental character of the Moors, to jealousy or to other similar passions that one probably owes the construction of these walls, which remind us more of the walls of a fortress than those of a garden'.[5] The inner face of the walls was covered with climbing plants 'rising and falling along the length of the walls which they cover like a closely woven mesh'.

Link, like the majority of foreigners, was only rarely invited to the homes of aristocratic families, and did not visit any sophisticated refined gardens where the walls were covered with glazed tiles, of which the gardens of the Counts of Mesquitela in Carnide are still an excellent example.

Surrounded by high walls, covered with climbing plants or 'surrounded with lemon and orange trees' [6] or glazed tiles, these gardens have remained since the sixteenth and seventeenth centuries as true architectural spaces which, in the words of Courtils, 'are more a room of greenery than true gardens' [7] (the concept of the garden as used here is the French or European one). The low walls forming benches and flowerboxes, the balustrades and the tiled pavement which were used to reinforce the architectural character of a place conceived as being one of comfort and relaxation, caused Beckford to describe the Ajuda Botanic Garden as having 'the appearance of a cemetery'.[8]

In England, especially from the eighteenth century onwards, a taste developed for the natural garden which was treated like a natural park, and which better corresponded to the nature and the climate of the country. It was thinking of the English parks that made Beckford react in the way he did to the formal and architectural character of Portuguese gardens. Although surrounded by high walls, the tendency was for gardens to be set out either on top of slopes or else spread out over them so as to take advantage of the beautiful views, to which Beckford was not indifferent: 'The garden is very pleasant and is situated on a rise full of plane trees, acacias, Indian cigar trees and other trees of a very gentle green, with flowers all round. At the top of this airy park rises an ample and majestic terrace with balustrades of a scintillating whiteness. I have never seen better hewn or chiselled balustrades than those which line the steps which lead from the wood to the terrace. The whole of the ample surface is divided into oblong marble flowerbeds, which contain a not very large variety of vanilla plants, aloes, geraniums, tea roses and the most common plants to be found in our green-houses. These heavy flowerboxes create a bad effect. They give this side of the garden the appearfance of a cemetery'.[9]

Months later, when he had visited the Quinta das Laranjeiras belonging to the Quintelas (another rich merchant protected by the Marquis), Beckford again referred to the garden saying 'it is a flat, dead and sandy thing. So full of immense urns and squat obelisks that it seems to be a churchyard full of tombstones'.[10]

The architectural character of the Portuguese garden, which was composed of terraces, was related to the geography and climate of the country. The hot, dry Mediterranean summers with little rain meant that watering techniques had to be developed and the land adapted to ensure a greater economy of water. Consequently, orchards were grown on terraces of different levels according to the slope of the land. From the highest point, on which the reservoirs and tanks which received water were normally situated, these terraces were provided with piping, fountains and small tanks. Located next to the supporting walls, the fountains and small tanks served as reservoirs for each terrace, thereby preventing water wastage.

The geographical conditions of the countries of central Europe and England were radically different. The abundance of water, even in the summer, ensured a green landscape without the need

200

for a watering system or adaptation of the land.

In the Mediterranean countries, especially in the summer, the stark contrast between the garden and the surrounding land, the presence of a cool and green place surrounded by a dry and burning nature, seems to generate a sense of magic.

Sintra, which for centuries was a favourite resort for foreigners, had a charming green landscape even in high summer. The warm, humid climate associated with the existence of an expanse of water encouraged the growth of exotic trees and plants. Laura Junot, who criticised everything in Portugal, was delighted by Sintra: *'The mountain appears to be covered with country houses: country estates which are charming refuges and whose orchards of orange and lemon trees make one think of brides' bouquets and whose woods are composed of India pines, banana plants and exotic trees from the island of Madeira'*.[11]

Besides their architectural character, that is the structuring into various terraces, eighteenth century Portuguese gardens also revealed an organisation which was subject to values of both a social and geographical order. Next to the house was the garden or box garden, a space which was always different from the other orchards and gardens that were laid out in a natural way, adapting themselves to the geography of the terrain.

It is like this that the gardens of the Quinta of the Marquis of Pombal in Oeiras appear today. The two small box gardens attached to the house are separated from the other spaces by steps which transform them into veranda-terraces.

The reduced size of the box garden is related to the private character of the place, in contrast with the orchard-gardens which are laid out below in a vast valley.

Although grand, these gardens are somewhat removed from the European layout which regulates the whole and Costigan referred to this after his visit to the palace: *'The gardens are very extensive and badly suited to recreation'*.[12]

The box gardens composed of one or more terraces do not differ much from those of the seventeenth century. The box is,

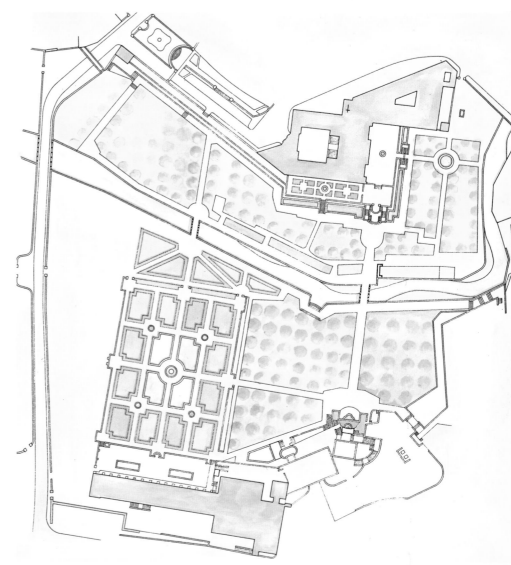

'...the gardens are very extensive and badly suited to recreation and one can see that there has been an attempt to make use of everything. The grounds are covered with orange trees, lemon trees and almond trees...' Costigan. 1778 [1]

Costigan's aesthetic standards refer to the concept of the English park, incompatible with the Portuguese tradition where orange and lemon trees, through their perfume, had had, ever since the fifteenth century, a symbolism and recreational significance unknown in Europe beyond the Pyrenees.
Plan of the gardens and view of the main staircase which links the box garden to the pleasure orchard.

Gardens of the Marquis of Pombal. Oeiras.

View of the approach to the palace as seen from the cascade. Set out on a different level, the box garden remains independent of the orchard-gardens, in a gradation of privacy and spatial hierarchy which determines a discontinuous layout of the gardens.

Gardens of the Marquis of Pombal. Oeiras.

therefore, cut into lower shapes without high pyramids, balls and other topiary shapes. The fashion for *rocaille*, which we mainly know about through engravings, appears in the box hedge design in the form of coils and asymmetrical curves, but the spatial structure did not undergo any significant transformation. Beckford's description of the gardens the Marquises of Marialva ordered to be constructed in the 1780s in their country retreat in Sintra can still be applied to a seventeenth century garden: *'Now it is a beautiful pavilion designed by Pillement and decorated with elegance, and it has a chess-board garden with statues and fountains. Closed in avenues of laurel and viburnum, cascades, arbours, pruned box and all the ornaments that the false taste of the Portuguese gardeners transform into something that is appreciated'.*[15] The so-called 'false' taste clearly reflects the contrast between the English-style natural garden and the Portuguese-style architectural garden.

In some cases, the different gardens seem to acquire a certain unity of layout by means of an axis which, from the centre of the house façade facing the gardens, organises the different spaces. This pathway appears in Queluz between the Pensil Garden and the cascade, but it can only be seen on a plan and is restricted to a small part of the whole of the overall layout of Queluz.

The garden of the Quinta das Laranjeiras is virtually the only layout to present a clear axis development line for the entire whole. The effect of continuity and spatial grandeur based on the rational layout of Le Nôtre is reduced here by the box garden which is directly connected to the house, which in turn is surrounded by railings and columns.

In general terms, the eighteenth century garden tended to remain as a concept of discontinuous space with a rigid hierarchy, and was composed of a series of interconnected gardens, each with a different level of privacy and formality of layout.

THE PLEASURE ORCHARD
and the reports of travellers

The most characteristic feature of eighteenth century Portuguese gardens, and one which was regularly referred to by all the foreigners who visited them, was the presence of orange and lemon trees. This tradition, which was first seen in the fifteenth century in the origins of the Portuguese garden, was, in its turn, to be found in an Islamic tradition of emphasising the value of the olfactory as well as the visual sense.

The various blossomings throughout the year, leaving a heady perfume in the air, ensured that these trees remained as one of the most typical elements of Portuguese gardens up to the nineteenth century.

Unfortunately, the majority of these gardens lost their orange and lemon trees in the nineteenth and twentieth centuries. The descriptions both of Dalrymple and Costigan who visited the gardens of the palace of the Marquis of Pombal in Oeiras are very specific about this. The former tells us: *'I had the opportunity to see the gardens of the Marquis of Pombal and the improvements made to it; there are cascades and great rows of orange and lemon trees, but they have been set out in a tasteless manner'.*[14] The latter, perhaps with even less sensitivity, states: *'The gardens* are very extensive and badly suited to recreation and one can see that there has been an attempt to make use of everything. The grounds are covered with orange trees, lemon trees and almond trees, and there is a large building in one part of the garden for silk-worms...' (15)

For the writers who had a more sensitive and poetic spirit, it was this aspect which charmed them the most: *'The lemon trees have been planted outside the high walls which surround the garden — some in flower, others bearing green lemons and others with already ripe fruit. On the inside of the wall, apple and orange trees are to be found, the latter with their branches hanging down under the weight of the fruit. And on all sides, one finds beautiful beds of flowers and many types of bush giving off perfumes. On the hill are some majestic cedars and the garden is decorated all over with marble figures which have been set out on numerous pedestals, which are also of marble, and they present a picture of varied and Romanesque aspect'.*(16)

Despite his refined English culture, Beckford frequently shows himself captivated by the charms of the orange and lemon trees and trellises of the gardens, when he writes: *'After dinner, I sat on the veranda talking...and enjoying the cool breeze that pleasantly blew through the leaves of the vines of the new small garden...'* (17)

In the country estate of Street Arriaga at Carnide (later on the estate of the Counts of Carnide), Beckford writes: *'Mr Horne and I, who were expecting to meet the group there...and spend the afternoon strolling with them among the vines and groves of lemon trees that surround the farm...'* (18)

The omnipresence of orange and lemon trees and trellises together with the concept of a markedly architectural garden composed of terraces, set out somewhat in accordance with the geographical conditions, gives us what will be the permanent basic characteristics of Portuguese gardens for the next centuries. One characteristic seemed to lose importance and herald decline.

'I had an opportunity to see the Marquis of Pombal's gardens and improvements; there are some cascades, and extensive rows of orange and lemon trees, but laid out without taste...'
Dalrymple. 1774 (II)

Orange and lemon trees are regularly referred to by travellers who have visited Portugal since the fifteenth century.

Above and left. *View of the cascade and entrance to the rose garden.*

Gardens of the Marquis of Pombal. Oeiras.

203

'...Four pointer hunting dogs of jasper, sitting...'
were referred to in the Pensil Garden, in the
Palace of Queluz inventory. Inventory 1761 (III)

*The taste for statues of pets was related to the nature of the
gardens, which were conceived to be lived in on a day-to-day basis
with intimate and domestic spaces.*

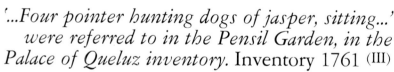

Terrace garden. Palace of the Marquis of Pombal. Oeiras.

Certain architectural elements, such as the summer house and the
lakes which functioned as strong space-polarising points of attraction, lost impact and size and contributed to a certain fluidity and
breaking-up of the layout of gardens.

THE DECLINE OF
THE ELEMENTS
which polarise space

During the sixteenth and seventeenth centuries, gardens which
were considered especially beautiful were given summer
houses, aviaries for exotic birds and lake-tanks which, due to their
monumental character in relation to the spaces in which they
were set, fulfilled a function which was to unify the organic layout

of the garden. Forming scenic backdrops within the gardens, as is the case with, for example, the lake houses in the gardens of Bacalhoa or Fronteira, with the lake of the Torres estate, or with the aviary of the Palace of Belém, these elements gave the space a special character which contrasted with the apparently disorderly character of the surrounding landscape.

The great lake of Queluz (the Jamôr Reservoir), despite its size and the richness of the decoration, possesses neither the location nor the framework necessary to establish the cohesion of the various gardens to be found around it. Hemmed in on one side by the presence of Jean Robillion's pavilion, the great lake lies along the banks of the Jamôr stream, independent of a common layout. This polarising effect was connected to the scale relationships between the architectural elements and the space. The monumentality of the lake house in the gardens of the Marquises of Fronteira comes from the small proportions of the box garden where the house provides a majestic and enveloping backdrop.

Cascades, which originate with the Queluz cascade, and which create a series of water effects, do not fulfil this function, it being found that they are incapable of creating sub-spaces for comfort and well-being around themselves. Their location at the end of

'...a parterre with statues and fountains...and every ornament the false taste of Portuguese gardening renders desirable...' Beckford. 1787 [IV]

Beckford was referring to the gardens of the Marquis of Marialva in Sintra, constructed a short time after those of Oeiras.

Terrace garden. Palace of the Marquis of Pombal. Oeiras.

Like a series of autonomous spaces, the gardens of the eighteenth century tended to be structured in one or more gardened terraces closely connected to the house, and separated from the rest of the complex.

Terrace facing west overlooking the ancient orchard-terrace, and the path to the garden facing south.

Gardens of the Marquis of Pombal. Oeiras.

vast avenues, as at Queluz and Oeiras, diminishes their polarising effect.

We know, however, that the cascade at Queluz was much bigger in the eighteenth century than it is today, being framed by two galleries with columns, balustrades and statues. The cascade in the Royal Gardens at Caxias, which are composed of various terraces is, without doubt, more monumental.

Cascades were used to recreate a natural atmosphere and thus heralded the fashion for the Romantic garden, where comfort and well-being were regarded as being less important than a scenic space to be enjoyed visually from winding pathways. At the end of a great cultural cycle, the gardens of the eighteenth century still possessed the last of the 'walks' set out in the form of long galleries or latticed arbours as we saw in the sixteenth and seventeenth centuries. These walks were conceived as specific spaces for strolling and conversing, the consequence of the layout of a garden composed of autonomous and hierarchical spaces. Next to these galleries and lattices were walls with benches and flowerboxes. The Great Lake at Queluz was also a late example of this ancient tradition. Beckford mentions a walk around trellises *'of vines, set in marble pillars...which connect the palace to the chapel'*. The author also stated that *'there is something majestic in this green gallery...'* [19]

The relationship with the chapel emphasised certain aspects connected with the end of the mass and the distant relationships between women and men. In the gardens of the Fronteira Palace, there is a walk in the form of a terrace which connects the house to the chapel. The dignity of these spaces — clearly evident in the Fronteira Palace — corresponds to their importance in romantic life, especially that of the aristocracy. It was here that young people sometimes exchanged looks or whispers with their beloved.

'...The gardens, which were very large, were in the rear of the palace... in four terraces connected by steps, and all the walls of the steps were covered with tiles...' Ayres. 1909 (V)

The author was referring to the former gardens of the Quinta de Pintéus. These illustrated the crypto-magic garden concept, the most decorated façades facing the gardens, like those at Queluz, without any of the aesthetic and domestic character being revealed on the exterior.

Detail of the south façade. Gardens of the Marquis de Pombal. Oeiras.

* * *

THE TRADITION OF THE DEAMBULATORY
and the public walk

As we have seen, the walk illustrates a concept of space and social relationship which radically separates it from the Europe of the eighteenth century where gardens were structured around a great axis which regulated the layout.

The total failure to identify with the concept of a 'public walk' is a prime reason for the continuation in the eighteenth century of the crypto-magic concept of the Portuguese garden.

When the Marquis of Pombal ordered a park to be created to mark the limits of his reconstructed Lisbon (Lisboa Moderna), following the great earthquake, the architect Reinaldo Manuel based the plan of the new park on the Portuguese tradition of the

the tiles reveal a sophistication and aestheticism.

Gardens of the Counts of Mesquitela. Carnide.

213

Surrounded by high walls, certain gardens in the eighteenth century still revealed a concept of spatial containment to which tile-work conferred an ambience of sensory fascination — a tradition in Portuguese gardens since the sixteenth century. Above. Wall facing south with a series of figures reproduced from engravings of ancient statues: Venus de Medici, Amazon, two groups of fighters, Apollo, Mercury, Centaur and Eros, Castor and Pollux, Mars and Mercury.
In the centre, designs symbolic of mathematics and history.

Gardens of the Counts of Mesquitela. Carnide.

214

'...Almost all the outskirts of Lisbon... are covered with gardens surrounded by high walls. It is unbearable to walk...between these high walls from which one can enjoy no view...'
Link. 1797 (VIII)

'...Presque tous les environs de Lisbonne...sont couverts de jardins entourés de hautes murailles. C'est une chose insuportable que de marcher...entre ces murailles élevées, ou l'on ne jouit d'aucune vue...'
These high walls corresponded to that particular concept of space in Portuguese gardens unknown to Link and Europe beyond the Pyrenees.
Left. Details of the D-shaped walls with figures symbolic of Asia and Africa.

Gardens of the Counts of Mesquitela. Carnide.

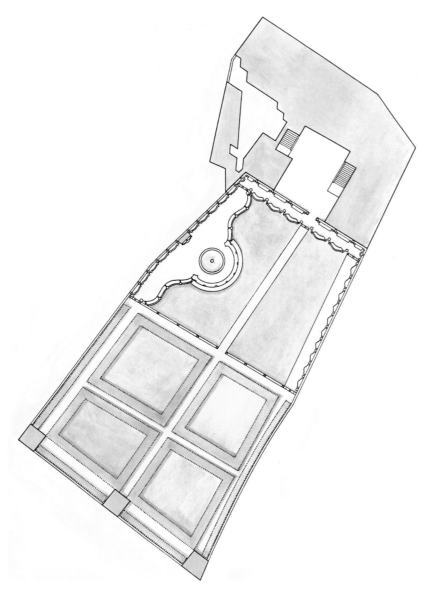

'The gardens of the farm, delimited in the ancient way... also underwent complete remodelling, adapting themselves to modern tastes, in the style of the English gardens'. Sousa Viterbo. 1909 (IX)

Although transformed in terms of their decorative vegetation, the architectural layout of the first garden remains, together with its paths bordered with flowerboxes, benches and fountains.

Quinta dos Azulejos. Lumiar.

with the almost complete abandonment of the majority of estates and gardens in the eighteenth century. In a letter written in 1909, Cristóvam Ayres described the ruins of the gardens of the Casa de Pinteus: *'The gardens themselves, which were very extensive, were to be found at the rear of the palace, on four levels connected by steps, and all the walls of the steps were covered in blue and white tiles, and there were also tiled figures, some of which were still attached to the ruins.*

'The lower level, to which one descends from a tile-covered terrace, with pictures depicting scenes from daily life, faces the west, all of which is surrounded by walls, benches and flowerboxes covered with tiles, and there is a stone tank, which is round in the middle, the whole being shaded by ash, poplar and other trees. All of this has disappeared, and the ground has been transformed into an orange grove. The design of the gardens and the kitchen-garden, which is called the capella, *and which goes down in terraces all the way to the river, and which in the past was also covered in tiles — on the steps, on the tank, on the walls, from top to bottom — must have been the work of an artist or artists of worth...'* [22]

Besides the interest in the description of a typical plan of an eighteenth century estate, the tile appears as a decorative element *par excellence* in both the gardens and the so-called *capella* kitchen-garden.

From the middle of the century onwards, other colours began to be used besides blue and white: yellow, green and purple, together with the development of the *rocaille* style.

The most sophisticated examples of this time came from the Rato factory: precision of design was combined with spontaneity of line. Considered by some art critics as *'a poor man's painting'*, the value of the tile is chiefly expressed through its architectural qualities.

Both tiles and shell-work possess characteristics that have made them popular with everyone, from the common man to the aristocracy, ever since the seventeenth century. In both cases, it is from poor materials that an infinity of effects and designs rich in spontaneity and poetry are obtained. Beckford, like Corsini a century before him, referred to shell-work. He described how, on his visit to the Convent of São José de Ribamar, he came across *'an almost hidden wall of bright decorative masonry composed of shells which a reverend brother, ten or eleven years before, had covered during his leisure hours. Glass beads, glazed earthenware saucers and plates, with the bottom facing outwards, were the main elements of this decoration.*

'I had already noted this tendency for decorative masonry using shell-work and glazed earthenware fragments in the house of a certain Mr. Devisme, whose garden in Benfica, about a league from Lisbon, eclipses all the celebrated lead statues, Chinese temples, winding rivers and old chapels of Bagnigge Wells, White Conduit House and Marylebone...' [23]

* * *

'It is more a room of greenery than a real garden...' Courtils. 1755 (X)

'C'est plutôt une sale de verdure q'un vrai jardin...'
Although Courtils was referring to the garden of the Convent of Mafra, the phrase could be applied to the majority of eighteenth century Portuguese gardens, as well as to the concept of an architectural garden and a garden of comfort and well-being, of which the Quinta dos Azulejos is one of the best examples.

Quinta dos Azulejos. Lumiar.

Their Excellent Majesties
Happily Reigning
Dom José and Queen N.S.
did this house the great favour of using it on
3 November 1753 and will repeat this
Honour with all the Royal Family

While António Colaço Torres wanted without doubt to dazzle the court with his gardens, the aesthetic option he took has given us one of the most typical examples of an architectural garden. Due to its architectural adaptation, forming frames, pilasters, capitals and columns, the tile-work of the Quinta dos Azulejos is the most complex example of this art in eighteenth century gardens.
Entrance walk and Europa fountain.
Quinta dos Azulejos.Lumiar.

THE QUINTA DOS AZULEJOS
and the tradition of the leisure and walk garden

Of the few examples of eighteenth century gardens that remain today with no significant alterations, the Quinta dos Azulejos is, without doubt, the most interesting.

Its value comes not only from its refined decorative treatment but also, and in particular, from its architectural conception. Courtils said of the gardens that they seemed more like *'a room of greenery than a real garden'*, in the sense of the European garden, conceived more in the form of a landscaped rather than an architectural order.

Surrounded by high walls totally covered in tiles, the gardens are closed in on themselves in a reserved atmosphere, without any contact with the exterior, and this not only transforms them into the clearest example of the eighteenth century Portuguese leisure garden, but also highlights the concept of crypto-magic space. The aesthetic principles which transformed Queluz *'into a medal with no reverse side'*,[24] where the most decorated façades face the gardens, without contact with the exterior, also appear here. The contrast between the exterior and the interior space — the interior being held to be sacred space, and the exterior profane and uncouth — which one observes in Portuguese gardens, is to be seen in the Quinta dos Azulejos in all its splendour, being, in the last analysis, close to the Mediterranean-Islamic tradition and not to the European tradition beyond the Pyrenees.

Besides the crypto-magic concept of space that one sees in the gardens of the Quinta dos Azulejos, another no less interesting fact can be observed in the layout of the garden. In terms of spatial structure we can still find, as at Bacalhoa or Fronteira, the value given by the 'walk'. The garden is formed by a first walk with columns, which suggests a hallway or antechamber, each walk having a set of fountains and arcades giving access to another walk which runs along the surrounding walls.

Once more, a central axis which governed the layout was rejected, since the visitor on entering is almost obliged, due to the richness of the decoration, to turn to the left or right and not go straight ahead.

The two walks which develop from the first are different, although symmetrically placed. The dissimilarity is due to domestic and not aesthetic factors. While one walk is protected from the sun by facing north, the other clearly faces south. This meant that the benches of the walk which faces north were placed against the wall, while those of the walk facing south were placed with their backs to the sun, but in front of the wall which has flowerboxes against it instead of benches. Anyone sitting on the benches of the walk facing south would be bathed by the sun and, as they have the surrounding wall of this walk for a view, the wall

Europa fountain. Quinta dos Azulejos. Lumiar.
Following pages. *Arbour surrounded by columns covered with tiles.*
Quinta dos Azulejos. Lumiar.

* * *

In the Portuguese tradition of the sixteenth and seventeenth
centuries, we still see in the eighteenth century the enhancement
of a space regarded as being a walk-deambulatory, as is the case
with the gardens at Bacalhoa and Fronteira. Transposed to a

rocaille *style, the spatial affinities, especially in the Oratory Walk*
in the gardens of the Fronteira Palace, are evident.

North and South Walk. Quinta dos Azulejos. Lumiar.

Detail of the low wall and flowerbox of the terrace-garden, with mid-eighteenth century tiles.

Quinta das Lapas. Torres Vedras.

naturally received greater decorative attention, there being concentrated here the Europa fountain and the arbour of columns.

The affinity with the gardens at Bacalhoa, also structured by three great walks along the walls and decorated with tiles, benches and flowerboxes, is evident. The similarity of spatial concepts, although with very different aesthetic models, extends to the polarising elements of the space. The features of the Lake House at Bacalhoa, between two walks, appear in the Quinta dos Azulejos in the form of the arbour with the Europa Fountain in front. A plan of the layout of the gardens at the beginning of the twentieth century indicated two small summer houses at the end of each walk, as is seen in the gardens at Bacalhoa with the Casa das Indias (Indias House) and the Casa das Pombas (House of the Doves).

The similarity of the two layouts as regards the structure of the space must be fortuitous, reflecting, therefore, the continuity of the concept over the centuries, despite the appearance of different styles.

Finally, the tile as a fine layer of shiny colours covers the whole of the space and is found in bands and strips on frames, columns, vases, capitals, bosses and panels. The effect and the fascination for the sensual is similar to that found in the gardens of the Fronteira and Bacalhoa Palaces, and is connected with an ancient tradition which can also be seen in Islamic gardens.

According to the commemorative stone that its first proprietor had engraved, the estate was visited, between 1753 and 1760, by the Royal Family, which will have led António Colaço Torres to dazzle the court with his estate and gardens.

An analysis of the tile-work reveals that the gardens were decorated in two distinct periods: the first in which the taste for blue and white was still in fashion, and the second in which yellow, green and white began to be used, thus damaging the unity and aesthetic balance of the whole.

In comparison, the gardens of the Counts of Mesquitela (today the Military College) in Carnide reflect a greater aesthetic quality. Unlike the Quinta dos Azulejos, these gardens seem to have been created in the same era, some time around 1755. Blue had not completely passed out of fashion and still predominated in relation to other colours. Since it could create greater dark-light effects, blue enhanced the value of the design and was used here for the different figures and central decorative bosses. Other colours were used along the borders and give the whole a more austere and refined effect.

In the eighteenth century, the gardens of the Counts of Mesquitela were decorated with marble statues, as is the case with the veranda-walk of the palace which looks out over the gardens. Various small pedestals of good *rocaille* design are still to be found dispersed at random in the grounds around the college building. Unfortunately, the statues have been lost.

Significantly transformed in the nineteenth century, both the gardens of the Quinta dos Azulejos and those of the Counts of Mesquitela are still two good examples of the concept of a leisure garden, surrounded by high tiled walls, a concept which was diluted during the Romantic period, due to the European aesthetic influence beyond the Pyrenees, and, especially, the fashion of the English-style garden-park.

'...In a summer house, near to the garden, I found in the shell-work that covers the interior walls, some pieces of coloured glass...'
Gabriel Pereira. 1909 (XI)

The architectural treatment of tiles in the first half of the eighteenth century, the Mannerist balustrade, and the shell-work interior of the summer house, are clearly related to the lake houses of the Marquises of Fronteira and Castelo Melhor.

Lake House. Quinta das Lapas. Torres Vedras.

'...and the entrance is in a very large courtyard with portals, surrounded by a wall, in which the bulls run...' Archive 1630 (XII)

While the archive refers to the Quinta da Bacalhoa, the entrance courtyard, closed in by high walls, of both this and other farms, reflects the liking of the nobility for bullfights, and this influenced the structure of the exterior spaces.

Entrance courtyard. Quinta das Lapas. Torres Vedras.

Opposite page: Box garden. Quinta das Lapas. Torres Vedras.

TYPICAL PORTUGUESE GARDENS

of the south in the eighteenth century

From the sixteenth century onwards, we see the simple fifteenth century orange grove of Portuguese gardens divided into two types of space: the first, a space-garden that is strictly private and intimately connected with the house, and the second, a pleasure orchard. As contemporary documentation confirms, the gardens of Bacalhoa and Vila Viçosa were structured in this way. The latter, due to its almost royal character, possessed more than one private garden — the Jardim da Duquesa and, at the rear, the Jardim das Damas.

In the second half of the seventeenth century, the construction of various large gardens, such as Fronteira, Castelo Melhor, Annunciada and Palhava, saw variations on this typical garden. The pleasure orchard was maintained, but the private garden was divided up into more than one space-garden, thereby giving it greater importance in social terms. The Large or Box Garden in the gardens of the Fronteira Palace, although enclosed at the time by high walls, acquired a scale and decoration that differentiated it from the typical space of the private garden. The need for a more private space seemed to determine that the Garden of Venus and the Oratory Walk became progressively more private and more richly decorative. The private garden is thus divided up, in terms of the typical garden, into two new types of space, although in a less obvious way: the ostentatious garden, with its clear social function, and the private garden. The fashion for shaped box gardens, introduced in the middle of the sixteenth century, is progressively concentrated in these spaces.

The typical garden, which was developed in the second half of the seventeenth century, can also be seen in the following century.

The gardens of the Belém Palace, which underwent major improvements under the Count of Aveiras, is structured around three types of space: the Jardim de Baixo (Lower Garden), the Jardim de Cima (Upper Garden), and the orchard. The Jardim de Baixo, which stretches out like a vast chess-board overlooking the Tagus, is decorated with fountains and statues and is, without doubt, the ostentatious space, and large reception rooms open on to it by means of a veranda-walk. The Jardim de Cima, which is smaller and clearly more subdued and reserved, is the private garden. The majestic aviary, in the shape of an amphitheatre which forms a backdrop, shows the importance attached to this space, as is the case with the Oratory Walk at the Fronteira Palace.

The constitution of these three typical gardens is determined by reasons of privacy and by a passion for spatial containment inherent to the concept of the garden in Portugal.

227

'Its ample surface is laid out in oblong compartments of marble... such ponderous divisions have a dismal effect...three large basins of clear water give it an air of coolness, much increased by the waving of plants and acacias...'
Beckford. 1787 (XIII)

Once again we see two opposing garden concepts: the more architectural garden of comfort and well-being and the more landscaped and natural walk-garden.

Royal Botanic Garden of Ajuda. Lisbon.

When, under Italian influence, the finely decorated box garden was created, the private garden moved to a more secluded location, without, however, it losing its special character.

It is without doubt this hierarchy of space which, in the eighteenth century, determined the constitution of a new typical space: the garden-terrace.

Because great value was put on dynamic effects, the Baroque period saw a fashion for staircases and, consequently, this led to gardens being made on various terraces. As we saw in Chapter VI, this concept of the garden and Baroque space only manifested itself in the large staircases in the north of the country. The Portuguese vision of the garden as a private and personalised space goes against the fashion for an overall vision of the layout of the whole and its spatial uniformity.

The garden-terrace, which was developed in the eighteenth century, was still used, however, as a transition space, and was unconnected with the remaining recreational spaces. In the eighteenth century, it was another version of the private garden, and although it lost its high walls, it maintained its privacy in relation to the orchard-garden and the exterior spaces. In the gardens of the Marquis of Pombal, the Quinta das Lapas in Oeiras, and in the Quinta do Freixo in Oporto, one can see garden-terraces attached to the façade of the house which constitute autonomous spaces in relation to the layout of the gardens.

The private high-walled garden, despite being less regular, continued to be used, and examples of this which are still to be found include the gardens of the Quinta dos Azulejos and the ancient gardens of the Counts of Mesquitela, in Carnide.

The eighteenth century gardens, especially in the centre and south of the country, were structured, in the majority of cases, in accordance with the individual interpretation of these four typical types of space. In Oeiras, the two garden-terraces adjoining the house were also, due to their decoration — statues, busts, pilasters and tiles — examples of the private and ostentatious garden. At the Quinta do Freixo, which we will look at in greater detail in the following chapter, one can see the formation of three terrace-gardens besides the pleasure orchard. One of the terrace-gardens, next to the west façade, possesses, due to its greater spatial containment and excessive decorative effects, the character of a private garden. The similarity of its spatial characteristics to those of the Jardim de Cima in the Belém Palace is evident.

At the end of the eighteenth century, the private garden and the importance given to a specific space for the ostentatious garden, resulted progressively in the loss of the clarity of its layout. The garden-terrace, which resolved problems of privacy with the exterior, became the type of space *par excellence,* and continued to be popular throughout almost all of the nineteenth century, especially in semi-urban pleasure farms and urban gardens. In numerous cases on the outskirts of Lisbon, Benfica, Carnide, Lumiar or in Oporto, on the slopes of the Douro, the garden-terrace developed with benches, flowerboxes and vases, and overlooking avenues and lanes so as to take advantage of the views.

* * *

228

instruido de semelhante processo pelo qual trabalho recebia cem réis para cada arratel de Anil purificado.

Desta administração nunca se me deo conta, porque o sobredito ministro tomou toda a si esta inspecção.

E não sei se se ajustarão contas com o Real Erario pelo valor do Anil recebido das companhias e daquelle que se vendeu, o qual no decurso de varios annos deve importar summas consideraveis. O que sómente sei a este respeito, é que na vespera da doença do jardineiro da qual fallezeo, que elle tinha recebidos alguns mil cruzados de huma partida de Anil vendida a Raimundo Pinto.

Extintas as sobreditas companhias pouco Anil depois veio a este Laboratorio, e fabricando-se já perfeito Anil no Brazil, cessou esta purificação.

Na casa poîs destinada a Laboratorio para conservarse as amostras das produções naturaes das colonias e os resultados das suas analyses e experiencias dei principio ao Museo com algumas produçoens naturaes daquelle que eu tinha formado neste Real Jardim e que dei de presente á Universidade de Coimbra, com outras daquelle que possuia em Padova e que veio para a mesma Universidade e com algumas e os armarios do Museo do capitam Vandeck.

Este Museo teve consideravel augmento pelo cuidado e zelo do sobredito ministro e principalmente com o que remeterão os quatro naturalistas meus dı ipulos que por este effeito de enriquecer o Museo, e fazer em consequencia a Historia Natural das Colonias S. Magestade mandou nellas viajar.

Por occasião de copiar-se huma collecção de riscos de plantas do Perú e Chyli, que vierão no Gallião que foi tomado pelos inglezes na ultima guerra, vierão da fundição tres habeis dessinadores, que unidos com dous outros que estavão no jardim para o risco do mesmo e que taobem trabalhavão em huma muito util obra para facilitar o estudo da Botanica, e consistia nas figuras de todas as frutificações dos generos das plantas athe agora conhecidas, derão principio com alguns aprendizes a actual casa do risco. As despezas que desde o principio se fizerão para este Jardim athe agora se pagavão na maneira seguinte:

O meu ordenado que S. Magestade o Senhor Rey D. Jozé me determinou no anno de 1764, e que se pagava na casa da moeda, passou o seu pagamento no Real Erario, como Director do Real Jardim Botanico; e no mesmo Erario se pagava taobem o ordenado do Jardineiro.

Os jornaes do caseiro e trabalhadores erão pagos pelo capitam Antonio Roiz por ser o mesmo caseiro que existia quando o jardim era huma quinta de frutta e hortalizes.

E as despesas das obras se pagavão no Real Erario pelas contas, ou folhas dos mestres sem fiscalização alguma.

Continuou o pagamento do caseiro e trabalhadores o Desembargador seu filho o qual tendo depois obtido de S. Magestade decreto para supraintender a todas as Quintas Reaes, quiz taobem considerar o Jardim Botanico como huma Quinta, e quiz tambem assumir a si o pagamento das obras, e por isso recebia sem distinção alguma o assignamento, ou consignação mensal pela despesa geral das Quintas, entre as quaes fez comprehender o Real Jardim Botanico, não havendo naquelle tempo Inspector, como o tem prezentemente, e como o jornal de alguns officiaes era muito modico, e os dessinadores não se podião computar entre os trabalhadores de huma quinta; assim determinou o ministro e secretario de estado do ultramar que os dessinadores recebessem o jornal da fundição e o argumento deste e dos jornaes de alguns officiaes do Jardim e Museo se augmentasse a titulo de comedorias pela secretaria do ultramar.

O total da despeza annual do Jardim e Museo depois da consignação feita ao desembargo importa em 3:038$800 réis, que com os 300$000 réis que o Desembargador aplica em obras ou que por isso se consinou em 3:600$000 réis, chegando assim a despeza annual sem computar os ordenados do Director e Jardineiro em 6:638$800 réis.

Devendo eu hir a Coimbra para reger as duas novas cadeiras de Historia Natural e de Chymica, estabelecer o Museo, Laboratorio Chymico e Jardim Botanico, entreguei a administração deste jardim ao jardineiro não deixando em cada anno no tempo das ferias vir huma ou duas vezes a esta côrte, e dirigir as operaçoens mais necessarias para concluir este jardim, que vagarosamente se hia continuando não obstante as enormes despezas que a titulo delle se fazião, as quais certamente para hum particular erão mais que sufficientes para formar tres similhantes jardins, mas que eu não podia obviar porque naquelle tempo não me era permittido sobre isso dar o meu parecer. Não deixando porém de continuar o commercio das plantas e sementes para augmento do mesmo jardim.

O jardineiro, Administrador na minha ausencia, tomando gosto ao governo independente pela protecção que tinha adquirido, chegou a pouco a pouco a não querer executar o que eu determinava em beneficio do mesmo Jardim e Museo, e deixando-se quaze totalmente da cultivação das plantas a qual era destinado, tomou

'The garden is a dead, sandy, flat place so full of huge urns and squat obelisks that it seems to be a churchyard of tombstones...' Beckford, 1787 (XVII)

Quinta das Laranjeiras. Lisbon

During the seventeenth and eighteenth centuries, the disposition of walls facing the gardens determined the construction of vast veranda-terraces. At the end of the eighteenth century, a unique decorative style emerged: a façade covered with tiles is integrated as a scenic trompe-l'oeil of the garden itself.

Above. *Façade decorated with Neo-classical tiles from the early nineteenth century.*

Quinta de São Mateus. Dafundo. Lisbon.

gosto para as conchas e outros animaes do Museo e a querer ser arquiteto, de maneira que deixou perder a maior parte das plantas, que certamente nos primeiros annos passavão de cinco mil especies, como aparece de hum catalogo do jardim, que já aprezentei não são muitos mezes ao Marquez Mordomo-mór.

ESTADO PRESENTE DO JARDIM

Contém sómente mil e duzentas especies de plantas.
As estufas têm os degraos, algumas columnas e janellas podres.
As pyramides para os vasos são muito altas.
Não estão feitas ainda as pequenas estufas para os Ananases.
No plano inferior ainda se devem pôr os cano de chumbo para fazer facil a rega, dos quaes a maior parte estavão feitos, e o dezembargador os mandou hir para a Quinta de baixo. Ainda estão sem plantas as divisões do plano inferior, nas quaes devem cultivar-se as plantas medicinaes, para as artes e economia.
O grande disproporcionado tanque que contra o meu parecer com tal antigo risco foi construido, está quaze acabado; nelle, não obstante os seus defeitos se admira a grande habilidade dos esculptores portuguezes.
O Viveiro das plantas era exausto, mas o Dr. Alexandre cuidou logo em fazelo plantar e semear.
As plantas todas, que estavam sem ordem alguma, agora se dispõem systematicamente.
A porta principal do jardim não está feita.
Não se fexou o terreno fóra do jardim donde está o tilheiro para os canteiros e algumas barracas, o qual deve servir para os estrumes e preparação de differentes terras similhantes, quanto he differente possivel, aquelles terrenos donde espontaneamente as plantas nascem, por ser todo o terreno do jardim puro saibro e terra argillosa vermelha.

LABORATORIO

Neste Laboratorio não se trabalha agora, e serve sómente para fazer-se algumas experiencias de Rapé, pelas quaes nelle existem muitas arrobas de folha de tabaco.

CASA DO RISCO

Nesta casa agora se riscão as plantas e animaes que recolheu o Dr. Alexandre nas suas viagens do Brazil.
Isto he o que posso informar da origem e estado prezente do Jardim Botanico, Laboratorio, Museo e da Casa do risco.
O que me parece respeito a este jardim e seus annexos estabelecimentos, porque se conservem e augmentem concluindo-se a Historia Natural das Colonias pelo qual principal fim o Senhor Rey D. Jozé deu principio a esta grandiosa obra, e com immensas despezas continuou S. Magestade.
Primeiro que tudo, simplifacar o pagamento das suas despezas que constão do mappa junto, no qual não entrão algumas maes do Desembargador.
Reduzindo-se a uma mensal consignação feita ao administrador de quatro centos mil réis, a qual quantia se devia tirar daquella que se faz ao Desembargador para todas as Quintas, ou entregar-se em cada quartel ao administrador hum conto e duzentos mil réis, o qual no fim do quartel desse o balanço, ou rol de todas as despezas documentado com os respectivos recibos o fiscalisado no Erario por hum official delle e assignado pelo seu prezidente se lhe passasse quitação.
Não sendo este hum simples Jardim Botanico, mas tendo annexo hum copioso e rico Museo e devendo-se nelle fazer a Historia Natural das Colonias, não he de admirar, que nelle annualmente se gaste doze mil cruzados, passando agora a total annual despeza de dezasseis mil cruzados quando M.ʳ de Visme gastava no seu jardim sómente quatro ou cinco mil cruzados cada anno.
He certo porém que esta despeza passados dous ou tres annos poderá chegar a diminuir quase a metade; porque neste tempo serão acabadas todas as obras do jardim sendo bem administradas, e então á proporção que se hirão diminuindo as despezas, se diminuirá a consignação descontando-se nos quarteis successivos o que hirá subijando da mesma.

Transcribed by Sousa Viterbo - *A Jardinagem em Portugal.* Coimbra. 1909. 2nd Series. Pages 98-108.

(This report describes the introduction in Portugal, as in the rest of Europe, of botanic gardens and their scientific and educational function.)

In the tradition of the terrace-garden, as is the case at the Quinta do Marques de Pombal, Oeiras, or the Quinta das Lapas, the tile is the element which indicates changes in taste at the end of the eighteenth century.
The influence of trompe-l'oeil painters such as Pillement can be seen in small design details.

Above and left. *Details of benches covered with tiles.*

Quinta de São Mateus. Dafundo. Lisbon.

235

THE LANES AND AVENUES
and trees of the New World

One of the most significant alterations to estate gardens in the second half of the eighteenth century seems to have been the introduction, albeit slowly, of a fashion for large lanes and avenues lined with tall, leafy trees. We find that during the seventeenth century and the first half of the eighteenth century there were pleasure orchards outside the walls which surrounded the gardens next to the house. This custom continued during the whole of the eighteenth century, as, for instance, on the estate of the Marquis of Pombal in Oeiras, or in the descriptions of Beckford or Ruders.

The taste for large avenues and leafy trees seems to be connected to the large landscape layouts on the estates of rich merchants protected by the Marquis. The Benfica estate of Devisme was described by both Ruders and, in more detail, by Laura Junot in her Memoirs. In both cases, one observes that the atmosphere of the gardens had a more natural character — that is, less architectural — as was the Portuguese tradition. At that time, the estate belonged to the Marquis of Abrantes, and Ruders mentions that *'while it is currently the property of the Marquis of Abrantes, it was created by the English merchant Devisme, famous throughout Europe for his fine taste for everything that is naturally beautiful. For the beautifying of the so-called "farm", or royal property, he spent incredible sums. Upon his retirement to England, he sold it to the aforementioned Marquis for 30,000 cruzados but, according to what people say, he only received a small part of what he had actually spent on it. With each step I took, what my eyes saw far exceeded anything I could have imagined, and I was left with no other feeling but complete admiration. And this despite the fact that these objects are just composed of houses, trees, plants, flowers, grottoes, lakes, brooks, valleys, hills, statues...'*[27]

Much transformed in the nineteenth century, the gardens of the Palace of Estoi retain various elements from the end of the eighteenth century. The staircase which connects the great entrance avenue to the lake platform hides a grotto of shell work with a sculpture of the Three Graces in the centre.

Above and right. *Staircases topped with the arms of the Carvalhais family and the shell-work grotto.*

Gardens of the Palace of Estoi. Algarve.

Although constructed in the middle of the nineteenth century, the gardens, with their fountains, staircases, benches, walls and encircling walls systematically covered in tiles, are a final example of the Portuguese tradition of the garden of comfort and well-being, conceived in a more architectural rather than landscaped form.

Above and left. *Fountain and niche decorated with shell-work and glazed tiles.*

Quinta da Assunção. Belas.

'...The lower terrace...was surrounded by walls, benches, and flowerboxes covered in tiles, and a stone tank... and it was all shaded by poplars, ashes and other trees...'.
Christovam Ayres. 1909 (XIX)

The author was referring to the former gardens of the Quinta de Pintéus which, compared with other gardens of the eighteenth century, suggests to us a typical space of that period, with landings, and staircases covered with tiles, of which the Quinta da Assunção is one of the last examples constructed.

Above. *Detail of tiled panel attributed to Luís Ferreira (circa 1850).*

Quinta da Assunção. Belas.

DESCRIPTION OF THE QUINTA DE PINTEUS GARDENS by Christovam Ayres, 1909

"Eu desejaria dar-te noticia circumstanciada dos jardins de Pinteus, que te interessasse, e que realmente deviam ter sido sumptuosos; mas o que existe nem ideia dá do que devia ter sido.

O que sobrevive á ruina, por um lado, e ás inovações de meu sogro, por outro, é apenas um pequeno terraço ajardinado, contiguo á casa de jantar, guardado por muros cobertos de bellos azulejos a côres, e com a frente aberta para o lado da frontaria do palacio.

Está alteado até ao andar nobre para se nivelar com a casa de jantar, que deita para esse jardim, por duas largas portas, ficando no rez do chão a cocheira, a cavallariça e o lagar.

Os azulejos que cobrem os muros são italianos, das mais finas côres, com quatro quadros correspondentes aos assentos do jardim, representando as estações do anno (graciosas figuras em azul), e ornamentação de flôres, principalmente girassóes e rosas, e de aves em diversas attitudes.

Nas côres predomina o rôxo, o azul e o amarello, em tons e cambiantes variados. Os assentos são ladeados de alegretes, todos guarnecidos de azulejos no mesmo sentido. Os canteiros são orlados de buxo alto.

Azulejos eguaes teve a casa de jantar, em altos rodapés, representando, segundo me consta, e ainda se vê nos restos dispersos, quadros campestres e de interior. O tecto era de madeira, apainelado, em fórma de caixão. Meu sogro, ha 50 e tantos annos, levado pela moda, arrancou os preciosos azulejos e substituiu-os por estuques!

Os jardins propriamente ditos, muito vastos, eram nas trazeiras do palacio, em quatro largos socalcos, ligados por escadas, e todos os muros das escadas forrados de azulejo azul e branco, entremeados de quadros com figuras, alguns dos quaes ainda conheci agarrados ás ruinas.

O socalco de baixo, para o qual se desce de um terreno azulejado, com quadros de costumes, voltado para o poente, era todo rodeado de muros, bancos e alegretes cobertos de azulejos, com um tanque de pedra, redondo, no meio, e todo ensombrado de alamos, freixos, choupos e outras arvores. Tudo isto desappareceu, e o chão converteu-se em laranjal. Os socalcos de cima tem oliveiras e chão de sementeira.

Na familia não ha, que eu conheça, documentos que tratem da construcção da casa; a tradicção que se conserva é que a casa de jantar, cosinha e parte accrescentada ao corpo primitivo, são do tempo de D. João V (a cosinha é forrada de azulejo simples que deve ser do Rato); e que sua crescença foi feita, creio que até em pouco tempo, para receber aqui aquelle rei, cuja memoria guardava, ainda não ha muito tempo, um banco de pau santo onde elle se sentara na cosinha, que fôra ver pela sua sumptuosidade.

Realmente ella é enorme, com uma grande lareira, dois vãos para grandes fornalhas, duas excellentes pias de pedra, etc.; hoje está sem tecto, que cahiu ha uns vinte annos.

O risco dos jardins e da horta fronteira, chamada "da capella", toda em socalcos tambem até ao rio, e outr'ora igualmente toda guarnecida de azulejos, nas escadas, no tanque, nos muros, de alto a baixo, deve ser de artista ou artistas de merecimento.

É tradicção tambem que as novas obras no palacio fôram contemporaneas das do convento de Mafra. No atrio da capella, a pia de agua benta, movel, em fórma de columna, tem um feitio de um longo buzio, que me dizem ser similar a outros specimens de Mafra.

É digna de menção tambem uma monumental cascata que está na casa de jantar, de marmore branco e côr de roza, com a bacia em fórma de concha, e o fundo, tambem *rocaille*, tendo em alto relevo a carranca de Neptuno, ladeada de duas sereias e dois golfinhos, jorrando agua por 5 bicas.

Na ala sul do palacio, na parte primitiva, conservam-se quatro grandes sallas com altos *lambris* de azulejos que suponho ser do seculo XVII, e que tenho andado a remendar e restaurar com os restos dispersos de antigas opulencias."

Transcribed by Sousa Viterbo — *A Jardinagem em Portugal (Gardening in Portugal)*. Coimbra 1909. 2nd series. Pages. 136-137.

(Although early nineteenth century, this description illustrates certain characteristics of eighteenth century Portuguese gardens with various spatial structures: ostentatious gardens and kitchen-gardens.)

Although revealing an out-of-date art form, the Quinta da Assunção perpetuated in the nineteenth century the Portuguese characteristics of an architectural garden and a garden of comfort and well-being which were prevalent between the fifteenth and eighteenth centuries.

Quinta da Assunção. Belas.

'...all of (the walls) are covered, and they appear to have beautiful inlays which try to provide a studied decorative effect without losing, however, their rustic character...'. Father Caldas Barbosa. 1799 (XX)

The design of the summer house, connected with the great lake water-mirror in front, continues the tradition of the polarising elements of space, as well as the tradition of comfort and well-being. Its structure reveals a clear affinity with the summer house and lake of the gardens of the Palace of Vila Viçosa, Bacalhoa, Fronteira and Carmo.
Above. *The summer house and the lake water-mirror.*
Right. *View of the curved access to the olive grove.*

Quinta da Assunção. Belas.

244

DESCRIPTION OF THE GARDENS
of the Quinta dos Senhores de Belas
by Caldas Barbosa, 1799

"Busquemos agora a porta que introduz a este Palacio. Ella se nos offerece aberta em meio dos já ditos Lagos, ostentando a antiguidade do mais que se respeita neste frontispicio. As suas ombreiras saõ de huma pedra lavrada, e em cada huma mostra duas columnas, sobre cujos capiteis vem descançar a arqueada verga, que se adorna dos convenientes florões que a affermoseaõ. Entre-mo-la, sem deixarmos comtudo de lançar os olhos para os dous gastos columnellos, que se antevem aos commodos poiares exteriores: hum destes columnellos ainda mostra hum resto da grossa antiga cadêa, com que algum tempo se coutava este Palacio Senhorial.

Entrados no seu pateo, que he de hum quadrado regular, o achamos por sima acompanhado da Varanda, que segue, e adorna as tres partes deste espaçoso quadro, e vai communicar-se ao edificio interior por dous córpos Salientes, que elle desta parte mostra no seu prospecto. Notaremos aqui que apparece elevado alli todo sobre largos, e esveltos arcos de pedra, que remataõ ponte agudos, o que dá bem a conhecer, com a antiguidade, a elegancia, e magnificencia da sua construcçaõ.

No meio das considerações que este objecto respeitavel suscitára, fomos chamados, e levados por huma pequena porta, que guardando similhante feitio, dá prompta passage, e introducçaõ ao arvoredo da Quinta. Huma especie de extasi me sorprehende no patim, que começa a descobrir-me a formosa multidaõ de verdes, e folhudas arvores. Tambem alli mesmo me encanta a agradavel confusaõ dos misturados suaves gorgeos, com que os passaros descantavaõ ainda a florida Primavera. Este canto era taõ vivo, e taõ poderoso na sua uniaõ, que naõ o abaffava o estrondo da larga torrente, que se precipita em hum Lago, que alli está visinho.

Este lago, que novamente me apparece, extende-se por 50 palmos de comprido, e na largura de 32 apresenta a sua frente para o meio da grande rua, que logo hiremos tambem ver, e medir. Trez columnas de ordem Toscana sustentaõ o largo canal, que remata em grossa bica, da qual o mesmo lago recebe continua a grande porçaõ de agoa que lhe compete"

DA MAGESTOSA RUA

"He tempo de deixar esta vista, que me enternece, para fartar os meus olhos nas magestosas alléas de frondentes, e altissimas arvores, que daqui estou entrevendo. Saio pois ao meio desta larga, e comprida rua, que por toda a sua extensaõ, que he de mais de 450 passos, se borda, por hum, e outro lado, de troncos de huma admiravel corpulencia, e desmedida altura. Muitos delles se admiraõ com a estatura de 150 palmos, e mais: Entre elles se respeitaõ freixos annosos, que contaõ 15 palmos de circumferencia de seu tronco: Muitos Olmos se apresentaõ com, 10; e, o que he mais para admirar, he apparecerem misturados hum grande numero de loureiros, que possaõ na sua circumferencia offerecer a medida de 7, e mais palmos.

Posso affirmar que esta rua apresenta, assim magestosa, mais de 180 destes ditos troncos respeitaveis, e taõ copados, que na largura de 30 palmos, que he a da rua, entrelaçaõ com os que lhe estaõ fronteiros de tal sorte os seus ramos, que a mesma rua apparece toda cuberta desta muito engraçada alta abobeda verde, raramente interrompida pelos raios do Sol.

Neste prospecto nada se via que irmanasse com a nobre arte, que ostenta a fachada exterior. O Terremoto de 1755 havia alli destrohido o que tantos Seculos respeitáraõ: Mas naõ se desordenou comtudo a Capella, que está defronte, a qual he, como mostra, contemporanea do resto do edificio. Por fóra mostra ella hua metade de oval, sostido, e atracado por seis pilastras de pedra, que se remataõ com huns floreados accafos. Estas pilastras saõ abraçadas pelo cordaõ da simalha, que corre em roda, e forma como hum geral colarete; offerecendo a altura desta simalha pela parte de dentro hum Terraço formado sobre a Abobeda da Capella, que ficando assim, dá huma Varanda commoda, para descobrir em roda muito da Quinta, e vêr muito a seu gosto todo o Jardim antigo da Casa que lhe está visinho. A Fonte, que orna este Jardim, he tambem

obra antiga. A agoa alli repuchada cahe de huma esfera em huma bacia gomeada, e dalli, por pequenas Carrancas que a lançaõ em hua maior, vem despejar-se no seu receptaculo, que he hum outavado gracioso".

DA OBRA DO REVERENDO
Felix José Lamprêa

"Que maravilhosa mudança vejo eu da parte da Serra! Este terreno que eu víra inculto, cuberto de aspero, rasteiro, e esteril Tojo, agora se mostra a meus olhos ondeando todo com a larga Seara, e do meio della brotaõ milhares, e milhares de viçosas Oliveiras, que affermoseaõ, e enriquecem esta agradavel encosta. Naõ deixaremos ignorado o Nome, e sem louvor a Pessos que fora instromento para tornar proveitoso este terreno, até entaõ bem pouco util. O Reverendo Felix José Lamprêa, (Beneficiado na Igreja de Santa Justa desta Cidade, e Cavalleiro da Ordem de Christo; natural de Serpa, e perito nestas Plantações, de que abunda a sua Patria), consultado sobre o aproveitamento desta grande porçaõ de terra, que o grande Genio do Solicito Conde mal soffria vêr taõ pouco aproveitada, he quem o delibera, contra o voto de todos, a encher esta ociosa Serra com este grande Olivedo, que affortunadamente vegeta, cresce, vai florindo, e promette encher as Tulhas do seu utilissimo fructo. Deixemos estas obvias esperanças, para continuarmos pela nova, e grande Rua, o nosso proposto caminho"

DAS ARVORES DO NOVO MUNDO

"Nós seriamos affaz prolixos se intentassemos individuar as diversas castas, e nomenclaturas de 400 Arvores, que por huma, e outra parte adornaõ esta maravilhosa, e bem delineada Rua. Acho porém muito necessario declarar, que a maior parte dellas saõ curiosamente trazidas de partes remotas, e escolhidas para a affermosearem. Muitas saõ producçaõ do novo Mundo, e trazem a sua origem do meio de diversas Nações. A Asia tambem vê aqui as que saõ oriundas do seu seio. Nem a Africa deixa de ter nesta Rua, vegetando, prole a que ella deo o natural principio; e entre as da Europa, que nos saõ Estrangeiras, amo aquellas que do Jardim do Infeliz Luiz XVI, aqui vieraõ acompanhar a outras.

Tornaõ aqui a apparecer-nos as Patricias Tuinantibas, entre os florigeros Azereiros: Os copados Sycomoros entremeaõ as Acacias amarellas, e brancas: Frondosos Platanos de Virginia, e Orientaes, daõ entre si accommodado lugar aos Estrangeiros Azedracos, e aos Sanguineos: Crescem tambem alli os ramalhudos Castanheiros da India; e os Tilholos fazem companhia ás Azarollas, que se adornaõ com o seu encarnado, e saboroso fructo. Tambem descubro na mesma Rua, entre as sempre verdes Alfarrobeiras, as nossas Nogueiras fructuosas, e tanto amigas deste terreno. No meio desta Rua perfumaõ de huma e outra parte o ar as bellas odoriferas Arvores que chamaõ do Paraizo. As Tintureiras que tem o nome de bellas Sombras, pela que daõ, crescem aqui, e fazem companhia a Ormeiros estranhos; e saõ misturadas estas arvores com os Trifólios de diversas castas, e com as differentes geraçoens de Freixos, que alli se encontraõ".

Finalmente crescem tambem nesta rica Rua as Rozas arboreas, que chamaõ de S. Francisco, que mudaõ côr com a mudança das horas do dia; e com ellas muitos Arbustos de igual estimaçaõ, e galantaria, e assim as plantas de que Flora cuida curiosamente para as aaprontar, e entregar ao util uso da proveitosa Medicina.

Entretidos com a alternada diversaõ que faz a aggradavel variedade do feitio do tronco das flores, e das folhas, que de huma, e outra parte eramos convidados a notar; passeámos, quasi sem o sentir-mos, o longo caminho de 650 passos que esta Rua tem de comprimento desde a porta, até este Lugar do Obelisco em que ora estamos.

DA PORTENTOSA CASCATA

Hum irregular Tanque, com graciosas sinuosidades se vê aqui, orlado, sem simetria alguma, destas pedras do lavor da Natureza. Do meio do mais profundo deste Tanque se erguem alguns mais grossos Penedos, que formando juntos hum pequeno Monte, mostraõ sobre elle Glauco, assim como o fingem os Poetas, já mudado „Por virtude da Erva poderosa.,, Meio Peixe, e meio Homem se vê alli erguido sobre a escamosa

Although the summer house is mid-nineteenth century, the taste for shell-work and tiles continued a tradition that only declined at the time of the Romantic garden.

Fountain in the Summer House.
Quinta da Assunção. Belas.

Cauda; e moftra-me o Corpo, em que o mefmo já louvado Efcultor exprime a força nervofa; e no bem apalpado dos mufclos fe conhece a groffaria natural, e até fe aviva o esforço que faz, para fegurar na rede, que aperta entre os nodofos dedos, os Peixes, que malháraõ nella. A cabeça defte Semi-Deos he notavel entre os admiradores da Arte. Os Cabellos, como efcorridos para a téfta, parecem gotejar a agoa que trouxéraõ de donde fe foppoem fahido. A Boca eftá aberta, naquella pofiçaõ em que fe coftuma vêr a do Pefcador que fe alegra com achar huma boa prêa. Todo o Corpo, longe de moftrar o lizo, e nedio do Homem farto, e defcançado, reprefenta o fecco de hum Trabalhador folicito: e o Ventre em vez de tufar para fóra de gordo, fe recolhe em rugofas dobras para dentro. As Coftas porém moftraõ a lizura que convem á fua pofiçaõ hum pouco curvada; dando a conhecer a fortaleza dos offos da fua formatura. Em fim, naõ fe exprime mais propriamente hum corpo affeito ao trabalho. O Rofto acaba de aperfeiçoar efta figura, exprimindo na applicaçaõ dos olhos o que em tal acçaõ fe devia efperar della; e moftrando nas feccas maçans, e na hirfuta crefpa barba, o natural defenfeite da fua laboriofa occupaçaõ.

Para bem vêr por todos os lados efta boa figura, me foi neceffario entrar pela abertura que á parte efquerda offerece o mefmo Tanque, e acabando de a vêr, me convidou a fobir mais o caminho, que por entre efta ageitada penedia me dirige a outra figura, que vejo mais em cima. Eftá ella; como fenhoreando toda efta Montanha, fentada diante de huma Cafa, trabalhada com arte, e formada de baixo de hum Arco da rufticidade da mefma pedra.

Parece-me vêr perfonalifada aqui a figura de hum Rio, que trabalharemos por conhecer. Efta refpeitofa laureada cabeça: efte remo, que, como divifa, tem alçado na efquerda maõ, em quanto com a potente dextra parece determinar ao efcamofo Delfim em que eftá recoftado, que defpeje fem ceffar a torrente de agoa, que cahida de tanta altura, pela larga boca, faz huma vifta muito aggradavel, certamente a defignaõ hum Rio com hum mando fuperior aos que vêmos correr. Notêmos o contínuo fom da fonora queda defta torrente, que faz harmonia com o manfo murmurio das gottas que por outra parte ou defcem juntas, ou feparadas efcorregaõ pela frente defta fingular Cafcata.

Efta figura que, como as duas, nos confirma no primor da Arte de quem as fez, vai com ambas, e com tudo o que fórma aquelle refpeitofo Obelifco, e efta portentofa Cafcata, comprovar perante a Pofteridade, que fomos veridicos, no que já diffemos do excellente Cyrillo Wolkmar Machado, quando no começo da defcripçaõ do Palacio de Lisboa deftes mefmos Senhores, démos a devída honra a feu pincel magiftral. Elle delineou eftas célebres obras; e a Razaõ, e a Natureza teraõ nellas que fazer admirar aos Vindouros a veracidade de quanto elle affim delineára.

DO PASMOSO BERNINI

Ao admirar a preffa, com que crefcêraõ eftes louros, e folhados, que alli fe femeáraõ, nefta agradavel ordem, muito depois do anno, em que eu primeiro entrára nefta. Quinta com feus Senhores, paffeando eftas fermofas banquetas, defcubro entre ellas preciofas, e admiraveis Eftatuas de hum rijo marmore branco.

Efta refpeitavel coloffal Figura, que até no venerando rofto expreffa a dignidade de hum Numen, he o célebre Neptuno, obra do pafmofo Cavalheiro Bernini: cuido que, fó com efte fimples narraçaõ, tenho feito o elogio da Obra.

DOS NOVOS JARDINS

Seja-me agora permitido dirigir os meus paffos á parte direita defta Rua, para ver os novos Jardins, que rafgou nefte terreno, dantes inculto, e defaffeitado, a curiofa Condeça. Naõ deixo de admirar-me nos graciofos variados debuxos, com que eftes trez Jardins faõ formados.

O primeiro, e mais proximo a efte lugar, de onde eu fahíra, tem a forma de hum triangulo, e moftra no meio huma Placa, ou Maffiço tambem em triangulo, cheio de varias, e diverfas flores. A fua fahida, e entrada he por huma pequena abertura, he feita em pequena rafgadura na alta Banqueta, que o cerca, fronteira a outro fimilhante, que moftra o outro Jardim, no qual atraveffando a Rua, eu devo agora entrar.

Devemos entrar no fegundo Jardim, que he hum quadrado longo, fem efcrupulofa regularidade. Acha-fe repartido em canteiros engraçados, em que, com flores, figuraõ plantas odoriferas. Os cheirofos, e lindos Morangaons, grandes, e pequenos, mais, e menos córados, augmentaõ a graça defte fegundo Járdim: no meio delle fe vê eftar formado, como huma Bacia, hum redondo, cheio de rafteiras plantas: Chorões de diverfas caftas o enchem, e matizaõ da variada côr das fuas flores, e orna-lhe o meio, fobindo do fundo acima, huma corpulenta ponte-aguda Tuia. No interior da

246

parede, que forma o verde Folhado, eftá defronte defta Bacia hum Sofá tambem ruftico, cujo affento, formado de larga cortiça, debaixo de huma accommodada cobertura, que lhe dão as mefmas plantas, que formaõ o efpaldar, he commodo ao eftudiofo que bufca fimilhantes retiros.

Entramos no terceiro Jardim, em que fe nota huma efpecie de labyrintho. Achaõ-fe nelle flores arvoreas, e fructos em pequenos mimofos arbuftos: nem há regularidade na difpofiçaõ deffas plantas, e ervas; como tambem na dos fructos, e flores. Por entre eftas voltas fe achaõ as cheirofas Madrefilvas, e pelas outras as amarellas Giéftas: aqui fe encontraõ as Rozas encarnadas: alli as que tem menos côr, e ainda as amarellas: mifturados com tudo ifto crefcem os Lyrios de toda as caftas; e fem certeza de lugar, os Perfeitos Amores, que tambem diverfificaõ em tamanho, e em côr: eftaõ daqui as pequenas Tangerinas mifturadas nefte redondo, com as cafcudas Toranjas: no outro apparecem cheirofas Limeiras, com folha de côr variada, e fazem companhia aos Limoens, que crefcem entre folhas rajadas. A florida Amendoeira, eftá acompanhando as eftranhas Pereiras: o Medronheiro mefmo tem aqui lugar junto da efcolhida Cereigeira: as Tuias parecem guardar aqui mais regularidade; e affim tambem as azuladas Maçarócas: finalmente efta compofiçaõ do Jardim he pouco ufada entre nós, e ouço que os Eftrangeiros chamaõ a ifto propriamente hum *Quodlibet*.

Dá regularidade a efte fermofo logradouro a parede de Cedros, que fegue, e affemelha a parede propria da antiga Capella. Em lugar que lhe cabe fe finge do mefmo Cedro a obra da Capella, e a porta que lhe iguála toma o mefmo feitio, accommodafe os ramos á altura, e dobras, com que corneja o exemplar, que quer affimilhar.

Por efta fingida porta fe entra no vaõ, que occupaõ Tintureiras, e alguma Tuinantiba: o chaõ porém, e em torno das arvores alaftraõ-fe as cheirofas Violas entermeadas das flores marchetadas, a que chamamos Amores Perfeitos, e os Francezes naõ paffaõ de as nonmear *Penfamentos*.

A parede do Palacio, que eu tinha vifto arruinada, e com hum concerto improprio, toma huma fórma ajuftada, e adaptada á Arquitectura antiga. Huma Varanda de pedra, rafgada em buracos fimilhantes aos que moftra a fachada exterior, com dous Gabinetes falientes dos lados, acaba de realçar efta figura. Efta Varanda he tractada fobre efbeltos Arcos de pedra, que com as fuas Pilaftras lhe daõ o parecer, e o refpeito de Gothica Arquitectura.

As Cafas melhoráraõ-fe, fazendo-fe regulares no feu interior: cobríraõ-fe as paredes, e mobilharaõ-fe as Sallas como convinha. O Jardim antigo, que pareceo pequeno affim cercado, teve de fe lhe arrazar huma parede, e continuando, e extendendo-fe chegar á primeira Rua, que do Cancello corre para a Cafcata. Efte accrefcentamento de Jardim precifou logo, para fe lhe dar regularidade, paredes de Louro, e de Folhado: e em huma mais alta, que fe encofta á Rua daquella entrada, fe practicou huma engraçada meia laranja, a quem affiftem dous vefejantes Iphis. Ficaõ porém dos lados defte Maffiço duas aberturas: a da direita fronteira á Rua do Pomar, que ainda agora vimos: a abertura porém da parte efquerda vem a fahir junto a hum novo Cancello.

Perdôem-me, fe eu naõ individúo muitas coufas defte Jardim affim augmentado. Eu mefmo temo atraveffá-lo outra vez, para entrar pela pequena porta de hum lado a invreftigar a virtuofa agoa, alli achada, e que, como diffe, he franca para todos. Eu temo, eu temo vêr o redondo Lago, em que perdi hum innocente Amigo, e os Senhores defta Cafa defgraçadamente hum amavel Filho.

Father Domingos Caldas Barbosa. *Descrição da Grandiosa Quinta dos Senhores de Belas*. Lisbon. 1799.

(Although totally lost to us, this estate and its vast gardens were described in such detail at the end of the eighteenth century that in this account we can see the passing of the formal seventeenth century style and the heralding of a pre-Romantic natural style. This is the case with the cascades and the summer houses constructed from volcanic rocks and wood.)

NOTES

1 Carrère. *Tableau de Lisbonne en 1796*. Paris 1789. Page 49.
2 6th Marquis of Alorna e Fronteira. *Memórias*. Lisbon. Vol. I. Page 12.
3 Carl Israel Ruders. *Viagem em Portugal 1789-1802*. Translation by António Feijó. Lisbon, 1981. Map XI. Page 123.
4 William Beckford. *Diário de... em Portugal e Espanha*. Translation by João Gaspar Simões. Lisbon. 1983. Page 49.
5 Henry Frederic Link. *Voyage en Portugal depuis 1797-1799*. Paris, 1803. Page 231.
6 William Beckford. Ibid. Page 41.
7 Courtils. *Une Description de Lisbonne en Juin 1755*. Lisbon 1965. Page 146.
8 William Beckford. Ibid. Page 46.
9 Idem. Page 46.
10 Idem. Page 162.
11 Laura Junot. (Duchess of Abrantes) *Souvenirs d'une Ambassade en Espagne et en Portugal entre 1808-1811*. Paris, 1837. Page 360.
12 Arthur William Costigan. *Cartas de Portugal 1778-1779*. Lisbon. Page 82.
13 William Beckford. Ibid. Page 87.
14 William Dalrymple. *Travels through Spain and Portugal in 1774*. London, 1777. Page 151.
15 Arthur Costigan. Ibid. Page 82.
16 Carl Israel Ruders. Ibid. Page 26.
17 William Beckford. Ibid. Page 41.
18 Idem. Page 57.
19 Idem. Page 77.
20 Carl I. Ruders. Ibid. Page 36.
21 Idem. Page 37.
22 Transcribed by Sousa Viterbo. *A Jardinagem em Portugal*. 2nd Series. Coimbra, 1909. Page 136-137.
23 William Beckford. Ibid. Page 41.
24 José Augusto França. Ibid. Page 264.
25 Arthur W. Costigan. Ibid. Page 76.
26 Father Caldas Barbosa. *Descrição da Grandiosa Quinta dos Senhores de Bellas*. Lisbon 1799. Page 16.
27 Carl I. Ruders. Ibid. Page 48-49.
28 Laura Junot (Duchess of Abrantes). Ibid. Page 210-211.
29 Father Caldas Barbosa. Ibid. Page 85.
30 Idem. Page 86.
31 Idem. Page 42-43.
32 Idem. Page 58.
33 Idem. Page 56-57.
34 Idem. Page 57.
35 João Baptista de Castro. Ibid. Page 451.
36 Transcribed by Sousa Viterbo. Ibid. Page 133.

Notes on Illustrations

I. Arthur W. Costigan. *Sketches of Society and Manners in Portugal,* London 1987. Page 81.
II. William Dalrymple. *Travels through Spain and Portugal in 1774*. London, 1777. Page 151.
III. Transcribed by A. Caldeira Pires. *História do Palácio de Queluz*. Coimbra, 1925. Volume II. Page 317.
IV. William Beckford. *Diário de... em Portugal e Espanha*. Translation by João Gaspar Simões. Lisbon, 1983. Page 87.
V. Transcribed by Sousa Viterbo. Ibid. page 136.
VI. William Beckford. Ibid. Page 41.
VII. Idem. Page 41.
VIII. Henry Frederic Link. French translation. *Voyage en Portugal depuis 1797-1799*. Paris. Page 231.
IX. Sousa Viterbo. *A Jardinagem em Portugal*. 2nd Series. Coimbra. 1909. Page 81.
X. Courtils. *Une Description de Lisbonne en Juin 1755*. Lisbon 1965. Page 146.
XI. Transcribed by the Count of Sabugosa. *Embrechados*. Lisbon, 1908. 5th ed. Page 11.
XII. Transcribed by Joaquim Rasteiro. *Quinta e Palácio da Bacalhoa em Azeitão*. Lisbon, 1895. Page 62.
XIII. William Beckford. Ibid. Page 46.
XIV. Idem. Page 46.
XV. Laura Junot (Duchess of Abrantes). *Portugal a princípios del siglo XIX*. Madrid. Page 132.
XVI. Transcribed by Sousa Viterbo. Ibid. Page 102.
XVII. William Beckford. Ibid. Page 162.
XVIII. Father Caldas Barbosa. *Descrição da Grandiosa Quinta dos Senhores de Bellas*. Lisbon, 1799. Page 41.
XIX. Transcribed by Sousa Viterbo. Ibid. Page 136.
XX. Father Caldas Barbosa. Ibid. Page 57.

THE GRANITE CULTURE
and the well-ordered gardens of the north in the eighteenth century

CHAPTER IX

In the north of the country during the eighteenth century, religious art was influenced by the Baroque in all its splendour. This art form spread from churches, convents, cloisters and episcopal palaces in urban and landscape designs, and one of the most interesting landscape layouts of Portuguese art was conceived at this time: the staircase.

Although not possessing the same grandeur, civilian architecture and garden art took on a fresh momentum, being influenced by religious art both in spatial concepts as well as decorative elements.

From the middle of the eighteenth century onwards, there was a growing interest in a more cultivated way of life, and this gave rise to a large group of manor houses and country retreats being built. In the north, the garden had played a secondary role in the evolution of Portuguese landscape design — the great layouts of the sixteenth and seventeenth centuries were almost exclusively situated in the south. Now, the northern garden acquired a new aesthetic ambience, side by side with other artistic expressions.

One of the greatest estates which resulted from this new taste for luxury, the Quinta de Freixo, was initiated by a rich churchman, the Dean of the Sé Cathedral, Oporto, Dom Jerónimo de Távora.

The Palace of Palmeira also took on the appearance of a princely residence due to the alterations ordered by the Archbishop of Braga, Dom José de Bragança, the illegitimate son of Dom João V. During the years he was Archbishop, between 1741 and 1756, Dom José gathered a court around himself which spent its time in elegant feasting and on religious ceremonies.

The strong resistance in the north to the Marquis of Pombal and his reforms contributed to the permanence of the ecclesiastic aesthetic and, with it, a certain traditional attitude to cultural life.

The fluctuation between the religious spirit and that of the courts, the effects of which were to be found in all aspects of social life, gave to gardens a sense of dynamic tension and scenic envelopment. Small terraces/landings divided into stairs; stone balustrades with balusters topped by pinnacles and pyramids; tall wall fountains with prominent curving and counter-curving moulded cornices; statues with robes that appear to be blowing in the wind, all sculpted out of the dark granite of the region, gave the space a formal density and dynamism that reflected the religious architecture to be found throughout the whole of the north.

Glazed tiles and shell-work, held by the south to be decorative elements *par excellence*, were almost non-existent here. Their aesthetic aspect — covering areas with a shiny surface — corresponded to a concept of static and crypto-magic space which contrasted strongly with the individualism of the north.

Much closer to the spatial concepts of central Europe, these gardens tended to divide up into staircases, structuring themselves around paths which governed the landscape layout. It was a tendency which was most dynamic in large staircases. In the majority of gardens, the focal points were not always the same, thereby diluting the effect of the rationalist outline of the whole.

The geographical conditions of the terrain, the taste for views and a certain life-style, all contributed to the end of this rationalist attitude.

On several occasions, Nazoni, because of his Italian aesthetic training, put the house in the centre of a garden axis, in the manner of Italian villas, a layout which seemed to disappear in face of the demands dictated by the requirements of his client. Sousa Reis, in his description of the gardens of the Freixo Palace, states: *'there is another reserved and closed in garden situated to the west'.*[1] This garden — today half in ruins — received, therefore, the most sophisticated treatment, being framed at the far end by a summer house with terraces with granite balustrades

Opposite page. *Detail of the terrace-garden with tower in the background.*
Quinta da Bouca. Felgueiras.

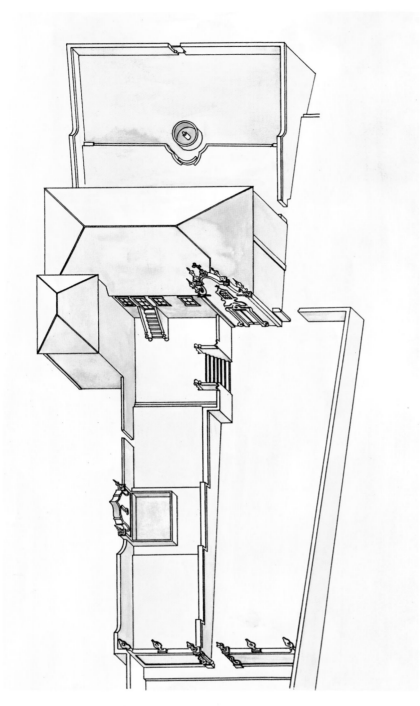

From his first civilian architectural works, Nazoni tried to introduce to the north of the country the concept of the European landscape layout structured around a great axis, in which the house was situated in the centre, as with Italian villas and French palaces.

Axonometric perspective of the house and chapel of Fafiães. Nazoni, circa 1735.

and pinnacles. In the centre, a monumental arch was designed topped by an enormous emblem *'which, due to its adornments, plays an important part in making this corner appreciated'.*[2]

The similarity of the spatial structure of this garden to the box garden of the gardens of the Fronteira Palace, framed by the lake house, or to the aviary garden of the gardens of the Belém Palace, is well known.

Instead of framing the end of the garden layout, thereby serving as the 'finial' on the whole, as was the case with Italian villas and French palaces, these buildings acted as majestic backdrops to small gardens.

Since the whole was autonomous, these gardens took on a special importance with their private reception areas and places reserved for the ladies of the house on a day-to-day basis.

It was in the Prelada Gardens that Nazoni managed to present the classic scheme, that of the house situated in the centre of a great axis which governed the landscape layout. An extensive avenue over four hundred metres in length descended from the palace by means of a valley which, as it rose again, used the enclosed area of the lake as a 'finial'. The classic European rules were applied but without any great aesthetic effect. The avenue was too long. We do not know if Nazoni planned a more architectural and grandiose conclusion for the lake area, as is seen in the curved entrance courtyard, since the estate was not completed.

It is interesting to find that Nazoni completely abandoned this plan in the Freixo Palace, constructed much later on, and adopted a discontinuous layout of garden-terraces without any continuity or direct link between them, in the purest Portuguese tradition.

It was not only in the Prelada Gardens that a plan for a landscape layout governed by a large axis was tried. One can clearly see an attempt to do the same thing in the Biscaínhos Gardens, as well as at the Palace of Queluz and the Quinta das Laranjeiras at Sete Rios, Lisbon. In these three cases, the axis can only be seen on the plan, as if the project had been badly interpreted or not followed. In all these gardens, the first garden next to the house is spatially closed in by balustrades, statues and portals, thereby creating a strong discontinuity between this space and the other terraces. The special care that was lavished on the first garden destroyed the effect of the spatial discontinuity and division of the overall structure of the layout, as was the case with the great European layouts.

Together with the creation of certain areas which were planned to be independent because of their more refined and reserved character, the terraces tended to extend in accordance with the ground conditions and especially because of the views.

At the end of the eighteenth century, Rebello da Costa considered the views to be one of the most important qualities of the estates in Oporto when he affirmed *'it is rare that there is no view over the river and the sea...'.*[3]

Although it has a very particular character, the consequence of the emphasis given to its qualities of size — the garden of the north was linked to that of the south by a resistance to rationalism. Characteristics that were more domestic and sensory in nature were regarded as being more important than characteristics of calculation and conceptualism, thus, for centuries, giving gardens throughout the country humanising qualities that were mainly enjoyed on the inside rather than contemplated from the outside.

Gorani, who visited Oporto in 1765, described the gardens of the country retreats: *'the small woods and gardens which surround them, respected by winter itself, constitute a charming spectacle. The orange and lemon trees there exceed in beauty all other trees. Of each one of these trees, one can truly say: il étale à la fois/et sa fleur et son fruit/prodigue de sens dous/sans cesse il reproduit'.*[4]

Although not corresponding to the omnipresent way in which these trees were set out in the gardens in the south, it is evident that they occupied an important place, although all trace of them has completely disappeared both in the north and south. Only in the gardens of the Alentejo region are they still found, perhaps in order to recall their importance in the origin of the Portuguese garden of the fifteenth century.

The detailed description of the eighteenth century garden of the Quinta da Prelada tells of the presence of pleasure orchards and kitchen-gardens and how they were an integral part of the gardens as a whole. Next to the house *'to the East, there is a orchard; in it there is a tank for water birds, and on one side a bird house'.*[5]

The description of the avenue that provides access to the enclosed space of the lake refers to the fact that: *'further on, and when this canopy of trees finishes, there is on one side a fountain with paths lined with orange and lemon trees. There is an eight-sided tank from which extend two avenues lined with hazels, the branches of which form tunnels. There are benches in these avenues. After this, there is a mirador from which run two avenues lined with trees of fruit containing stones'.*[6]

These different pleasure orchards remind us of the disappointment felt by Arthur Costigan on his visit to the gardens of the Marquis of Pombal at Oeiras in 1779: *'The gardens are very extensive and badly laid out for pleasure purposes and one can see that there was an intention to make use of everything. They are covered with orange trees, lemon trees and almond trees...'.*[7]

Corsini on his visit to Oporto refers to the small woods, and Rebello da Costa spoke about their importance in the gardens: *'Rare is the estate that does not have within its walls copious and leafy chestnuts, oaks and other great trees...'.*[8]

The contrast between garden and enveloping nature — interior and exterior space — which is seen in the south up to the nineteenth century is almost unknown in the north.

An old Celtic tradition of the cult of the forest led to an opening up of the garden, in which the wood was used as a structural element of garden layouts in the north.

Another characteristic element to be found throughout Portugal were long trellises, supported on heavy granite pillars in the north. In more sophisticated cases, there were carved stone benches and pillars were transformed into columns; these were found in favourite places for spending hot summer afternoons and for enjoying beautiful views. The Solar de Mateus Gardens still have an extensive trellis with benches and columns in the shape of long, thin balusters. Although completely disappeared from the gardens of the Quinta de Vila Flôr, the avenues were also decorated with long trellises. The Quinta, which was constructed with noteworthy magnificence in the eighteenth century, is the only civilian construction specifically referred to in

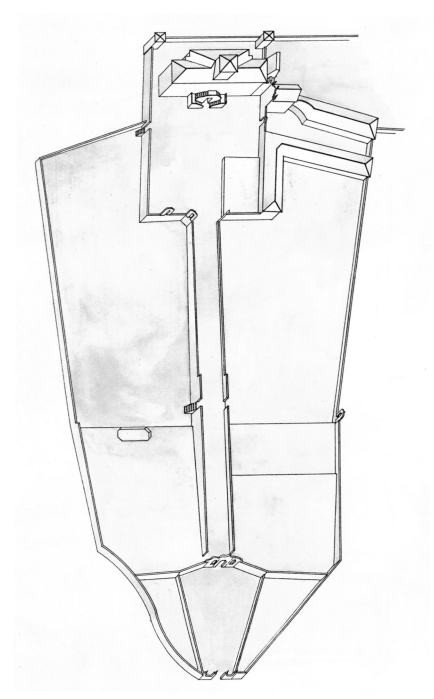

The landscaped layout of the exterior spaces of both the Quinta do Chantre and the Quinta de Ramalde took the form of a great axis only tenuously. Nazoni's clientele, closely linked to the ecclesiastical class, seemed to allow the development of an approach axis to the house as long as it did not extend into the garden.

Axonometric perspective of the Quinta de Chantre. Nazoni, circa 1745.

'...going up the Douro, one sees here and there on the slopes estates with their parks. The principal·ornament consists of carefully tended trellises which are placed on terraces facing the sea, the Douro, or some beautiful valley'.
Tollenare. 1816 [I]

'...en remontant le Douro, et sur ses bords, on voit çá et la quelques quintas avec leurs parcs. Leur principal ornement consiste en trellis très bien soignés et plantées sur des terrasses vers la mer, où vers le Douro, ou vers quelques belles vallées'.

Detail of the Freixo Palace with the Douro in the background.

the Parochial Memoirs of the City of Guimarães. The description refers to *'wide lanes, some of which are covered with trellised vines and lattice work...'*[(9)] These trellises are featured in an engraving of Guimarães in 1747 with the estate in the background, spreading out along different narrow terraces and with the palace above. The aforementioned lattice-work appears along the supporting walls which suggests that many others must have disappeared during the decline of the majority of these large houses in the nineteenth and twentieth centuries.

On the slopes of the hills, taking advantage of the wide views, the gardens were set out on terraces to ensure a greater economy of irrigation water. The water was pumped up to the highest points and, from tanks and wells, it was gradually distributed to the different terraces on progressively lower levels. Fountains, lakes and wall fountains functioned as water reservoirs for the areas or terraces on which they were found, either retaining or distributing water according to the many different needs. The plumbing was generally by means of granite pipes laid on the surface, the durability and resistance of which means that in many cases they are still in good working order.

The granite spouting fountains and the tall granite wall fountain, with the curves and counter curves of their shells, dolphins, moulded cornices and niches, clearly characterise the Baroque taste of the north.

The great water-mirror of the south with its calm and restful ambience contrasts with the monumental wall fountain of the north, a taste which was to be found from the seventeenth century onwards in the Maia Gardens of the Bishops of Oporto as well as in the Simães Gardens, near Felgueiras, or in those of the House of Avintes.

VARIATIONS BETWEEN
the garden of comfort and well-being, the walk garden

As a result of first approaching and then distancing themselves from the art of the south, the gardens of the north acquired a special character of their own that was due more to a formal and volumetric nature than to a radically different concept of space.

Staircase design was generally restricted to the religious Baroque art of the north, as such staircases are not generally found in private gardens. Their layout, which was set out with much precision on the great axis of the staircase which developed along a pathway of decorative elements right up to the temple, was dictated more by great religious aspirations than by the needs of a conceptualist nature.

The resistance of Nazoni's clientele to accept his landscape layouts is well known.

The gardens of the Quinta de Vila Flôr are practically the only example of a clear transition of the layout of staircases in religious gardens to secular or pleasure gardens.

The series of three great terraces framed by stone balustrades with pinnacles and statues and connected by staircases clearly reminds us of the staircase, also in Guimarães, of the Convent of Santa Maria da Costa.

The undeniably aesthetic and monumental effect of the whole, seen from far off, was not, however, repeated elsewhere.

It is the different paths for crossing the gardens and which divide up into stairways, trellises and walks, that clearly reveal an approach by the gardens in the north to the concept of a garden whose structure is based on paths, although without the rational character of the European garden layouts.

It is this affinity with northern Europe — which was never seen in the south — which determined both the design of the great approach avenues to the house and the importance given to the tall box-lined lanes, topped by high pyramids, balls and arches. At crossing points and in certain areas, the box grew freely, to a great height, forming a roof. In the continuation of the axis at the small box garden of the Mateus Manor House, one can still see today a monumental construction with very old box bushes which are shaped on the outside but which form an enormous tunnel. Box covered lanes also exist at Insua and Oliveira do Conde.

Finally, camellias, which are almost unknown in the south, occupy, together with box, a privileged place in the northern taste, which tends more to the formal and grandiose; they are to be found everywhere, even in the Beira Alta region, and they remained a typical element of northern gardens until the nine-

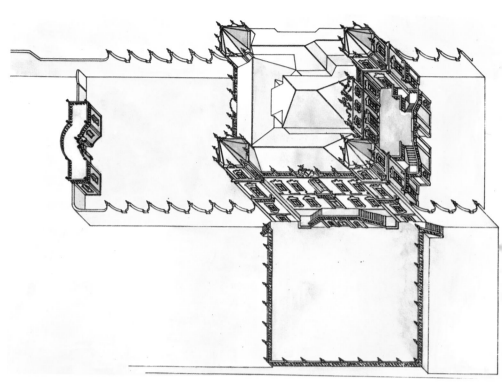

'...together with the beautiful garden which is in front of the south part...there is another reserved and closed in garden to the west which, due to its adornments, makes this enclosed space most appreciated...' Sousa Reis. Nineteenth century (II)

The author clearly defines here two typical types of space, the private garden and the ostentatious garden, clearly revealing a concept of garden and exterior space which is based more on domestic and hierarchic than rational values and on an overall landscape layout.

Above. *Axonometric perspective of the Freixo Gardens and Palace.*
Nazoni. circa 1750.

The emphasis on the number and volume of decorative elements in the space, which was to be seen in the north of the country in the sixteenth and seventeenth centuries, was maintained with large wall fountains being the most visible element of this trend — in eighteenth century gardens.
Above. *Wall fountain of the Saraiva Reffoios family at the ancient Casa da Vela.* Guarda.

253

'...a majestic and grandiose quinta with obelisks, gardens, cascades, pyramids, labyrinths, and a great lake which surrounds a castle-style house that stands in the middle on a small island...'
Rebello da Costa. 1799 (III)

Above and right. Great lake and access staircase, with the Fonte do Cágado (Turtle Fountain) in the centre.

Quinta da Prelada. Oporto.

teenth century. Biscainhos and Insua possess notable camellias shaped in the form of summer houses, a tradition which has existed since the appearance of the first camellias brought to Europe by the Portuguese at the end of the sixteenth century.[10]

The aesthetics of the eighteenth century gardens in the north — like those in the south — continued during almost the whole of the nineteenth century, a new concept of the garden with new recreational habits and spatial concepts only really appearing at the end of the nineteenth century with the Romantic garden.

THE GREAT FOUNTAINS
and the taste for decorative items in the north

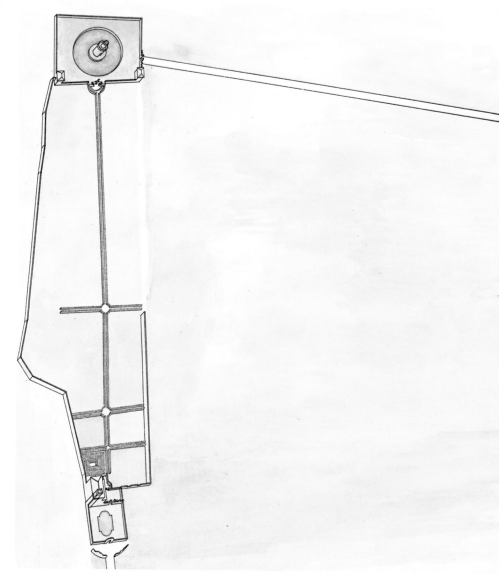

From the end of the sixteenth century, we find that gardens in the north reveal a clear tendency to emphasise certain volumetric and dynamic aspects in their exterior spaces. A taste for large avenues, both those which approach the house as well as those which extend from the gardens into the woods, indicates a dynamic sense of space that is unknown in the south. In contrast to this aspect, which was analysed in detail in the concept of the crypto-magic spatial concept of the south, is the concept of dynamic and directional space which has become standardised in the north.

Besides the great avenues, this spatial concept also has a tendency to place greater value on large sculptural elements which accentuate the dynamic value of the space. The large wall fountains of the Casa de Simães, Fiães, or of the Convent of Tibães, are examples of a seventeenth century art which, while mannerist in design, was already Baroque due to its scale.

In the eighteenth century, the gardens and exterior spaces of the large manor houses and estates in the north, together with the religious staircases, continued to accentuate this effect in wall fountains and doorways decorated with coats-of-arms and sculp-

'The first entrance, which is 756 feet long, starts next to the pyramids... two pedestals are to be found at the end of this first entrance... and a little distance away from the end are two large half-orange shaped spaces, the walls of which are carved from stone, as are their benches...'
Description 1753 (IV)

It was in the Quinta da Prelada that Nazoni conceived his plan of the great landscape layout structured around a single axis.

Axonometric perspective and entrance gate of the walled-in terrace.
Quinta da Prelada. Oporto.

'...discover the house and garden of Vila Flor, which is a short distance away (from Guimarães)...It is admirable in its architecture and grandeur and the construction of the garden...' Parish Records. circa 1750 (V)

The description is confirmed by an engraving of Guimarães of 1747 with the palace in the background, in which the garden, formed by three terraces with a kitchen garden-orchard at the side, clearly recreational, appears.

Façade of the House of Vila Flor and engraving of Guimarães. Casa de Vila Flor. Guimarães.

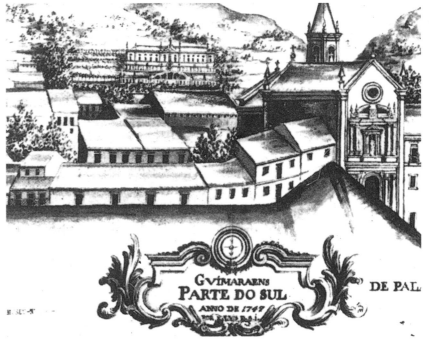

GVIMARAENS
PARTE DO SUL   DE PAL
ANNO DE 1747

tural elements. In the north, gardens were used especially as spaces for walking and as recreational pathways, and this contributed to the transformation of these great wall fountains into polarising elements of the space which, while possessing a strong urban flavour, are meant to be seen from afar.

The fact that they were conceived either for the perception of movement or for the perception of the whole, explains why, in the majority of cases, there was a certain lack of aesthetic quality in the sculptural details. The value was more spatial, the detail being only of secondary importance.

Their location was rarely to be found in spaces of comfort and well-being. Instead, they were located at the end of avenues or else where avenues crossed, in the centre of squares or on box terraces.

According to a 1753 description of the great access avenue to the lake in the Prelada Gardens: *'there is, in the fourth part of this avenue, an eight-sided tank of water and around it runs the width of the same street. It has a pyramid in the middle which shoots water into the air through two openings, and at the bottom of the tank is a set of water spouts'.*[11] This lake is surrounded by *'some freshly-painted stone seats'*,[12] but one gathers that the aesthetic value of the tank and the pyramid was markedly scenic in nature and for the benefit of those who were strolling along the avenue, while the benches permitted a small pause during the walk.

In other cases, the taste for scale is seen in the form of lakes, with large sculptured figures, in the centre of box terraces, as may be seen in the Biscaínhos and Vila Flor Gardens. In both cases, the scale of the sculptures is related more to the garden as a whole than to the enclosed space which surrounds the lake. The gardens of Vila Flor, besides a monumental fountain in the courtyard and the lake with various bowls on the first terrace, possesses, according to a description of the time, on the lower terrace *'two giant lions standing up and which are holding in their hands a shell, in which they catch the water...'.*[13]

More characteristically northern, however, are the tall granite wall fountains, decorated with a profusion of scrolls, moulded cornices, pilasters, niches, stone coats-of-arms, emblems and statuary. It is here that one can see much more clearly the direct influence of the ecclesiastical aesthetic to which the gardens of the north were closely connected. The wall of the fountain, with its pilasters and scrolls, reproduces in stone the structure and decorative forms of carved altars. In São João de Ver, near Vila da Feira, the fountain of the Casa da Torre is divided into three niches in which images of saints bordered by pilasters are to be found, as if it were really the altar of a church.

The gardens of the Counts of Santar also possess a monumental fountain with a large stone coat-of-arms in the centre and a gargoyle below. On each side, in glazed tiles, are two arches with horsemen dressed in seventeenth century costume, in imitation of the horsemen of the Casa do Lago at the Fronteira Palace. Although dated 1790, the tiles were painted at the beginning of the century by José Maria Pereira Cão who also restored, on the orders of Dom Carlos I, the Great Lake at Queluz.

The fountain of the Saraiva Reffóios family at Guarda is without doubt the most grandiose example of this fashion in eighteenth century Portuguese gardens. Although removed from its original site, the Casa da Vela on the outskirts of Guarda, the

'...which is composed of wide avenues, some of which are covered with trellises or arbours of ingenious manufacture, and has a beautiful garden'. Parish Records. circa 1750 (VI)

Plan of the gardens of Casa de Vila Flor. Guimarães.

'...two steep stone staircases under which are two fountains which have water issuing from stone figures...' **Parish Records. circa 1750** (VII)

Situated on the axis of the gardens, the staircases enhanced the sense of dynamic movement of the space.

Above and right. Staircases in the gardens of the Casa de Vila Flor. Guimarães.

fountain rises up in a monumental scenic effect of pilasters, scrolls, pinnacles and low relief carvings, and the three sea monsters, from the mouths of which issue jets of water, suggest certain almost surrealist themes introduced by Nazoni, as in the staircase rail of the Sé Cathedral in Oporto.

THE FASHION FOR TRELLISES
and the tradition of the deambulatory

T he strangest characteristic of the estates on the outskirts of Oporto, according to Tollenare in his *Notes Dominicais,* were their extensive trellises: *'...one cannot find imposing palaces, but going up the Douro, on top of the steep slopes, one can see here and there estates and their parks. The main decorative form consists of well-cared for trellises which are placed on the terraces facing the sea, the Douro river or else some beautiful valley. These trellises are, at the same time, useful, since they provide wine and permit one to stroll in the shade. They are held up by granite prisms whose six faces are parallelograms and which are shaped with such skill that it excites my curiosity, since it must be difficult to raise these pillars without breaking them, as they are pieces of granite four inches thick and they are frequently fifteen to eighteen feet in height...'*[(14)] Unfortunately, Tollenare did not visit more sophisticated gardens with trellises supported on columns, such as those to be found today in the gardens of the Mateus Palace.

From the description, one can clearly see that these trellises had the recreational function of a walk, which we have seen also existed in the south since the fifteenth century, and Tollenare in his description of his visit to the Quinta de Fiães makes special

'...this (garden) continues the pattern of many flights of carved stone steps, with stone figures, and with carved pyramids.' Parish Records. circa 1750 (VIII)

Basically composed of a succession of landings, inter-connected by flights of steps, the gardens of Vila Flor are the most visible example of the influence of religious staircases on secular architecture.

Above and left. *Succession of terrace-gardens and view of the staircases.*

Gardens of the Casa de Vila Flor. Guimarães.

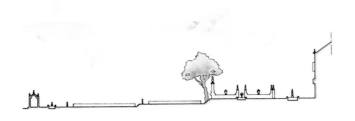

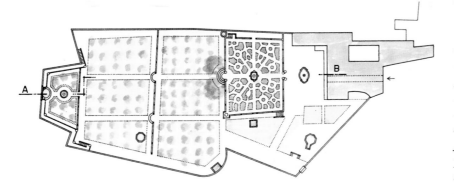

The effect of depth and spatial continuity expressed in the great development axis of the layout of the gardens only has significance on a plan. As in the south of the country, on the Quinta das Laranjeiras, or in Queluz, the ostentatious garden is closed in by walls and gates to create an autonomous space with no relation to the whole.

Plan and cross-section of the gardens of the Biscaínhos Manor House. Braga.

reference to its Mediterranean character: *'the gardens possess the French "parterres" and the delicious trellises of the south (midi)'.*[15]

While one can attribute a tradition of walk-deambulatory to these trellises, their ordinary aspect sets them apart from the walk-deambulatory of the south which, as we have seen, occupies the most privileged place in the garden, from the sixteenth century at the Quinta da Bacalhoa and the Fronteira Palace, till the eighteenth century at Queluz and the Quinta dos Azulejos. We cannot, however, deny that the trellises of the Mateus Gardens possess a certain grandeur, or that the benches between the columns seem to resemble those of the typical walk in the south, which was used for strolling along, relaxing and conversing. The importance attached to the trellis of the Prelada Gardens is also evident. The great avenue which connects the house to the great lake is composed of a long trellis which, although it has a certain grandeur, does not possess the decorative refinements of gardens in the south. The 1753 description states: *'At the end of the stairs, which come out in the middle of the two gardens, there is an avenue which is 1,290 feet in length and ten and two-thirds feet in width. A large part of the trellis of this pathway is composed of octagonal-shaped wooden bars set on stone columns of the same shape: it is covered with layers of vines and has box four feet in height along the edges, and trees on either side'.*[16]

The style of the decorative elements of the walk-deambulatory is not very evident in the Prelada Gardens despite the octagonal-sided columns. As was the case with the gardens of the south, the lack of tiles covering flowerboxes, benches, vases and niches gave a more natural atmosphere than an architecturally refined one, as we can see, for example, in the Quinta dos Azulejos.

THE TERRACE-GARDEN
of estates in the north of the country

One of the characteristics of the gardens of the north in the eighteenth century was, without doubt, the fact that they were structured in the form of terraces. While this feature is also apparent in the south, in the north it appears more systematically and in a different form. In the south, the garden-terrace is connected with the need to create a hierarchy among the garden spaces, thereby establishing areas which are grand and more secluded in contrast to others which are to a certain extent less grand and more public. These grander areas are situated next to the house in small gardens of comfort and well-being, encircled by low walls, with benches and flowerboxes, and open up into larger areas: the pleasure orchards. In the north, terrace-gardens seem to be more the result of geographical influences and a desire to take advantage of the views than the need to hierarchise the space.

As Tollenare tells us: *'the country (the north), being very mountainous, offers increasingly picturesque views each step we take...thousands of streams cut the country in all directions, spreading their freshness, and the beautiful bubbling sound of their waters which are an invitation to rest and poetry...*[17]

The enjoyment of these beautiful views, an indispensable quality on any pleasure estate, led to the locating of the house and the outside spaces on the top of slopes and hills. The sharply sloping land resulted in the formation of terraces, with most of the agriculture in the region being carried out along the same lines.

Terrace-gardens thus naturally suggest a taste for views and an adaptation of the terrain. Finally, the more dynamic man of the north, with his much stronger personality, always revealed himself to be much more courageous and individualistic in relation to life and the universe than the man of the south, and this resulted in more aesthetically strong and Baroque effects by use of terraces with staircases and balustrades.

Such effects, which are best seen in large religious staircases, can also be found on diverse estates, especially in the gardens of the Quinta de Vila Flor in Guimarães. A special case, these gardens illustrate practically the only layout which carries over into civilian architecture the linear development of the staircase. By means of a strict axis, which extends from the centre of the façade facing the gardens, they are organised into three landings interconnected by staircases. Thick buttresses support the landings which are bordered by balustrades with spires, pyramids and

The large sculptural elements in the centre of lakes, in fountains and portals show themselves to be a particular characteristic of the gardens of the north, and camellias shaped into the form of summer houses accentuated this trend which first became popular in the seventeenth century.

Above and left. *Details of the ostentatious garden at the Biscaínhos Manor House. Braga.*

states. In both the gardens of the Quinta da China and the Casa do Ribeiro on the banks of the Douro, as well as in the gardens of the Mateus and Santar Palaces, the value attached to staircases and pathways laid out along the lines of the development axis on various terraces of the gardens is evident.

Together with the dynamic and volumetric nature of the landscape, these garden-terraces acquire with the façade of the house a scenic value that is meant to be seen from a distance, without any of the characteristics of the gardens of comfort and well-being in the south. The intimacy of the garden-terraces of Oeiras, Lapa or Queluz, no sign of which is visible from the exterior, and where the façade functions as an element of the composition of the space, is not felt in the north.

The façades of the great manor-houses in the north are designed to be seen from a distance. The light-dark contrast between granite and white-washed wall, the thick pilasters and corners of the walls, the frames of windows that jut out, give the façades a grandeur which extends to the exterior spaces. The garden-terraces of the north do not possess the intimacy and spatial containment of those in the south, and acquire a more monumental and scenic character, both for the observer from a distance and for the visitor.

The lack of intimacy between the gardens and the house seems, on the other hand, to create ambivalence as regards the veranda-walk, which is a semi-exterior space, as we have seen in the south. The seventeenth century veranda, with its thick Tuscan columns continues in the eighteenth century with a roof as an integral part of the house and the interior spaces, with no hint of being interconnected with the gardens.

THE LEAFY AVENUE
and large trees

As may be seen from Rebello da Costa's description, large trees and woods have always had a significance and importance in the layout of the recreational spaces of the estates in the north that was unknown in the south. Only at the end of the eighteenth century, due to the influence of the botanic gardens and because of certain changes in taste and living habits, does one notice in the south a significant increase in the number of large-sized trees. The north, however, had always had an affinity with the forest since its environment was always green, even in summer.

Enveloping the estate, the wood was normally used to form the great approach avenue to the house. Even today, at the Quinta da Bouça, near Felgueiras, the wood forms, between the entrance gate and the house, an extensive and long avenue which terminates at the entrance courtyard, in the centre of which is a huge fountain.

The most significant example of the importance placed on a wood forming an approach avenue to the house is to be seen at the Quintas da Prelada. This began with two enormous pyramids (to be found today 'in the Passeio Alegrete, at Foz do Douro) from which stretched an avenue 237 metres long. A small change in direction at the end, where there were two new pedestals top-

Above and opposite. *Summer house in a corner of the box garden and detail of the central lake.*

Garden of Biscaínhos Manor House. Braga.

263

'...The country houses are, for the most part, surrounded by thick bushes which, climbing to the tops of the roofs, present the eyes with pleasant labyrinths sprinkled with jasmine...'
Rebello da Costa. 1789 (IX)

Gardens of the Quinta da Bouça. Felgueiras.

ped by statues, signalled the beginning of a new avenue, 214 metres in length. These two avenues terminated in a curving courtyard, which still exists today, where the great entrance doorway to the walled-in terrace was located.

The Quinta de Freixo was also encircled by a leafy wood in which avenues and cascades were to be found. Sousa Reis, in his notes for the history of Oporto, mentions that: *'on the inside, you go up to the second floor, and walk towards the back exit of the building where you will be fascinated, once you pass through the door-way, by a semi-circular area around which stone benches are set against the windows which form it and shelter it, all of which end in friezes and which are hemmed in by pilasters of carved and polished granite, and on either side of the afore-mentioned area are extensive lanes covered with branches which partly run alongside the Palace, and then continue past it as they are very long, the lanes of which, in the North, are bordered with a wall covered in tiles, there being cascades here and there whose coolness offers a pleasant and delightful stay on hot days...'* [18]

In the Beira region, the Quinta da Insua is today perhaps the most significant example of an eighteenth century wood planted for recreational purposes. Significant work was carried out on the wood and the palace at the beginning of the twentieth century (1908) which bears the hallmarks of the architect Nicola Bigaglia, but where avenues cross at one point in the wood, a circular area is formed and around this are seats bearing the date 1775. A letter describing the farm, written by its owner in 1909, refers to the fact that *'the walled and tree covered part covers an area of approximately forty hectares, and is enclosed by a wall two to three metres high and is bordered by approximately four hundred cypresses, twenty-five to thirty metres tall, set apart at equal distances. The main avenues are 4.40m wide so that they can easily accommodate carriages. These avenues are all wooded, the most notable being one avenue lined with box which forms an arched dome, which was planted in 1775 in a straight line three hundred metres in length; one formed by cedars of Bussaco, probably of the same date: one of palm trees and another of oak trees'.* [19]

At the end of the nineteenth century, the estate was the object of a study by Marques Loureiro who published an article in the 'Jornal de Horticultura' in 1890. A comparison made between the trees analysed and Father Caldas Barbosa's description of the Quinta dos Senhores de Bellas at the end of the eighteenth century, as well as the *Notes de Tollenare* in 1816, constitutes a rich base of study for an analysis of the introduction of exotic trees into the country.

THE TYPICAL GARDEN
OF THE NORTH
during the eighteenth century and first half of the nineteenth century

In both Rebello da Costa and Tollenare's descriptions one can see two typical types of recreational space: the garden-terrace in the form of the 'parterre Français', and the wood. Besides these two types of space which are still perfectly visible today in many

'...very rare is (the quinta). which does not have inside its walls copious woods of leafy chestnuts, oaks and other noble trees...' Rebello da Costa. 1789 (IX)

Above. *The approach to the house; the avenue terminates in a terrace, with a fountain in the centre around which is a low wall with benches.*
Left. *View of the staircase providing access to the garden.*

Gardens of the Quinta da Bouça. Felgueiras.

Together with woods and pleasure orchards, the gardens of the farms of the eighteenth century tended to form a particular space, like that of the terrace-garden, decorated with box and statues: the ostentatious garden.

Garden-terrace with view of the central tank.

Quinta da Bouça. Felgueiras.

gardens in the north of the country, Gorani refers to another when he writes *'...the orange and lemon trees there have a greater beauty than all the other trees'.*[20]

The Quinta de Vila Flor, which stands to one side of the three box garden terraces, possesses a large orchard-kitchen garden. In an engraving of 1747 of the southern part of the city of Guimarães, the Palace of Vila Flor appears in the background with trellises bordering this orchard-kitchen garden, which is clearly integrated in the group of spaces used for the estate's recreational purposes.

In the case of other eighteenth century gardens, one can see a recreational area separated from the box garden and the wood. The Biscaínhos Gardens, at the point where the first box garden ends, extend over three terraces which, beginning at a high entrance gate, drop downwards to end at a summer house, with columns and a small garden encircled by a balustrade. Despite being greatly restored at the beginning of this century, the Mateus Gardens possess an extensive area for a pleasure orchard-kitchen garden in front of the southern façade. Ancient granite gutters are to be found all over the ground of the different terraces, water coming from the ancient tank which is surrounded by elegant granite columns.

While in the north the orchard-kitchen garden did not have the·significance and importance it acquired in the south, it must nevertheless be considered a third type of typical garden in terms of the structure of exterior spaces in the north. Unfortunately, this space was that part of the estate which was always most damaged during the decline of great eighteenth century gardens which has taken place since the nineteenth century. For example, the Prelada Gardens, which we have frequently referred to as they are not only those which are the most minutely described, but, according to the document, are *'the best in all these provinces'*, were totally destroyed in the 1980s to allow for the passage of a main road from the city of Oporto. Reference to other examples would be the subject of a lengthy and depressing book.

The division of the sixteenth century walled garden into a reserved garden and an ostentatious garden which occurred in the south in the seventeenth century onwards, was not seen in the north. In this granite culture, the garden was never regarded as being a private space rigorously separated from the exterior and its physical surroundings. In the eighteenth century, when exterior spaces took on a greater importance in the social life of the country, we find a specific representational space being defined — the ostentatious garden. Only in rare cases, in both the south and north, is the reserved garden, as the most noble place in a garden, to be seen, but when it is it always reflects the influence of the south.

The most significant example of the division of exterior spaces into ostentatious gardens and reserved gardens is to be found in the Freixo Palace. Next to the principal façade, which faces south and looks out over the Douro, one finds, on a terrace, the garden framed by balustrades on three sides. The doors and windows of the large rooms open on to this garden and Sousa Reis states: *'as soon as we see the main façade that faces South, if we can call it the "main" façade since the others are just as impressive, and the beautiful garden that is to be found in front of it, we immediately consider it to be imposing and majestic...'*[21]

Above and left. *View of statues and gargoyles in the terrace-garden.*

Following pages. *Terrace-garden overlooking vine covered valleys.* Quinta da Bouça. Felgueiras.

Positioned on one of the most prominent points, the reservoir tank distributes water to the different gardens and pleasure orchards which are spread out over the lower levels. Granite gutters channel water to different areas, as can still be seen in the Mateus Gardens.

Above. *Tank with fountain and main avenue of the pleasure orchard.*
Right. *View of the gardens laid out over different terraces.*

Gardens of the Mateus Manor House. Vila Real.

'...the main avenue has on both sides vegetable gardens and orchards, bordered with box...'. Description of 1753. [X]

Although referring to the gardens of the Quinta da Prelada, the description defines the importance of the pleasure orchards which appear side by side with the box gardens.

Above and left. *Views of the box garden and pleasure orchard avenue.*

Gardens of the Mateus Manor House. Vila Real.

The author was referring to the effect of the façade and garden seen from the river. Bearing more relation to the façade than to the overall layout of the exterior spaces, is another garden that is completely independent of the ostentatious garden: the reserved garden. Sousa Reis clearly defines it: *'There is another closed and reserved garden, facing the west, whose adornments make this enclosed space highly appreciated'.*[22] Besides its more private character, this garden, on account of the monumental belvedere which marks one end, appears as the important space, in line with the southern tradition. Another house with a reserved garden is that of the Palace of Palmeira, near Braga, on the banks of the Cávado river. Its similarities with the south, in terms of its aesthetic and domestic qualities, are evident. As has been said, this palace was transformed when it was adapted as the country retreat of archbishop Dom José de Braganza, the illegitimate son of Dom João V. In Lisbon, Dom José was used to gardens that were fundamentally designed for comfort and well-being, and which Courtils would define as being more rooms of greenery than true gardens (as the term was understood in France). While the ostentatious gardens extend along the banks of the Cávado river on various terraces, between the house and the river, a long terrace is formed on the lowest level surrounded by a high narrow balcony. Ilídio Araújo wrote of this: *'...around this terrace runs a narrow balcony paved with slabs, protected from the side of the river by a parapet of thick parpen stones, and in the interior there is a thick box hedge, so that while one enjoys an atmosphere of privacy in the garden, by climbing up on to the surrounding narrow balcony one can look at the view along the course of the river and its banks...'.*[23]

These examples therefore reflect more a cultural cross influence between the north and the south than a specific type of reserved garden. Besides the wood and the pleasure orchard, in the gardens of the north, when the garden as such is formed by various terraces, only next to the façade facing the gardens is a private space defined: the ostentatious garden.

* * *

'(One) of the most notable being an avenue of box, forming a tunnel, planted in 1775, which is three hundred metres long in a straight line...'
Manuel de Albuquerque. 1909 (XI)

Although the author was referring to his Quinta da Insua, the box avenue of the Mateus Manor House reflected the same eighteenth century taste.

Above and right. *Box avenue forming a tunnel.*

Gardens of the Mateus Manor House. Vila Real.

'*...A long bower of vines supported by marble pillars leads from the palace to the chapel. There is something majestic in this verdant gallery...*'
Beckford. 1787 (XII)

The trellis of the Marialvas Palace, Marvila, has disappeared, but one can imagine it from descriptions of the grandeur of its proportions.

Above and left. *Trellis on granite balustrades and fountain.*

Gardens of the Mateus Manor House. Vila Real.

273

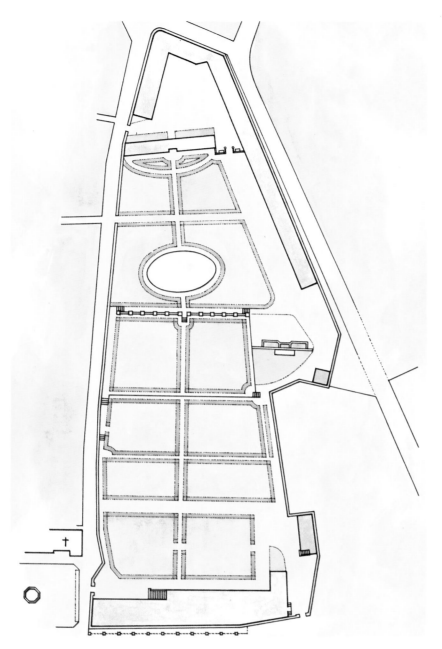

A SHORT DESCRIPTION
OF THE GARDENS
of Vila Flor, Guimarães

I n the parochial records written for the *Chorografia Portuguesa* in the middle of the eighteenth century, the gardens of the Vila Flor Palace were worthy of a special description, and one which no other house in Guimarães merited.

From the description, we can deduce that the trellises, which have now disappeared, were very similar to the large trellises with high pillars in the form of balusters that are to be found in the gardens of the Mateus Palace.

"Descobre-se a casa e jardim de Vila Flor, que dista pouco, a qual é de Thadeu Luís António Lopes de Carvalho e Camões, fidalgo da Casa Real, senhor dos Coutos de Abadim e Negrelos. É esta admirável em sua arquitectura e na grandeza e fábrica de jardim, que se compõe de dilatadas ruas, cobertas algumas de latadas ou parreiras, com engenhos fabricados, tem primoroso jardim. Um vistoso chafariz do qual se comunica água para os demais... mais debaixo duas custosas escadas de pedra se acham duas fontes emanando água por figuras de pedra e da parte de fora nas primeiras arcadas da entrada deste jardim, que estão com grandeza, vem a referida água ter seu fim pela boca de dois agigantados leões que em pé sustentam suas mãos umas conchas, donde pela boca apanham a água. São estes de pedra feitos com primor. Contém o âmbito deste muitas (?) escadas, assim lavradas, com vultos de pedra e com suas pirâmides lavradas".

Tem uma fonte de Santo António, "onde estão umas torres pequenas" a que chamam vígias de guerra, "cuja fábrica toda está com o melhor primor da arte e tem vistosa recreação, faz este a melhor vista para esta freguesia e vila".

Transcrito por *Castelo Branco. Guimarães nos meados do séc. XVIII.* Braga. Pág. 255.

(Although short, this description points out the influence of the ecclesiastic aesthetic in Portuguese gardens in the north of the country.)

* * *

Although much restored at the beginning of the twentieth century, the gardens are structured in a series of terraces bordered by box avenues which terminate in a large lake with eighteenth century balustrades. This is an identical structured to that at the Biscaínhos Gardens.

Above and right. *Plan and view of balustrades.*

Manor House of the Counts of Santar. Beira.

DESCRIPTION OF THE GARDENS
of the Quinta da Prelada, 1753

With the exception of the great axis which governs the whole of the layout, the Quinta da Prelada does not reveal any special characteristics in its gardens which differentiate it from the large country retreats in the north of the country. Its size, however, does indicate a large number of characteristics and elements which we find in many estates in the north — from its large avenue of carved granite pillars (also to be found in the gardens of the Solar de Mateus) to its fountains, lakes and statuary (also seen in the gardens of Biscaínhos and Vila Flor) and its great lake, summer houses and wood.

Within this ambit, the description made in 1753 for the *Geographical Dictionary* by Father Luís Cardoso is of particular importance on account of the degree of detail with which he describes the different parts of the landscaped whole.

While the terrace-gardens between the house and the gardens is relatively recent, the lemon trees against the house illustrate an ancient tradition referred to in eighteenth century descriptions.

Manor House of the Counts of Santar. Beira.

"No lugar da Prelada há uma quinta que passa pela melhor destas províncias; a sua entrada principal é no lugar do Carvalhido, freguesia de Cedofeita, aonde faz um largo de 360 pés de comprimento e 43 de largo; no fim dele se elevam duas pirâmides de figuras triangular assentadas sobre três bolas de pedra; elas têm de altura 30 pés e dois terços, acabam em ponta aguda com uma torre em cima, que são as armas dos Noronhas; as bases que as sustentam têm de alto 10 pés (*).

Pegado às pirâmides começa a primeira entrada que tem de comprimento 756 pés e pouco mais de dois terços, e de largura 35 pés; este caminho que corre bastante do Nascente para o Norte está bordado de árvores silvestres postas ao nível. No fim desta primeira entrada se levantam dois "pedrastais" de 10 pés de alto, e também acabam com a figura de uma torre. E aqui retrocede o caminho para o Nascente aonde faz uma carreira, até à porta, de 678 pés de comprido e 25 de largo, também copada de árvores silvestres. No fim desta entrada (rua), e um pouco apartadas da porta, há duas grandes meias-laranjas, de pedra lavrada com seus assentos. A porta é de relevo e tem 8 pés de largo e pouco mais que 13 de alto, mas o escudo das armas, que sobe 8 pés, lhe serve de remate.

Dentro de um pátio de 120 pés de fundo e 113 e 1/3 de largo, e tem em um dos lados uma fonte. As casas estão começadas com o risco de Nasoni e só a galeria que fica para o mar está acabada com uma torre que franquearam no cunhal da parte do Poente, e que faz vista para o pátio... Esta obra há-de ter a largura do pátio e de fundo 40 pés com torres quadradas nos cantos.

Nas escadas que descem para a quinta tem em um dos seus pátios uma fonte que faz a figura de um bruquel com a cabeça de Medusa, lançando água pela língua, e cabelos que transformados em cobras, deitam pelos olhos a água. Para a parte da quinta e debaixo da galeria das casas há um jardim de árvores do Norte e de espinho; a sua figura é oval e no meio tem um grande tanque redondo de água. Em correspondência deste jardim há outro irregular, mas de bom risco com árvores de boa vista e bem tratadas. Tem um tanque oitavado com uma estátua da Aurora sustentando em um dos braços uma cornucopeia por onde saem alguns registos de água. Esta figura está sentada em um delfim pegando-lhe na cauda com uma mão. Para o Nascente fica um pomar de fruta de espinho doce; nele há um tanque para as aves anfíbias, e em um dos lados uma casa de pássaros.

Pegado ao segundo jardim há um labirinto de buxo, que tem 72 pés e 3/4 por lado; a arte lhe fez com algumas figuras do mesmo buxo, mais vistosa a simetria.

No fim das escadas sai pélo meio dos dois jardins uma rua que tem de comprimento 1290 pés e de largo 10 e 2/3. Grande parte desta carreira é coberta de madeira em oitavo, e assentada em colunas de pedra da mesma forma; ela é coada de vides e bordada de buxo de 4 pés de alto com árvores por um e outro lado. Na quarta parte desta rua há um tanque oitavado de água e na volta dele corre a largura da mesma rua. Ele tem no meio uma pirâmide que lança por dois registos água para o ar, e no assento do mesmo tanque um jogo de águas. Neste sítio há alguns assentos de pedra

'...The thrust and weight of the current of the lakes and tanks of ever present water work some water-wheels...' Rebello da Costa. 1789 (XIII)

The trend towards large sculptural elements in the gardens extends throughout the Beira region. Despite an inscription bearing the date 1790, the tiles were painted by Pereira Cão at the beginning of the century, perhaps replacing other much older ones.

The arches are clearly replicas of the horsemen in the lake house at the Fronteira Palace. The faces, however, are portraits of the different members of the House of the Counts of Santar at the beginning of the twentieth century.

Monumental fountain.
Manor House of the Counts of Santar. Beira.

pintados a fresco, e por ele corre para um e outro lado uma rua com o mesmo ornato. As espaldas dos assentos são guarnecidas de azereiros para fazerem sombra. *Mais adiante e quando se acaba esta abóbada de árvores, para um dos lados há uma fonte com ruas de limoeiros e laranjeiras.* Segue-se um oitavado donde saem duas ruas guarnecidas de aveleiras, fechadas em volta redonda. Nestas ruas há assentos de laurestins. Segue-se um mirante donde nascem duas ruas guarnecidas com árvores de fruta de caroço.

A rua principal, acompanham por uma e outra parte, quartos de hortaliças e pomares bordados de buxo. As ruas que ficam encostadas aos muros são guarnecidas de alecrim, salva e outra erva cheirosa, e os mesmos muros tecidos de limoeiros que cobrem parte de uma delas.

Vai a rua principal ter a um pátio onde se forma uma escada de dois lanços; no meio do pátio está uma fonte que é um cágado que lança água pela boca, e ela cai em uma grande concha. Servem de ornato àquela figura dois rapazes com semelhança de monstros, e este sítio é obra "Moyzaica".

Subindo pelas escadas se dá em uma planície irregular, porque o seu fundo é de 210 pés e a largura, na parte por onde se entra, de 303 e 1/3. Nela há um lago artificial, e perfeitamente redondo: o seu diâmetro é de 465 pés e a água tem 4,5 de fundo. No meio dele está uma ilha aonde se levanta uma torre de dois corpos — a sua figura é redonda; a primeira tem em volta 85 pés e de altura 25 e 1/4 (nas ameias segue a forma mourisca); o segundo corpo sobe 18 pés e 3/4 e a grossura é de 44 pés e 1/4. O mastro aonde se põe uma bandeira é de 46 pés e 2/3. Da ponta do lago à ilha há 48 pés.

Na testa deste terreno há uma fonte bruta com a figura de Polifemo: ela tem na cabeça uma grande pedra e dos pés lhe... um golfo de águas que vão para o lago. De fronte desta figura e no meio do lago está uma estátua que representa Asis; esta lança água pela boca e veias dos braços, e na ilha há outra estátua de Galatea.

Todas as figuras, que são de pedra, estão muito bem cortadas. Nos dois lados do lago que fazem vista para a quinta, estão duas casas de campo. Todo o mais terreno tem plátanos, cedros, aciprestes, e outras árvores, e os muros cobertos de limoeiros.

Para a parte do Nascente, no mesmo sítio, há um pórtico com duas janelas, por onde se entra para a mata que esta quinta tem, e é capaz ainda para caça grossa.

Deste pórtico nascem três grandes ruas que por si mesmo se vão separando, e a do meio vai ter a um pórtico de figura oval que está na estrada de Viana e Galiza, e deste mesmo pórtico nascem outras três ruas que vão ter às portas da quinta. Alguma delas tem de fundo 1166 pés e 2/3, e de largura 40 pés; outras 525 pés de comprimento e 33 e 1/3 de largo. Todas elas são guarnecidas de árvores silvestres. A quinta terá de âmbito quarto e meio de légua, e dela é o senhor D. António de Noronha Menezes Mesquita e Mello, fidalgo da Casa Real.

Transcrito por Sousa Viterbo. *Dicionário Histórico e Documental dos Arquitectos.* Imprensa Nacional, 1904, Vol. II pág. 191-193.

(Although these gardens are almost completely lost today, the precision of this description means we could almost reconstruct them in their entirety. Besides the structure of gardens, avenues and woods, we can also see the different species of plants used at this time.)

'...A great, flat space before the garden in front of the villa is laid out in dismal labyrinths of clipped myrtle hedges, with lofty pyramids rising up from out of them'. Beckford. 1789 (XIV)

Great pyramids of shaped box, introduced in the seventeenth century, continued in Portugal throughout the eighteenth century, as can be seen in Beckford's description of the gardens of the Palace of the Children of Palhavã.

Façade facing south and gardens.
Manor House of the Counts of Santar. Beira.

DESCRIPTION OF THE GARDENS
of the Quinta da Insua

Although somewhat briefly, the estate was described at the beginning of this century by its proprietor, Manuel de Albuquerque, at the request of Sousa Viterbo. The house and park had undergone recent work designed by Bigaglia, but the owner refers to the work prior to this. The great walled-in wood, which extends along a vast slope in front of the house, although it underwent alterations in the time of Bigaglia, was part of the initial layout of the gardens. Its planting seems to be connected, like that of the Belas estate, to Brazil, since while Dom António Castelo Branco had been the governor of Pernambuco, Luís de Albuquerque de Melo Pereira e Cáceres — one of the first owners of the house — was Governor and Captain-General of Mato Grosso, between 1771 and 1790. The Insua wood seems, however, to have fewer exotic trees than those referred to by Father Caldas Barbosa in Belas which is linked to ancient tradition in the north of the country, where the wood occupies a more important place in gardens than in the south.

Besides the description of Manuel de Albuquerque, the wood was also described by Marques Loureiro years before in the magazine 'Horticultura Prática', nº 1, Oporto, 1890, which gives the various species of trees in the wood.

It is also interesting to note that in his letter Manuel de Albuquerque does not make special reference to the camellias shaped into the form of summer houses, as is the case in the Biscaínhos Garden, which suggests that this practice was common at the time.

A description of the gardens of the Quinta da Insua, by Manuel de Albuquerque, in 1909:

A respeito da quinta e jardim, que é o que interessa a V., direi o seguinte:

A parte murada e arborisada tem approximadamente 40 hectares, fechada por um muro de 2 a 3 metros de alto e orlada de Cyprestes em distancias iguaes em numero de 400 approximadamente, e 25 a 30 metros de alto.

As principaes ruas têem 4m,40 de largo (4 varas) de fórma que póde ser percorrida facilmente de carruagem. Essas ruas são todas arborisadas, sendo as mais notáveis uma rua de buxo, formando abobada, plantada em 1775, com 300 metros de comprido em linha recta; uma de Cedros do Bussaco, provavelmente da mesma data, uma de Palmeiras, uma de Avelleiras e outras de Carvalhas.

Tem abundancia de agua, tendo um lago na parte mais elevada da quinta, vários tanques e chafarizes.

O jardim é um traçado geometrico, como era uso na epoca; todos os canteiros rodeados de buxo, representando cornucopias, vasos, leques, etc. É curioso ter sido sempre esse buxo tosquiado com todo o cuidado e sem intervalo de um anno desde a sua plantação, unica fórma como se explica a sua perfeita conservação.

Tem paredes de buxo, murta e cedros, com fórmas rigorosamente geometricas, etc. Consta que o cargo de jardineiro tem sido sempre exercido pela mesma familia, dos Thiagos. Eu já conheci tres gerações e não deve isso ter concorrido pouco para a perfeita conservação dos jardins.

A quinta da Insua está situada na freguezia do mesmo nome, concelho de Penalva do Castello, districto de Vizeu, a 15 kilometros da estação do caminho de ferro da Beira, Mangualde e 29 de Vizeu e ligada por excellentes estradas para esses dous pontos.

Ainda dentro da propriedade, mas fóra da parte murada, passa o rio Coja, pequeno affluente do Dão, atravessando uma matta de carvalhos; ultimamente foi alli construida, ou para melhor dizer, appropriada, uma penedia que alli ha para uma gruta

Camellias shaped into small summer houses, box-lined paths, garden terraces set out in a sequence of landings, and a leafy wood which surrounds the quinta, make the Insua Gardens the most complex example of the landscape layout that remains today in the Beira region.

Façade overlooking the gardens and view of the gardens.

Quinta da Insua. Penalva do Castelo. Beira.

dedicada a Nossa Senhora de Lourdes, que fica na margem do rio e onde ha uma romaria no ultimo domingo de setembro.

Desejando mais algum esclarecimento fico com o maior prazer ao dispor de V., e subscrevo-me com a maior consideração, — de V. mt.º att.º ven.ᵈᵒʳ e obg.ᵈᵒ — *Manuel d'Albuquerque*"

'The garden is a geometric outline... All the flowerbeds are surrounded by box representing cornucopia, vases, fans, etc.... It is curious that this box has been clipped with all possible care every year since it was planted...' Manuel de Albuquerque. 1909 (XV)

Detail of a fan shaped from box in one of the garden-terraces. Quinta da Insua. Penalva do Castelo. Beira.

(Although it is written in the twentieth century, this description points out that the gardens, and especially the beautiful wood, of this house were constructed in the second half of the eighteenth century).

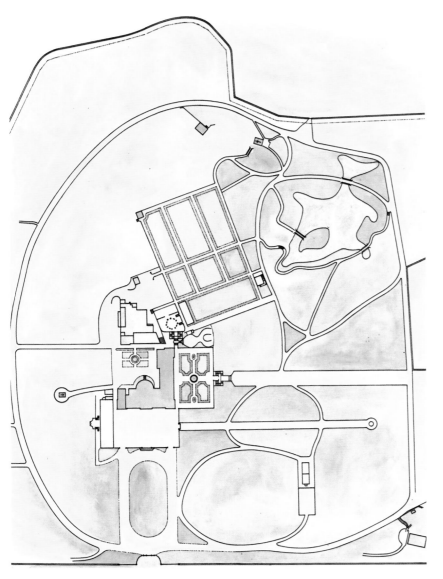

PLANTS, FLOWERS AND TREES
noted by Tollenare, 1816

The fact that Tollenare specifically named the typical species of the gardens makes these notes particularly interesting, especially if we compare them with other authors such as Caldas Barbosa or Marques Loureiro.

Les arbres qu'on rencontre le plus souvent dans la campagne sont:

— 1º Le *Pinus maritimus* et le *Pinus pinea*. C'est celui-ci qui fournit l'excellent sapin qu'on emploie pour la construction des navires. L'un et l'autre s'élèvent jusqu'à 60 pieds. On les sème, ou plus souvent ils se sèment d'eux-mêmes. Chaque année on les éclaircit en détruisant les plus faibles, et on coupe les branches inférieures dès que l'arbre a 5 à 6 ans. La première année, les petits pins étaient à 6 à 8 pouces les uns des autres. Lorsque, à 20 à 25 ans, ils ont à peu près atteint leur croissance, ils sont distants les uns des autres de 12 à 20 pieds. On n'en extrait ni résine, ni goudron.

— 2º Deux sortes de chênes. Une espèce, qui diffère peu de la nôtre, mais que je ne saurais déterminer ([a]), est petite || et rabougrie. Elle sert souvent d'appui à la vigne qui probablement s'oppose à son développement. Mais les individus mêmes qui ne la reçoivent pas sont d'une médiocre grandeur. Ils portent des galles d'une grosseur considérable: j'en ai vu qui avaient près de 2 pouces de diamètre. La seconde espèce est le subrier (*Quercus suber*, arbre à liège). J'ai vu quelques individus qui avaient 80 pieds de haut: mais en général, ceux qu'on rencontre sur les montagnes sont faibles comme ceux que j'ai vus sur les montagnes calcaires de la Provence du côté d'Hyères. Le liège qu'ils produisent est peu estimé; cependant on l'exporte.

— 3º Des châtaigniers, surtout sur les bords du Douro. J'en ai rencontré qui, pour leur beauté, pourraient rivaliser avec les nôtres. Sur les côtés du Douro, on voit des châtaigneraies qui sont d'un grand produit. On les coupe tous les cinq ans. Malgré la douceur du climat, il y a cependant des hivers assez sévères, sinon pour les geler totalement, du moins pour les retarder d'une année.

— 4º Quelques peupliers et saules, mais en petit nombre, dans les campagnes. On voit souvent le saule pleureur autour des habitations.

L'oranger et le citronnier ne se rencontrent que dans les endroits cultivés, dans les jardins autour des maisons du riche et du pauvre.

Je n'ai point vu de hêtres, ni de charmes. Ce n'est que dans les jardins que j'ai vu le tilleul.

Above. *Constructed at the end of the eighteenth century, the estate and its gardens underwent improvements and alterations during the nineteenth century, as can be seen from the Romantic area around the great lake. The large avenues of leafy trees which grow around the terrace and box garden continue an eighteenth century fashion.*

Right. *View of the large entrance gate.*
Palace of Brejoeira. Monção.

'The estate of the Marquis of Marialva also serves as the meeting point, on a lawn in front of the house, for passers-by. Stretches of grass and lawns are so rare in Portugal that coming across one is a delightful occurrence...'
Tollenare. 1816 (XVI)

'La quinta do marquês de Marialva sert aussi de rendez-vous aux promeneurs qui s'y réunissent sur une pelouse devant la maison. Les prairies et les pelouses sont si rares en Portugal que la recontre de celle-ci est un événement gracieux...'.

Above and left. *Entrance terrace and main façade.*
Palace of Brejoeira. Monção.

Detail of the north garden decorated with old camellias.
Palace of Brejoeira. Monção.

Les arbres qui ornent les jardins sont: des poiriers, pommiers, pêchers, cerisiers et pruniers, mais de mauvaise qualité; des lauriers dont on || fait des murailles de verdure (il y en a de plusieurs sortes); des *Melia azedarach*; des lauriers-roses d'une grande hauteur; quelques *cyprès pyramidaux*; quelques ifs taillés à l'ancienne mode française; enfin des treilles, des figuiers, des orangers et citronniers. Le *Magnolia grandiflora* et le tulipier de Virginie, quoique assez abondants, sont encore considérés comme des arbres précieux.

Dans presque tous les quintals ou jardins, les carreaux de terre sont cultivés en maïs. On n'y voit point d'espaliers et peu de légumes. Près de la maison se trouve ordinairement un parterre français orné d'assez belles fleurs; mais je n'en ai point encore vu qui me fussent très étrangères. Le caprier, si abondant en Provence, est si rare ici qu'on me l'a montré dans un jardin comme une curiosité.

Je réserve cette place vide pour noter les autres arbres que je remarquerai.

Arbousiers dans les montagnes. Sureau. Quelques espèces de cornouiller que je ne connais pas. Très peu de peupliers de Virginie. Frêne. Olivier. Troene.

J'ai cherché dans mes promenades à découvrir quelques plantes qui ne fussent pas communes dans notre France. Soit défaut de connaissances, soit parce que la nature fournit ici les mêmes productions végétales qu'en France, j'ai toujours rencontré des genres qui m'étaient connus; je ne suis pas assez habile pour dire que ce soient les mêmes espèces.

Voici la note des plantes que j'ai recueillies jusqu'à ce jour. Elles ne m'ont pas paru valoir la peine d'être conservées dans un herbier puisque la France les produit à peu près toutes ou du moins les mêmes genres. Pour m'y reconnaître, je les ai classées méthodiquement avant de les jeter par la croisée.

ACOTYLÉDONES.

Je connais peu cette classe. Partout j'ai vu des mousses et des agarics. Je n'ai pas encore trouvé de nos champignons mangeables. Fougères, mâle et femelle; polypodes, scolopendre sur les murailles. *Equisetum*, mais d'espèces que je crois différentes.

MONOCOTYLÉDONES.

Massettes et rubans d'eau (*Typha* et *Sparganium*). [*Tremella*.]

Scirpes (*Scirpus*) et carex (*Carex*); et souchets (*Cyperus*) près du Douro.

Dans les Graminées, ce sont toujours les flouves, *Alopecurus, Holcus, Elymus* (celui des sables), brome, fétuque, *Poa, Dactylis agglomerata, Avena*, peu d'*Hordeum murinum, Lolium*. Ne pouvant faire des longues recherches, je me suis borné à reconnaître les genres et j'ai toujours cru trouver les mêmes espèces qu'en France. Il faudrait || un botaniste plus exercé que je ne le suis pour assigner les différences. Il y a ici très peu de prairies. Peut-être y en avait-il plus autrefois: la culture du maïs a tout envahi.

Joncs. *Sagittaria sagittifolia* dans les ruisseaux.

Les yucas se trouvent dans les jardins, les aloès se rencontrent çà et là sur des murailles, mais évidemment plantés.

Les asphodèles, très communes dans les bas-fonds près des bords du Douro.

Iris germanica. Je crois avoir vu la *pseudo-Acarus*. Je n'ai pas trouvé le safran, mais on le dit commun.

Orchis, celle qui pue.

DICOTYLÉDONES.

Nymphea, nénuphar, dans les bassins de quelques jardins.

Aristoloches, *Azarum* ou cabaret dans des ruisseaux.

Lauréole (*Daphne*) très abondant; j'en ai vu sur les bords de la mer une espèce que je ne connais pas.

Lauriers dans les jardins cultivés.

Rumex dans les jardins cultivés.

Salsola de plusieurs sortes à São João de Foz, et salicorne; plusieurs espèces de *Chenopodium* et d'arroches, entre autres le *Chenopodium Bonus Henricus*.

L'herniole, autant que je peux croire.

Plantago, moins abondant que près de Nantes. [Abondant depuis.]

Statice, mais près des jardins, d'où peut-être il provenait.

Anagallis, la variété bleu et rouge. Lysimachie, autant que j'aie pu reconnaître à la feuille, la *Lysimachia nummularia*; elle n'était pas fleurie.

Rhinanthus, crête de coq.

Le frêne, le troene, l'olivier.

Dans les Labiées: romarin; *Salvia pratensis*; bugle pyramidale; lavande dans les jardins; lierre terrestre; *Lamium amplexicaule, Stachis palustris, Ballotta* et *Marubium*, autant que je peux croire; mélisses, plusieurs espèces très odorantes; thym; basilic (cultivé); *Brunella*.

Anthirinum, muflier; *Digitalis purpurea* très abondant.

Hysciamus nigra très abondant; *Verbascum nigrum*; *Solanum dulcamara*; *Lycium*.

Echium vulgare, consoude. Je n'ai vu ni la bourrache ni la cynoglosse.

Je guettais les liserons (*Convolvulus*), dont nous avons plusieurs très belles espèces de Portugal; je n'ai encore rien rencontré.

Je n'ai point vu la pervenche. *Laurier-rose dans les jardins, quelquefois dans les haies.*

Asclepias.

Beaucoup de jolies bruyères; celle qui prédomine dans les landes est la *cinerea*, mais avec des fleurs beaucoup plus grosses que chez nous.

Je me perds facilement dans les semi-Flosculeuses jaunes quand je n'ai pas de livre. *Crepis virens, Taraxacum; Tragopogon.*

Flosculeuses. *Cardus acanthoides, Onopordium; Centaurea nigra.* Je n'ai point vu la tanaisie.

Radiées. *Bellis pulchra; Solidago*, camomille.

Scabiosa, une petite espèce qui ne ressemble pas à la nôtre.

Gallium verum.

Chèvrefeuille, dans les haies.

Hortensia, dans les jardins du riche et du pauvre.

Je n'ai pas encore vu le sureau. [Je l'ai vu depuis.]

Cornouiller, dans les haies; la *sanguinea*.

Je n'ai vu que quelques très grands ombellifères que je ne connais point. *Daucus carota* dans les prairies, mais très peu.

Plusieurs sortes de renoncules.

Fumeterre.

Raphanus raphanistrum; Sinapis nigra; Erysimum (du moins je crois que ce l'est). C'est près de la mer que j'ai vu cette plante. *Iberis, Thlaspis bursa pastoris.* On dit que l'*Isatis tinctoria* est commun. Je ne l'ai pas encore vu. [J'en ai trouvé beaucoup sur la rive du sud.]

Reseda luteola.

Caprier (curiosité dans un jardin).

Hypericum perforatum.

Orangers et citronniers (cultivés).

Melia azedarach, dans les jardins.

Beaucoup de géranium.

Malva sylvestris.

Magnoliers, tulipiers, dans les jardins.

Tilleuls, dans les jardins.

Les violettes sont passées; on les dit rares.

Dianthus, seulement dans les jardins.

Lin, cultivé.

Joubarbe, sur les murs.

Plusieurs saxifrages.

Cactus, assicoides, dans les jardins.

Volant d'eau.

Fuschia, très abondant dans les jardins.

Myrtes, grenadiers, *idem*. Je ne vois pas de grenadiers dans les haies comme en Provence, [mais le myrte.]   *Roses, dans les haies et dans les jardins; Agrimonia eupatoria.* Je n'ai encore vu ni la potentille, ni la tormentille, ni la benoîte (*Geum*). Ronces, fond des haies, *Rubus fructicosus*.

Acacia, très fréquent; plusieurs sortes dans les jardins.

Ajonc, fond des bruyères, *europoeus* et *nanus*; genêt, *Genista*, aussi celui *tinctoria*; lupin, *Ononis* (arrête-boeuf); *Melilotus; Trifolium*, cultivé et petites espèces dans les champs; luzerne, *Medicago*, et *Lotus corniculatus; Dolichos; Viscia sativa*; fèves, pois, haricots, cultivés; *Cicer*.

Sumac, abondant.

Noyer, peu abondant.

Je ne vois ni fusains (*Evonimus*), ni *Celastron*, ni *Prunus* dans les haies. Ni nerprun (Ramnées).

Mercuriale, moins abondante que chez nous; euphorbe, une espèce gigantesque, [plusieurs autres]; *buis, dans les jardins.*

Je n'ai pas encore vu le bryone; [vu depuis]. On cultive toutes sortes de melons, et citrouilles, courges.

Figuiers; mûriers.

Quelques pariétaires; point de houblon; peu d'orties; [j'en ai trouvé depuis]; chanvre, cultivé.

Tank with large granite statue in the north garden.
Palace of Brejoeira. Monção.

Gardens in the north of the country are noted for the number and volume of decorative elements, of which the fountain is one of the most characteristic.

Rocaille fountain. Convent of Grijó. Oporto.

Orme, rare.
Salix. Salix cinerea; peuplier *tremula*; je ne vois point le peuplier d'Italie.
Ni de l'hêtre, ni de noisetier, ni d'érable, ni de platane.
If. Buis, dans les jardins. Point de genévriers.
Pinus maritimus, Pinus pinea. Point de sapin. Quelques mélèzes.

Ceci est un aperçu bien léger sans doute, mais il suffit pour faire voir que la nature ici ne diffère pas très essentiellement de ce qu'elle est près de Nantes. Des recherches de plantes ne me paraissent devoir présenter du nouveau qu'à des botanistes très habiles.

L. F. de Tollenare, *Notes Dominicales Prises Pendant une Voyage en Portugal et au Brézil en 1816, 1817 et 1818,* Paris 1972. Fundação Calouste Gulbenkian, pág. 50-53.

DESCRIPTION OF GARDENS
by Rebello da Costa, 1789

B esides referring to the most important estates of Oporto, Rebello da Costa gives us some general characteristics which are important elements in defining the typical exterior spaces on estates in the north of the country during the eighteenth century.

"Não lhes são necessárias cautelas para evitarem o rigor da neve ou o ardor do Estio. Em tôdas as estações do ano as laranjas, limões, limas, cidras, alfaces, couves, etc. crescem e sazonam-se completamente. Muitas destas quintas dilatam-se por Massarelos, Vilar e Cedofeita. Raríssima haverá da qual se não goze vista de rio e mar; raríssima a que não tenha, dentro dos seus muros, copados bosques de frondosos castanheiros, carvalhos e outras árvores pomposas. Os lagos e tanques de água perene são nelas frequentíssimos, de sorte que, com o impulso e peso da sua corrente, trabalham alguns moínhos e azenhas.

As casas de campo são, pela maior parte, rodeadas de espessos arbustos que, trepando até o cume dos telhados, representam aos olhos agradáveis labirintos semeados de jasmins, martírios e muitas outras flores, cuja variedade e cheiro suavíssimo é o encanto dos sentidos. Os ingleses, franceses, holandeses, hamburgueses, e outras famílias estrangeiras comerciantes, são os que arrendam estas quintas e nelas vivem a maior parte do ano; mas os portugueses reservam para seu uso e divertimento as melhores e as mais custosas. Tais são: da parte do nascente, norte e poente, a das *Virtudes*, pertencente à viúva e filhos de José Pinto de Meireles, Cavaleiro professo na Ordem de Cristo, que se inclue no bairro de Miragaia e é de um preço e valor tal que, só os muros que a cercam e formoseiam, custaram muito mais de vinte mil cruzados; a do *Pinheiro*, enriquecida com uma aceada capela, de que falarei no capítulon seguinte, e na qual se principia a edificar uma grande casa em figura de palácio, pertencente a João António Monteiro e Azevedo, Cavaleiro professo na Ordem de Santiago; a dos *Carvalhos*, imediata ao Mirante dos Ingleses, a José Ribeiro Braga, Cavaleiro professo na Ordem de Cristo, e a seu irmão António Ribeiro Braga; a de *Santo Ovídeo* a Manuel de Figueirôa; a da *Prelada*, quinta majestosa em grandeza, obeliscos, jardins, cascatas, pirâmides, labirintos e um grande lago que, rodeia uma casa acastelada que está no seu centro firmada sôbre uma pequena ilha; pertence a D. Manuel de Noronha e Menezes, Fidalgo da Casa Real; a da *Fonte*, em Cedofeita, aos filhos de Domingos José Nogueira; a do *Bom Sucesso*, a António de Sá Lopes.

Seguem-se as três quintas de Vilar, pertencentes, uma, a Vicente Pedrossen, outra a Manuel Francisco Guimarães, e a outra a Nicolau Kopke, Cavaleiros professos na Ordem de Cristo; a do *Regueirinho* em Massarelos a Joaquim Kopke.

Não falo na Quinta dos Arcos, em que mora Gabriel Herault, e na do curioso horto botânico, em que assiste Francisco Bearsley e em outras mais, porque não habitam nelas os próprios donos portugueses.

Segue-se para o nascente a de *Sacais*, sita no campo da Oliveira, e de que é senhor Nicolau Francisco Guimarães, Cavaleiro professo na Ordem de Cristo; tem a sua Casa de Campo magnífica e proporcionada ao grande páteo interior, sôbre que forma três fachadas, com janelas de cristalinas vidraças e portas correspondentes umas às outras;

uma asseada capela, dedicada a Santa Bárbara, medeia entre as duas fronteiras que faceiam, uma com a Quinta do Prado, outra com a rua pública ou entrada principal da cidade, em que pega a quinta de António José Guimarães, Cavaleiro professo na Ordem de Cristo, irmão do sôbredito, e que em tudo lhe é igual, ou seja na situação e grandeza, ou na bondade e mimo dos seus frutos.

As que estão à borda do rio Douro são: a do *Prado*, pertencente aos Excelentíssimos Bispos do Pôrto, que não a estimam tanto como a Quinta de Santa Cruz, cuja extensão é incomparàvelmente maior e tem servido de assunto ao delicioso canto das Musas; a da *Chiná*, pertencente a João Lopes Ferraz, que na grandeza da sua casa, do seu terreno, jardins, árvores e muros tem poucas semelhantes; a de *Campanhã*, pertencente a D. António de Amorim da Gama Lobo; a do *Freixo*, à viúva e filhas de Vicente de Noronha Cernache, quinta na verdade digna de um príncipe, tanto pela majestade do seu Palácio, como pela magnificência dos seus jardins, estátuas, etc.; a do *Sardão*, que fica da parte meridional do Douro e de que é senhora a Viúva de José Bento Leitão, Cavaleiro professo na Ordem de Cristo; segue-se a Quinta dos *Fiais*, sita na freguesia de S. Pedro de Avintes, pertencente a Pedro Van-Zeller, Cavaleiro professo na Ordem de Cristo, rico e acreditado comerciante nesta Praça e nas principais do reino e nações estrangeira. As casas desta quinta têm cento e setenta e oito palmos de frente, aberta em multiplicadas janelas envidraçadas, que formam o superior andar; e no inferior estão as portas que dão entrada para os armazéns dos frutos, quartos dos criados e outros cómodos precisos. Esta longa fachada remata-se em dois quartões correspondentes em altura e em formalidade igual, que realçam a beleza de todo o edifício. No quartão da parte esquerda está a capela dedicada a Santo *Inácio*, muito decente e própria para celebrar-se o incruento Sacrifício do Altar. Duas formosas escadas de pedra bem polida, uma da parte do norte, outra do sul, rematam-se em um asseado pátio que franqueia a passagem para tôdas as salas, e por baixo dêle estão as cavalhariças e cocheiras. Tem na frente um terreiro ou praça, que ocupa em quadra os ditos 178 palmos, e em um dos seus lados um grande tanque com três grossas bicas.''

Agostinho Rebello da Costa. *Descrição da Cidade do Porto*. 1789. Pages 66-69.

NOTES

1 Transcribed by Ilídio Araújo. *Arte paisagística e arte dos jardins em Portugal*. Lisbon, 1962. Page 190.
2 Idem. Page 190.
3 Agostinho Rebello da Costa. *Descrição da Cidade doPorto*. 1789. Page 66.
4 Gorani. *Portugal, A Corte e o País nos anos de 1765 a 1767*. Translation, preface and notes by Castelo Branco Chaves. Lisbon, 1945. Page 128.
5 Transcribed by Sousa Viterbo in *Dicionário Histórico e Documental dos arquitectos engenheiros...* National Printers, 1904. Volume II. Page 192.
6 Idem. Page 192.
7 Arthur W. Costigan. *Cartas de Portugal 1778-1779*. Lisbon. Page 81.
8 Agostinho Rebello da Costa. Ibid. Page 66.
9 Transcribed by Castelo Branco Chaves. *Guimarães em meados do séc. XVIII*. Braga. Page 255.
10 The camellias in the gardens of the Counts of Campo Bello, Gaia, have been the object of recent studies by American scientists and have proved to be the oldest camellias to have come directly from the Orient at the end of the sixteenth century and the beginning of the seventeenth century.
11 Transcribed by Sousa Viterbo. Ibid. Page 192.
12 Idem. Page 192.
13 Transcribed by Castelo Branco Chaves. Ibid. Page 255.
14 Tollenare. *Notes Dominicales Prises Pendant une Voyage en Portugal et au Brézil en 1816, 1817 et 1818*. Paris. F.C. Gulbenkian. 1972. Page 48.
15 Tollenare. Ibid. Page 48.
16 Transcribed by Sousa Viterbo. Ibid. Page 192.
17 Tollenare. Ibid. Page 48.
18 Transcribed by Ilídio Araújo. Ibid. Pages 190-191.
19 Transcribed by Sousa Viterbo. *A Jardinagem em Portugal*. Coimbra, 1909. 2nd series. Page 68.
20 Gorani. Ibid. Page 68.
21 Transcribed by Ilídio Araújo. Ibid. Page 190.
22 Idem. Page 190.
23 Idem. Page 207.

Notes on Illustrations

    I. Tollenare. Ibid. Page 48.
   II. Transcribed by Ilídio Araújo. Ibid. Page 190.
  III. Agostinho Rebello da Costa. Ibid. Page 66.
  IV. Transcribed by Sousa Viterbo. *Dicionário Histórico e Documental dos arquitectos...* National Printers. 1904. Volume II. Page 192.
   V. Transcribed by Castelo Branco Chaves. *Guimarães nos meados do séc. XVII*. Braga. Page 255.
  VI. Idem. Page 255.
 VII. Idem. Page 255.
VIII. Idem. Page 255.
  IX. Rebello da Costa. Ibid. Page 66.
   X. Transcribed by Sousa Viterbo. *Dicionário Histórico e Documental dos arquitectos*. Page 192.
  XI. Transcribed by Sousa Viterbo. *A Jardinagem em Portugal*. Coimbra, 1909. 2nd series. Page 68.
 XII. William Beckford. *The Journal of ... in Portugal and Spain 1767-1788*. London, 1954. Page 96. Translation by João Gaspar Simões. National Library, Lisbon 1983. 2nd ed.. Page 69.
XIII. A. Rebello da Costa. Ibid. Page 66.
XIV. William Beckford. Ibid. London, 1954. Page 49. Portuguese translation B.N.L. Page 43.
 XV. Transcribed by Sousa Viterbo. *A Jardinagem em Portugal*. Coimbra, 1909. 2nd series. Page 68.
XVI. Tollenare. Ibid. Page 135.

THE CONCEPT OF
THE SCENIC GARDEN
and the decline of the pleasure garden

CHAPTER X

The scenic garden only became known with some difficulty in Portugal, as the exponents of the Romantic garden presented it as the antithesis of the Portuguese tradition of the pleasure garden. Their love for both nature and the forest suggested a unity between the garden and the surrounding landscape, which was difficult to achieve in a Mediterranean climate of dry summers with water shortages. The Portuguese pleasure garden, treated as a rigorously delimited space of one or more terraces, economised on the use of irrigation water, especially in the summer, and this permitted the creation of a small cool and green oasis of nature, surrounded in the summer by a landscape that was dry and burnt by the sun.

In Portugal, the most significant examples of the Romantic garden are restricted almost exclusively to two areas: Sintra and the north of the country. Climatic reasons are evident. The abundance of water in these two areas stems from an environment of thick woods and clearings, streams and lakes, that was in perfect harmony with the Romantic taste. Laura Junot, on arriving at Sintra at the beginning of the nineteenth century, describes it thus: *'The way nature changes here is a paradise...on every side are streams of pure and abundant water, on every side meadows and shade, on every side houses built with a truly charming graciousness that harmonises with the beautiful landscape of the valley...Next to the houses, one sees one of the most charming trees for a landscape, the strawberry tree (Arbutus unedo), as well as the carob (Ceratonia siliqua). One also finds the* Phyllirières *and* Myrica faga. *A true paradise! A perfumed paradise!'* The micro-climate of Sintra also permitted the culture of exotic plants *'...pine woods, banana plants and exotic trees, mainly from Madeira, which the English and the French have made indigenous, in this land loved by the sun...'.*[1]

The main European influence in the country was to be found in Sintra and on the outskirts of Oporto. Sintra, since the middle of the mid-eighteenth century, had been transformed into the summer resort of rich foreign merchants living in Lisbon. On the other hand, Oporto, whose export business, and in particular that of port wine, was controlled by the English, underwent a strong English cultural influence from the eighteenth century onwards. Rebello da Costa, in 1789, when he described the estates on the outskirts of Oporto, mentions that: *'The English, French, Dutch, Hamburgers, and other foreigners are those who rent these quintas and live on them for most of the year...'*[2] The foreign merchants were looking on the outskirts of the city, and especially on the banks of the Douro, for the estates with thick woods and abundant spring water of which Rebello da Costa wrote and which reminded him of the leafy parks of northern Europe.

In Sintra, from the middle of the eighteenth century onwards, the estates of the old aristocracy were also acquired or rented by rich foreign merchants.

The recorded life of Monserrate and its gardens began when it was rented by Devisme to the Melo e Castros.[3] In other cases, the merchants bought properties on which to build houses without the inconvenient Portuguese idiosyncrasies, which irritated the foreigners of the time so much.

With radically different aesthetic standards and spatial traditions, the large Portuguese residences, from the fifteenth to the sixteenth century, continued a spatial structure incompatible with European taste. Seteais, which was built by a wealthy Dutch merchant, Gildemeester, is separated from the road by an extensive gardened terrace, unlike the majority of Portuguese estates which are to be found next to the road, facing inwards on to the gardens and surrounded by high walls. This particular aspect is specifically

Opposite page. *View of the mock Greek-Roman temple ruins.*
Gardens of the Quinta dos Lagos. Sintra.

mentioned by Tollenare when he writes about Seteais in 1816, the Palace being the property of the Marquises of Marialva at the time: 'The estate of the Marquis of Marialva also serves as the meeting point on a lawn in front of the house for passers by. Stretches of grass and lawns are so rare in Portugal that coming across one is a delightful occurrence...'[(1)]

Because of their special climate and geography, and because of the strong European influence in the area, Sintra and the region of Oporto are, in Portugal, two focal points for the development of the Romantic garden which rarely attained, as it did in northern Europe, the extent and grandeur of true landscape layouts.

THE PICTURESQUE GARDEN
and the origin of the Romantic garden

At the beginning of the eighteenth century, a wave of ideas from England, mainly expressed in poetry, flooded Europe and led to the birth of the Romantic garden on the Continent. From James Thomson came the 'Seasons' which led the way for a whole school of poetry such as Gray's 'Elegy in a Country Churchyard' and Goldsmith's 'The Deserted Village'. Abandoning the classical rules of composition, this lyrical poetry took nature as its central theme, praising it as a mythical symbol of beauty and perfection.

Its Scottish roots revealed an ancient Druidic tradition of the forest gods, which was never lost either to catholicism or, later on, classicism.

The cross-influence between landscape poets and landscape art was apparent from the early days of the movement. The gardens at Castle Howard and Stowe were made in the first half of the eighteenth century, at the same time as the publication of the first poems by Thomson, Collins and Gray. It is interesting to find that the layout of these two park-gardens presents a natural plan with the formal discipline of classical gardens, while the architecture of the house and the pavilions, temples and bridges follows traditional rules.

Gothic revivalism in architecture as well as a Chinese influence came much later on, the landscape layout being the forerunner of the movement in the area of fine arts. There is, however, an influence from the painting of Poussin, Claude Lorraine and Constable in the conception of these park-gardens. While the classical garden from the time of the Italian renaissance to the formalism of Le Nôtre was closely connected to architecture, the aesthetic of the Romantic garden took on a pictorial nature.

The gardens can be seen in a succession of images and from different viewing points and it is at times difficult to know if certain aspects were studied to suggest a painting or if they were inspired by paintings. The effects of perspective were influenced by the works of landscape artists. Each image tended to be marked by a foreground of high trees whose shady part gave way to a second plan of smoother tones made up of clearings, valleys, lawns, lakes and streams. At the bottom, in shades that became progressively bluer as they stretched into the distance, small temples, arches and bridges appeared, wisely placed on slopes or the top of small hills.

Nature appears, in its most significant elements, in a setting which, although rigorously constructed and programmed, looks as natural and spontaneous as possible. In the curve of a stream or path, there unexpectedly appeared landscape painting views. The perspective, as seen in terms of a long vanishing line (avenue or main axis), is substituted by the aerial perspective made by overlaying progressively more diffuse and distant planes.

Together with painting, this new concept of landscape was influenced by the Chinese tradition of a deep understanding of the aesthetic. At the end of the seventeenth century, William Temple wrote about the originality of Chinese gardens, which he called the 'artificial jungle', and the natural harmony of *sharawaldgi*: beauty without apparent order. This influence later appeared throughout Europe in everything that was exotic or picturesque as a result of the studies and books of William Chambers: *Design of Chinese Buildings, Furniture, Dress, Machines and Utensils,* published in 1757 and *A Dissertation on Oriental Gardening,* of 1772.

The affinity between the Romantic park and Chinese garden was, therefore, apparent. For Chinese culture, nature was the beginning and end of everything: the immutable eternity. For European culture, in the early days of Romanticism, nature was the beginning and a return to the origins of Jean Jacques Rousseau, but not the end.

NOSTALGIA
in the concept of the Romantic garden

At the beginning of the industrial revolution, between scientific empiricism and illuminism, Europe found itself on the threshold of a great historical era. Nature was seen more as a force with ancient origins, a nostalgia for an irredeemably lost past. In contrast to the Chinese garden, the Romantic garden was progressively impregnated with the nostalgia of time. Following the Graeco-Roman temples at Castle Howard, Stowe or Stourhead with their timeless classicism, the parks begin to be filled with chapels, Gothic towers, Turkish and Chinese pavilions, medieval bridges, courtyards and triumphal arches.

With an increasing emphasis on the Romantic spirit, these constructions took the form of ruins, reinforcing the effect of nostalgia and the passage of time, in line with excessive sentimentalism which characterised the second Romantic school. What fascinated Byron on his visit to Monserrate in 1811 and what inspired him to write the celebrated poem of *Childe Harold*, was the state of abandonment and mystery which Tollenare described with equal enthusiasm: *'I was surprised by the view of an elegant castle, constructed in Gothic style and surrounded by beautiful gardens. I went towards it with the idea of asking permission to visit it. The main gate was open and I entered without meeting anybody. The deepest silence reigned over the entrance courtyard. I climbed up to the landing at the top of the stairs...nobody. I entered the house: complete silence! I went into all the rooms, which were decorated with taste and magnificence, but in a state of abandonment and ruin capable of inspiring the coldest romanticism...'.*[5]

If we consider how Monserrate had been allowed to fall into decay, this fascination with the effect of time, also expressed in the romantic taste for collections and antiques, and which can be seen in Byron and Tollenare, still had no echo in nineteenth century Portugal. The value of the past and of time in Portuguese culture had, for centuries, a definite Oriental affinity, a significance more mythical than historical, and while England and northern Europe constructed false ruins, as Tollenare stated: *'The Portuguese let everything fall into ruin instead.'*[6]

The writer continues: *'In our country, these ruins, if not guarded, would soon have everything stolen from them by the active farm workers of the neighbourhood. Here, nothing is touched, the doors and the railings rot in their iron hinges'.*[7] In the yearnings in the Portuguese soul for that which is long gone, the past was something irredeemably lost and rapidly transposed to an area of myth and legendary memory — Sebastianism. Especially in the centre and the south of the country, the garden was, for centuries, a space-symbol of a lost or promised paradise that had no similarity with the earthly world or nature. This vision, which continued an ancient Hellenic-Islamic tradition, regarded the garden as an oasis, whose desert was dangerously waiting to cover it at each and every moment. In contrast, the Romantic garden clearly continued a Druidic tradition of the cult of the forest and of mother nature.

Portuguese resistance to the Romantic garden was thus based on two reasons. On the one hand, a clear unsuitability to the climate and orography, and on the other hand the fact that its space-time concepts continued a radically contrasting cultural tradition.

The Romantic Garden marked the supremacy of northern Europe as the nucleus from which culture spread outwards to Mediterranean Europe. The European centre of gravity shifted permanently to the north from the eighteenth century onwards, when it also became, at the same time, the centre of political and economic decisions. The adoption in Portugal of the Romantic garden was thus delayed until the second half of the nineteenth century, coinciding with a gradual loss of cultural identity and a weakness for everything that came from the north of Europe.

When the eminent gardener-botanist Ernest Bergman visited Portugal at the end of the nineteenth century, his eulogies fell on two foreign undertakings: Pena Park and Monserrate Gardens. The first is connected with a German prince, Ferdinand von Saxe Coburg Gotha, the second with a rich English merchant, Francis Cook, who was later made Viscount of Monserrate.

'Beautiful trees, and of the rarest species, cover part of the range of hills... great water tanks or lakes, in imitation of natural ones, have been built on those heights both for recreational and irrigation purposes'.
Arquivo Pitoresco. 1858 (I)

Artificial lake with an island tower.
Pena Park. Sintra.

PENA PARK
and the artist-king

Reflecting the Portuguese resistance to the Romantic garden and its landscape layout is the fact that the two most important exponents of this garden art were foreigners: Ferdinand von Saxe Coburg Gotha and Francis Cook. The first was responsible for Pena Park, the second for the gardens of Monserrate. The fact that both are in Sintra is not a coincidence. It was there, as we have seen, that the strongest cultural influence of the foreigners who had settled in Portugal was concentrated, attracted by a micro-climate and the geography of the place.

Ferdinand ordered the plans of his palace-castle from a German — Baron Von Escheweg. The works, which began in 1844, continued to 1849, and during this period the construction of the park was also initiated. The *Arquivo Pitoresco* confirms that: *'the construction of the new royal palace began in 1844 but is not concluded yet, although work is being done on it constantly...In 1847, a circular road was built around the building; and land was levelled for the installation of a battery of four cannon. At the same time, the improvement of the surrounding walls and the lands which have been successively acquired by leasing, has been progressively carried out with the greatest intelligence and solicitude'.* [8]

Ferdinand had sent from Europe, and in particular from the Black Forest, different trees, which gradually covered an area of Sintra's range of hills *'...beautiful trees and of the rarest species, cover this part of the Sintra hills, which also has on its highest*

'...decorated with white statues, jets of water falling into scintillating marble basins, the house seems to be a silver feather fallen from the turban of a sultan...an illustration from the stories of the Thousand and One Nights...'
Princess Rattazzi. 1879 (II)

'...ornée de blanches statues, de jets d'eau retombant dans des vasques de marbre étincelant, elle semble une plume d'argent tombée du turban d'un sultan...l'illustration des contes merveilleux des Milles et une Nuits...'.
The idea of another space and another time is to be found here, and accentuates one of the characteristics of the Romantic garden.
Above and right. *View of the palace and balustrades overlooking a landscape scene on various levels.*

Gardens and Palace of Monserrate. Sintra.

part extensive green pine woods'.[9] The steep slopes, which we know about from drawings and engravings dating back to the sixteenth century (from the drawings of Duarte d'Armas), were transformed: *'The enormous boulders, of which we can virtually say the hills are constituted, have almost disappeared under the dense vegetation, the growth and expansion of which have been admirably favoured by the natural coolness of the climate and the abundance of water...'*[10]

Later on, in 1880, Marques Loureiro visited Pena Park, which was still the residence of Ferdinand II, and was surprised by the richness and variety of its plants and trees: *'One is really surprised. The trees are admirable. They have tall, thick trunks, which seem to be centuries old...for instance the Balantium antarcticum, the Alsophila australis and also the Cyathea dealbata, a tree ennobled by its immense tripinnate foliage'.*[11]

The steep slope, the height of the cliffs and the exposure to wind, suggest more the creation of a central European wood than an English park of clearings covered with grass and in which small clusters of trees and streams appear.

The park possesses an irregularly shaped lake with a small island in the middle from the centre of which a medieval tower rises. The *Arquivo Pitoresco* describes it for us: *'...both for recreational purposes and to facilitate irrigation, great tanks, or imitation lakes, some of which are of notable size, have been constructed on those heights. The largest has an average length of 540 hand spans, 120 in width and 10 in depth and has a capacity for 407,500 of water...'.*[12] On one of the few flat areas of the park is the entrance, forming a clearing, where there are flowerbeds into which the foundations of the walls and the guard-house extend. René Bazin, who had already visited the palace and the park in the time of Dom Carlos, wrote: *'Une barrière coupe une avenue; c'est l'entrée du parc royal...nous traversons des jardins abrités, minutieusement tenus, où les fleurs sont vives encore, un bois de mimosas côtoyant un ruisseau très clair, un bois de citronniers, un autre de camélias géants, puis un corridor vôuté et tournant qui donne accés dans le palais...'.*[13]

Enveloped in thick fog, with paths over which trees form a dome-like cover, high cliffs, and an imposing palace-castle that seems to be out of a fairy story, Pena Park corresponded to the mythical atmosphere of a Romantic legend.

THE LUXURIANT CLIMATE
of Monserrate Gardens

While the climate of Pena Park evokes medieval legends of knights, goblins and princesses, the atmosphere of the Monserrate Gardens takes us to the Orient, reminding us of the stories of the Thousand and One Nights. In both cases, however, it is the evocation of myth and historical memory that constitutes the essence of these gardens.

In the second half of the eighteenth century, the wealthy merchant Gerard Devisme rented the property to the Melo e Castro family and constructed on the ruins of the house a new palace in

'...we passed along a lane shaded by all types of trees from the south of Europe, the rarest of leaves forming a roof above our heads...I began to walk slowly, for fear that this virgin forest would disappear with the strange sound of my footsteps, as in the fairy tales...'
René Bazin. 1875 (III)

'...nous suivons l'allée qu'ombragent des arbres de toutes les essences meridionales; les feuillages les plus rares se croisent au-dessus de nous... je commence à marcher tout doucement, de peur que cette forêt vierge ne s'évanouisse au bruit étranger de mes pas, comme dans les contes de fées...'

Under the direction of the landscape architect Birt, plants and trees were ordered from all over the world for Monserrate, where the climate provided the conditions in which they could adapt perfectly.

Gardens of the Palace of Monserrate. Sintra.

'It is a virgin forest, a wild garden unlike any other I have ever seen. I found myself living in Brazil for an hour, I searched for the golden-crested macaw, I thought of tigers, I heard the tinkling of fountains and I drank in the heady perfumes so full of life and the sun, which make one drunk like champagne...'

René Bazin. 1875 (III)

292

the medieval taste, the project being designed by Oliveira Bernardes. William Beckford, during his brief stay, rented the property, thinking to settle in Portugal. But he changed his mind, and left the country, and the palace returned to a state of gentle south European decline. It was in this atmosphere of being lost in time that Byron visited Monserrate and considered it one of the most beautiful places in the world. Both the novel *Vathek*, written by William Beckford at Monserrate, and Byron's poem *Childe Harold*, must have influenced Francis Cook when he rented the house in

the middle of the nineteenth century.

Years later, in 1863, Francis Cook finally bought the estate and decided to transform the palace and gardens, giving them the same Oriental atmosphere of the Thousand and One Nights that William Beckford was to create in *Vathek*. Princess Rattazzi was not indifferent to this when she wrote in one of her letters: *'Tout ce qui peut captiver, séduire, charmer, est réuni dans cet Eden que ne manque de visiter aucun voyageur, curieux de voir l'illustration des contes merveilleux des Mille et une Nuits'.*[14]

'C'est la forêt vierge, un jardin sauvage tel que je n'en ai pas vu d'autre. Pendant une heure j'ai vécu au Brésil, j'ai cherché les aras à huppe d'or au sommet des laines, pensé aux tigres, écouté les sources et bu les lourds parfums, petris de vie et de soleil, qui grisent comme du champagne...'.

Above and left. *View of the park seen from the terrace and chapel ruins.*
Garden of the Palace of Monserrate. Sintra.

The gardens of the Quinta da Regaleira formulate in a Romantic way the concept of the traditional Portuguese garden of comfort and well-being. They are structured in a series of spaces interconnected by pathways, and differ from the concepts of virgin forest, as at Pena Park, and exotic park garden, as at Monserrate Gardens.

Above and right. *Aerial view and detail of garden bench.* Quinta da Regaleira. Sintra.

294

Besides an architect, Francis Cook also contracted in London a landscape architect, Birt, for the layout and setting out of the gardens. He ordered plants, trees and flowers from almost every part of the world which, in the exceptional climate, adapted themselves perfectly and are today unique examples. Three third century Etruscan mummies were bought in Rome to decorate the grottoes and the ruins of a chapel. The waters of a small stream were diverted to create a cascade which falls between large boulders and exotic plants. Next to the south façade a vast English-style lawn is framed by rare trees which end at the so-called 'naturally-shaped lake'.

In contrast to Pena Park, Monserrate Gardens reflect a careful study of the effects of perspective and viewing points. Different paths are studied in accordance with the scenic possibilities of the place, now opening up on to clearings and landscapes, while at other points closing in on cupolas of luxurious vegetation or passages hewn out of tall rocks.

Despite the favourable climate and the mythological poetry in which Monserrate was enveloped, it was no coincidence that René Bazin wrote: '...the rarest of branches form a roof above our heads; vines run from branch to branch and purple bunches of grapes hang down everywhere. I began to walk slowly, for fear that this virgin forest would disappear with the strange sound of my footsteps, as in the fairy tales...it is a virgin forest, a wild garden unlike any other I have ever seen. I found myself living in Brazil for an hour, I searched for the golden-crested macaw, and I thought of tigers, I heard the tinkling of fountains and I drank in the heady perfumes so full of life and the sun, which make one drunk like champagne'.[15]

GARDENER-BOTANISTS
from abroad

At the beginning, the Romantic garden was closely connected to the concept of a great landscape layout in which the main concern was for scenic effect. The composition of the plans and viewing points, the structure of the paths and natural elements — wood, lake, stream, clearing — superimposed themselves on the value or rarity of botanic species.

As word spread through Europe of the concept of the English park, we see a gradual decline in scenic and landscape effects, while the variety, rarity and exoticism of the plants becomes more important. The landscape architect gave way to the gardener-botanist, and the great parks tended to take the form of botanic gardens.

While the gardens at Pena and Monserrate may be considered as lying between these two extremes, the difficulty of putting into practice in Portugal the principles of the great landscape layout led to a tendency to opt for the botanic garden. The first example in the nineteenth century comes to us from the 1st Duke of Palmela who, for about twenty years, employed from Paris the bota-

For the decoration and construction of the gardens, the architect Luigi Manini resorted to sculptors in Coimbra from the Free School of Art and Design who had worked for the Palace of Buçaco. The statuary created by the team led by José Fonseca can be found throughout the garden in the form of fountains, benches, balustrades, urns, tables, columns, belvederes.

Above. *Detail of fountain.*
Garden of the Quinta da Regaleira. Sintra.

Although laid out in the Portuguese tradition, the gardens of the Quinta da Regaleira did not dispense with a green English-style lawn beside the house, as at Monserrate, albeit on a more intimate scale.

Above. *Lawn seen from the Neo-Manueline belvedere.* Gardens of the Quinta da Regaleira. Sintra.

nic gardener Rosenfelder to set out and take care of the gardens of his Lumiar Palace. This estate, which possessed a botanic garden at the end of the eighteenth century, was compared at the time to that of the Marquises of Angega.

Besides Rosenfelder, the nineteenth century saw a long list of botanic gardeners whose names remain connected with the management, conception and remodelling of the most significant Portuguese gardens of the Romantic period.

The Count of Farrobo employed the Frenchman Pierre Maurier for about forty years to remodel the gardens of his Quinta das Laranjeiras at Sete Rios. This estate, which was constructed around 1780, was visited by William Beckford[16] and is today the Zoological Gardens of Lisbon. Pierre Maurier, who was the head gardener of the Quinta das Laranjeiras until his death, and who was known as 'Pedro of Laranjeiras', was also involved in the remodelling of the Quinta de Santo António on the outskirts of Torres Novas. Known as the Quinta da Torre, the estate remains part of the property of the family of the Marquises of Foz.

Frederick Welwitsch who, at the time he visited Portugal in 1839, worked for a company involved in the gathering of plants on the island of Cape Verde, had a doctorate in medicine from the University of Vienna, Austria. Welwitsch sensed a rich field of investigation in Portugal and in 1840 he was nominated Director of the Royal Botanic Garden at Ajuda. After the death of Rosenfelder in 1844 he was also nominated to the post of Director of the garden of the Palace of Lumiar. In 1853 the government sent him on a scientific voyage to Angola,[17] which was linked to his botanical interests and he remained in Africa for eight years. His departure obliged the Dukes of Palmela to appoint another botanist, Jacob Weiss, who was working for the Jardin des Plantes in Paris[18] at the time, to be Director of the gardens at the Lumiar Palace. Besides being in charge of these gardens, Jacob Weiss was also charged by José Maria Eugénio de Almeida to plan and lay out the park of his palace in São Sebastião de Pedreira. In 1860[19] a rich capitalist bought a palace from the descendants of the French architect Fernando Larre who had worked for Dom João V. The estate, which extended right up to the Duque de Avila Avenue, was gradually reduced as the city council expropriated land. The park was once the zoo and city fun fair and what remains of it are now the gardens of the Calouste Gulbenkian Foundation, which have been completely transformed, while the area around the Palace of the present Marquises of Vilalva has been planted with trees. This building, ancient coach-houses and annexes, were converted to living accommodation at the time of the sale of the palace to the government. The encircling walls, with sentry-boxes and gates, are the remains of the original park.

The regular appearance of foreign names in the management of the majority of the parks and gardens in Portugal emphasises the state of cultural and aesthetic dependence in the country. However, the gardeners' lack of knowledge about Portuguese traditions is referred to by Sousa Viterbo, in 1905: *'...our gardens cannot nor should be the exact reproduction of the gardens of the north...in a country in which the orange tree and the grape vine flourish in the open air, as well as other plants that are not only ornamental but useful too, they should not be systematically put to one side, as is the case, and substituted by others which at times only have their exoticism to recommend them...'* [20]

At a national level, the Gomes de Macedo family of Oporto extended their floral business to the layouts of some Portuguese gardens. João José, son of the gardener of the Quinta da China, whose gardens were famous in the second half of the eighteenth century, was the first gardener for the Oporto City Council. In this position, he was responsible for the layout of the public gardens of São Lazaro,[21] which were later remodelled by the landscape architect Emílio David. Besides São Lazaro, João José remodelled the gardens of the Quinta da Prelada, as well as those of the Counts of Ferreira at Bonfim.

But it was with his son, José Gomes de Macedo, that the family reached a high point. Thanks to his excellent education, which extended to music and painting, José Gomes designed various garden-parks in the Oporto region. According to Sousa Viterbo,[22] his stamp can be seen on the gardens of the Viscounts of Proença Vieira, at Vilar do Paraíso, as well as on the gardens at Sacaes and Dourado at São Mamede de Infesta, Godinho at Matosinhos and Santa Luzia at Guimarães.

The Gomes de Macedo family did not create a school of their own in Portugal, perhaps because of the mania for following northern European fashions — for everything with this origin was synonymous with quality.

In 1865, the firm operating the Crystal Palace in Oporto contracted the landscape architect Emílio David to design and run its gardens. In Lisbon, the Count of Burnay contracted M. Spalla to direct the construction of the gardens of his palace at Junqueira which he wanted to be like those of the Viscounts of Condeixa who had hired Nogré in Paris to manage the family property at Cernache.

In Oporto Emílio David designed not only the gardens of the Crystal Palace but also, according to Sousa Viterbo,[23] the Cordoaria Gardens, the Ribeiro de Faria Garden in Rosário Road and Heroísmo Road and that of the Baroness Seixo in Cedofeita Road. While both the Crystal Palace and the Cordoaria Gardens have been significantly altered, the gardens of Baroness Seixo can still be seen with their original layout. Besides the gardens of the Counts of Burnay, the making of which he directed between 1882 and 1883, Spalla was involved with the gardens of the Viana family in Sintra, and those of the Duff family, who were related to the Burnays.

Nogré, after the remodelling of the Cernache estate, directed various works on the outskirts of Lisbon, such as the garden-park of the Challé Biester, which at the time was called the Quinta Velha, work on this beginning in 1887.

As we have seen, the majority of private individuals in the nineteenth century opted for foreign garden designers to lay out their garden-parks, and the government and official bodies followed their example. The Estrela walk bears the stamp of Bonard, who was helped by a Portuguese, João Francisco, who is referred to in the *Arquivo Pitoresco* of 1858.[24] Remodelled later on, it was the Frenchman Ernest Pissard who took over the garden design in the last decade of the nineteenth century. Finally, the layout of the Avenida de Liberdade was put out to international tender in 1887,[25] and the work given to Henri Lusseau.

* * *

The belvedere, together with the summer house, reappears as a fundamental element of the Portuguese garden, enhancing aspects that are more domestic than merely visual. The garden here is considered to be a space to be enjoyed from the inside.

Gardens of the Quinta da Regaleira. Sintra.

Due to it's ability to evoke legend and myth, the mock ruin is one of the most significant elements in the Romantic garden. It bestows on the garden an ambience of mystery which the soul of Romantic man needed.

Above and right. *Mock ruin of a classical temple and plan of the whole.*
Gardens of the Quinta dos Lagos. Sintra,

THE GARDENS OF SINTRA
described by René Bazin, 1894

The eminent French writer René Bazin, on a brief visit to Portugal, visited Sintra, devoting a chapter to it in his book *Terres d'Espagne* under the title *The Gardens of Sintra*.

Lisbonne, 13 octobre.

"Cintra est un nid de verdure, une station d'été très élégante, dans une toute petite sierre hérisée d'arbres. qui s'élève à peu de distance de Lisbonne, suit une ligne parallèle au Tage, et finit dans la mer. La cour y passe près de trois mois, de juillet à la mi-septembre, et descend, quand la chaleur s'apaise, vers le château de Cascaes, où elle habite jusqu'aux premiers jours de novembre".

"Le paysage est romantique à souhait. En une heure de chemin de fer, à travers une banlieue pleine de jardins, de villas et de moulins à vent dont les ailes de toile dessinent une croix de Malte, ou atteint le pied de la montagne. Là commence l'enchantement. Vue d'en bas, la montagne est toute bleue; elle porte au sommet un grand château qui paraît, lui aussi, fait avec de l'azur, et qui tord ses murailles autour de toutes les pointes de roche, qui dresse, en plein ciel, la silhouette la plus compliquée de tours rondes et carrées, de terrasses crénelées, de coupoles revêtues de faience et luisantes vaguement. On monte à cheval ou à âne, et, dès qu'on a dépassé la village de Cintra, la forêt vous enveloppe, forêt de sapins mêlés d'ormes, d'eucalyptus et de bouleaux. Le chemin se plie en lacets; le lierre roule en cascades aux deux bords; on aperçoit, entre les branches, des plaines qui se fondent peu à peu et pâlissent à leur tour; des sources coulent à travers bois; l'air salin se perfume de résine; des colonies de lis roses s'épanoussent aux rares endroits où le soleil peut toucher la terre.

"Jusque-là nous avons, mon compagnon de voyage et moi, marché en route libre, sans rencontrer personne, sur le sol commum des rois et des charbonniers. Une barrière coupe une avenue: c'est l'entrée du parc royal. Un jardinier, en bonnet de laine, nous introduit et nous explique que les équipages, même ceux de la cour, ne pourraient sans danger gravier les pentes qui nous séparent du château, et que le roi et la reine, en descendant de voiture, doivent monter à âne pour achever le trajet. Nous traversons des jardins abrités, minutieusement tenus, où les fleurs sont vives encore, un bois de mimosas côtoyant un ruisseau très clair, un bois de citronniers, un autre de camélias géants, puis un corridor voûté et tournant qui donne accès dans le palais, des terrasses, des chemins de ronde, une chapelle froide et battue par le vent de mer; enfin, par une échelle, nous grimpons au sommet de la grande coupole jaune: toute la sierra est à nos pieds, dentelées, touffue, énorme haie de verdure allant droit vers la mer que le soleil met en feu; au bas de ses deux pentes, à gauche où le Tage coule au loin, à droite où s'étendent des plaines, il semble qu'il n'y ait plus de végétation, mais seulement des terres nues, entièrement plates, d'une même

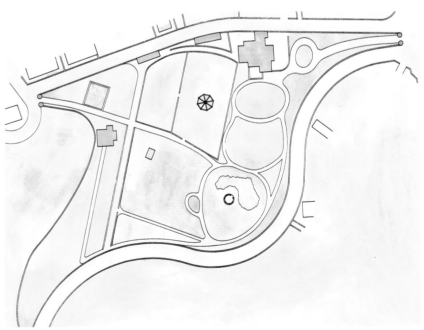

teinte lilas, que perlent çà et là des semis de maisons blanches, et d'où le regard, las de lumière confuse, revient vers la forêt fraîche.Vers les cimes, fuyantes au-dessous de nous, qu'illumine le scintillement des pins, vers les ravins d'ombre où se devine un détour de sentier.

"Et ce n'est pas encore la merveille de Cintra. Un ami nous a conseillé de visiter la villa Cook. Du haut du château de la Pena, j'ai aperçu, dans les frondaisons qui entaillent le bord de la plaine, la masse pâle d'un palais arabe. Il nous faut descendre près de six cents mètres de pente, tantôt à travers les bois, tantôt dans des lits de ruisseaux, ou entre deux murs tapissés de lierre et coiffés de branches de cèdres. L'air s'attiédit et se charge d'aromes puissants, mystérieux, qui font chercher du regard des arbres inconnus. Les eucalyptus trouent de leurs grandes gerbes glauques le vert noir des sapins. Un palmier dresse au-dessus d'eux son bouquet de plumes. Voici une maison de garde, une toute petite barrière, et une allée qui s'enfonce en pente raide sous les arbres enchevêtrés.

"C'est bien le palais de Monserrat, la villa Cook", me dit un homme qui passe, à cheval sur un âne minuscule et chargé de fagots, les jambes traînant à terre... Lady Cook! on m'a parlé d'elle à Lisbonne:

Mais, une fois de plus, la chance me servit bien. Nous suivons l'allée qu'ombragent des arbres de toutes les essences méridionales; les feuillages les plus rares se croisent au-dessus de nous; des lianes courent d'une branche à l'autre et retombent em grappes violettes ou pourpres.Je commence à marcher tout doucement, de peur que cette forêt vierge ne s'évanouisse, au bruit étranger de mes pas, comme dans les contes de fées. Les sous-bois sont pleins de mousse. Il y a una grande lumière en avant, et, quand j'ai franchi un pont de bois, je vois que cette lumière est une façade blanche, au milieu de laquelle s'ouvre une porte au faîte ajouré, semblable à celle des mosquées, et que sur le seuil deux femmes sont debout, près d'une balustrade qu'enveloppent des géraniums. Elles sont en noir. Les fées ne portant jamais le deuil, autant qu'il m'en souvient d'après d'anciennes lectures, je comprends que nous sommes en présence de la châtelaine et d'une de ses parentes ou amies. Mon compagnon de route s'est avancé, et comme il parle très facilement l'anglais, je l'entends qui demande l'autorisation de visiter le parc. La dame qui lui répond est grande, mince, encore jeune de visage malgré ses bandeaux de cheveux gris. Elle a dû être fort belle, d'une beauté poétique et rêveuse. Et elle a des yeux clairs, énergiques. Le dialogue se poursuit une minute. Elle apprend que je suis écrivain. Le souvenir da sa réputation littéraire, de ses articles, de ses conférences, du *Woodhull and Claflin Weekly*, plaident sans doute auprés de lady Cook, en faveur des deux inconnus; elle a le bon goût de ne pas même s'informer si je suis partisain de l'émancipation: elle nous invite à visiter le palais. Par le couloir de style oriental, orné de colonnes de marbres rares, de statues, et d'une fontaine au milieu, nous pénétrons dans une série de salons qui sont plutôt des musées que des appartements de réception. Les vieux japon, les vieux chine abondent, non pas les modèles de bazar, mais des pièces de toute beauté, d'un rose ou d'un vert tendre à désespérer les porcelainiers de Sèvres. L'Inde, la Perse, l'Asie Mineure, l'Afrique, sont représentées par des meubles, des stores, des tentures, des idoles dorées, des armes, des ivoires, des vases émaillés de la grande époque arabe, de ceux dont le vernis enferme, dans sa transparence nacrée, tous les reflets de l'arc-en-ciel. Un contraste drôle: devant les cheminées, qui sont aussi des oeuvres d'art, et dans chacune des pièces, on a disposé un rang de potirons et de courges, qui achèvent de mûrir à l'abri.

L'aimable propriétaire de Monserrat, malgré le soleil, malgré une promenade projetée, veut encore nous montrer une vallée de son domaine. "Vous allez voir mes fougères!" nous dit-elle. Nous repassons près des lianes fleuries, nous tournons à droite. J'entends des coups de pioche. Sous bois, au bord d'une cascade embarrassée de feuillages, nous saluons M. Cook, vieil Anglais à barbe blanche, qui surveille la transplantation d'une fougère arborescente haute de cinq ou six mètres et grosse comme un mât de navire. Il est coiffé du large panama des planteurs. IJ nous indique la meilleure route à suivre pour voir le plus beau coin du parc. Alors, ayant pris congé de nos hôtes, nous descendons seuls, les pieds dans les lacis de lierre et les touffes de pervenches, sous la voûte découpée à jour des fougères qui emplissent le ravin. Des palmiers, des cocotiers, des caoutchoucs, des poivriers leur font suite. Ils forment une épaisse forêt. Des racines barrent les sentiers; des troncs morts de vieillesse ou brisés par le vent, couchés sur des fourrés verts, dorment leur sommeil sans plus toucher la terre qu'au jour des premières sèves.

C'est la forêt vierge, un jardin sauvage tel que je n'en ai pas vu d'autre.

Pendant une heure j'ai vécu au Brésil, j'ai cherché les aras à huppe d'or au sommet des lianes, pensé aux tigres, écouté les sources et bu les lourds parfums, pétris de vie et de soleil, qui grisent comme du champagne.

René Bazin. *Terres d'Espagne*. Paris. Pages 208-215.

(René Bazin makes special mention here of the ambience of mystery and magic felt in gardens where nature is present as an active element.)

Relegated to a secondary position, the tile appears here decorating a façade of a greenhouse. The spontaneity of line and the freshness of the colours indicate the revival of a great Portuguese aesthetic tradition.

Above. *Tile panels with monogram of Amélia de Morais, patroness of the house, and the chronogram of 1907, the date of the construction of the house and garden.*

Quinta dos Lagos. Sintra.

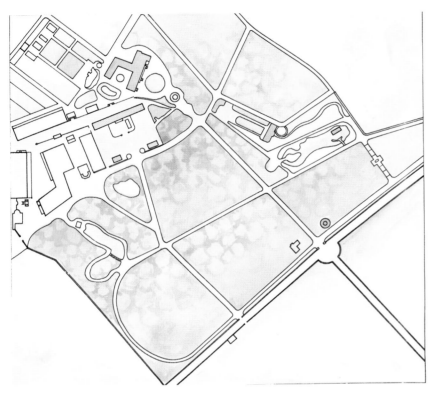

'The orchards, gardens and wood are worth visiting for the way in which they are set out, and for the beautiful viewing points they provide. The main avenue...is bordered by magnificent conifers and enormous cork oaks and oaks of majestic size'.
José Marques Loureiro. 1882 (IV)

Plan of the Quinta da Aveleda.

A DESCRIPTION OF THE BOTANIC GARDEN
of the Dukes of Palmela
at the Lumiar Palace, 1875

With the growing taste for rare and exotic plants, the nineteenth century saw the garden at Lumiar rival the Royal Botanic Gardens at Ajuda and those at Coimbra in the rarity of its trees, particularly in its rare collection of palm trees. The garden, which by the end of the eighteenth century equalled the botanic gardens of the Marquises of Angêja, was, in the following century, the object of much careful attention from the Dukes of Palmela. The 1st Duke during King Dom João's reign began by employing Rosenfelder from Paris in the 1820s and, for the rest of the century, first Frederick Welwitsch and then Jacob Weiss occupied the position of Director.

"Poucas milhas distante de Lisboa, para o interior, está situada a povoação do Lumiar, que passaria talvez despercebida aos habitantes da capital se não fosse o palacio do duque de Palmella com os seus bellos jardins, o que a salva do esquecimento e lhe dá uma reputação, que já se estende além das fronteiras portuguezas. Ha uns quarenta annos que o avô da actual duqueza lançou os fundamentos d'esta adoravel vivenda. N'aquelle tempo os jardins em Portugal estavam na sua infancia, e não é para admirar que dentro em pouco o do Lumiar occupasse o logar de honra, e que passo a passo se tornasse o modêlo do bom gosto na escolha e arranjo das plantas exoticas. O exemplo foi seguido e não tardou que se creassem por diversas partes excellentes jardins debaixo de todas as condições necessarias. O Lumiar, todavia, conservou-se sempre no seu plano superior, e se algum dia se escrever, desde os seus lineamentos, a historia dos progressos da horticultura portugueza, esperamos que não ficará no olvido, nem a influencia d'aquelles jardins no passado, nem as suas admiraveis condições no presente.

Não ha duvida que para este resultado se deve immenso ao gosto que os actuaes duques téem pelas cousas horticolas, mas é um acto de justiça da minha parte não esquecer o louvor que merece o snr. Jacob Weiss, que durante mais de trinta annos tem sido o jardineiro em chefe, e em todo esse periodo mostrou sempre grande zêlo e profundos conhecimentos, o que tudo tem concorrido para o florescimento em que as cousas presentemente se acham. Não se passa nenhum anno em que elle não introduza alguma planta nova ou rara, ou deixe de fazer alguns melhoramentos importantes no Lumiar e nos outros jardins ducaes. Não me é possível deixar de o considerar como o primeiro entre os jardineiros portuguezes.

O fallecido dr. Welwitsch esteve por algum tempo ao serviço do primeiro duque antes de partir para a Africa, e foi com o maior interesse que eu, vendo n'outro dia um herbario de plantas cultivadas no Lumiar, nótei o resultado da sua estada n'estes jardins, e por este herbario não só formei uma boa ideia da riqueza da flora exotica n'aquelle periodo, mas pude comparar o estado dos jardins no passado e no presente. Outr'ora cultivavam-se aqui muitos arbustos e arvores de pequeno porte do Cabo e da Australia, mas as variedades mais delicadas, especialmente as pertencentes ás *Leguminosas*, *Ericaceas* e *Proteaceas* desappareceram, por causa da nociva influencia das aguas calcareas. O logar d'ellas foi occupado por outras plantas mais pomposas e não menos interessantes. Passando em revista a rica e luxuriante vegetação do Lumiar, principiarei pela collecção sem rival das *Palmeiras*.

Posso afiançar que estas não téem rival, quer se considere o numero das especies, quer a belleza dos specimens. A maior parte d'ellas foram plantadas em 1856, e bastaram apenas 19 annos para as tornar, de pequenas que eram, em robustos exemplares, o que prova que muitas *Palmeiras*, ainda as que são dos paizes mais quentes, quando bem tractadas, adoptam voluntariamente Portugal como sua segunda patria.

O exemplar da *Juboea spectabilis* no Lumiar é, em altura, inferior ao das Necessidades. O tronco tem apenas trinta pés d'alto, e a circumferencia mede na base 14 e 1/2 pés. A altura do tronco do *Chamoerops Ghiesbreghtii* é quasi de treze pés, e a circumferencia na base 3 pés e 3 pollegadas. A do *Chamoerops excelsa* é entre 20 e 21 pés, tendo a cirumferencia na base 3 pés e 9 pollegadas approximadamente. Este individuo produz todos os annos grande numero de sementes ferteis e podemol-o considerar como o antecessor de centenares de exemplares em variados estados de crescimento, que adornam actualmente muitos jardins portuguezes, tanto publicos particulares. As *Palmeiras* téem tendencia, mesmo sendo cultivadas, para variar. Isto parece certo depois d'uma demorada observação d'esta planta e da sua progenie.

300

porque muitos exemplares, provenientes d'ella, differem no habito, no vigor do crescimento e até na textura mais ou menos compacta das folhas. O saber se o *Chamoerops excelsa* e o *C. Fortunei* são realmente duas boas especies, ou se a ultima se deve considerar uma variedade distincta da primeira, é isto talvez mais um assumpto de imaginação, de que uma questão scientifica. Quando, porém, se acham collocadas lado a lado como n'estes jardins, e sendo quasi eguaes em vigor, é verdadeiramente difficil affirmar onde é que está a differença que existe entre ellas.

O tronéo da *Livistona sinensis (Corypha)* mede 13 pés d'alto e tem de circumferencia na base 4 pés. Com as suas folhas largas e bellas cobre uma superficie de quasi 45 pés de circumferencia. Os exemplares da *Livistona australis (Corypha)* abundam no Lumiar, mais sendo plantados muito depois das outras *Palmeiras*, ainda não podem apresentar identicas dimensões. A *Phoenix leonensis* Lodd. *(P. spinosa)* é uma graciosissima especie, posto que de moroso desenvolvimento, approximando-se alguma cousa no *habitat* com a *Phoenix reclinata.* O tronco mede 13 pés de alto: as folhas mais erectas accrescentam-lhe mais 9 pés e 6 pollegadas. A *Copernicia sp. Bahia* é uma especie que attinge pequena altura; compacta e de singular belleza; fórma um grande tufo e augmenta de anno para anno. A *Rhapis sp.* é muito distincta da *Rhapis flabelliformis,* que, tanto aqui como nas Necessidades, não vae muito bem. Pelo contrário, outra especie sem nome, talvez a *Rhapis aspera,* está perfeitamente á vontade n'estes jardins e póde ser indubitavelmente considerada como uma das mais notaveis *Palmeiras* anãs.

As especies acima mencionadas formam um grande grupo, e estão plantadas com tal arte, que se podem admirar no seu conjuncto, ou contemplar em particular a belleza de cada uma. Em todo o caso, o visitante ficará conhecendo a difficuldade de encontrar em outra parte tão esplendida collecção como esta.

Magnificos exemplares do *Chamoerops tomentosa, Seaforthia elegans* e *Sabal umbraculifera,* crescem em outras partes do Lumiar, não fallando do *Chamoerops humilis* e do *Phoenix dactylifera,* que são aqui tão communs, que não merecem especial menção.

'...furthermore, one finds a small garden with different palms and agaves which are already well in flower... as well as many avenues in the wood, like the lanes of a great landscaped garden...we mention only the avenue which, beginning at the lake, leads to the main house'.
Marques Loureiro. 1882 (IV)

Gardens of the Quinta da Aveleda.

'There is also a large greenhouse with a dome and gallery, which contains valuable plants, mainly palms and ferns. Among the former we noted a tall example of Caryota urens, *some beautiful examples of* Terinax parviflora, chanuaedoreas *and various betel nut palms and coconut trees.'* Edmund Goeze. 1876 (V)

The greenhouses contained the most delicate and tropical plants, and became an essential element of the Romantic garden.

Greenhouse of the gardens at the Necessidades Palace.

Ultimamente chegaram do Rio de Janeiro alguns alguns exemplares fortes da *Oreodoxa regia,* mas duvido que se dêem bem n'este clima, ainda que se escolham logares abrigados, como os que ha n'este jardim.

Trepadeiras de toda a casta cobrem os muros e as gradarias: entre ellas a *Bougainvillea brasiliensis,* merecendo especial menção uma variedade obtida aqui de semente e justamente denominada *Bougainvillea Palmella.*

Esta magnifica quinta ducal não era a principio tão extensa; actualmente compõe--se de quatro pequenas quintas, que medem talvez ao todo 125 acres. Terraços com bellas vistas, cheios de taboleiros de flores, alternam-se aqui com doces valles e pittorescas ladeiras. Encantadoras grutas e lagos, onde se espaneja a *Bambusa gracilis* e a *B. nigra,* dão realce ao composto geral, desenhado com muita pericia.

Edmond Goeze. *Jornal de Horticultura Prática.* 1875. Pages 230-235.

THE GARDENS AND WOODS
of the Quinta da Aveleda, 1882

Entre à estação de Penafiel e a de Paredes, a 30 kilometros do Porto ou hora e meia de caminho de ferro, encontra-se a quinta d'este nome, magnifica e importante propriedade pertencente ao snr. Manoel Pedro Guedes.

Situada, na sua maior parte, na freguezia e arrabaldes de Penafiel, e uma pequena parte na freguezia de Guilhufe, tem por annexo uma grande propriedade chamada Quinta de Cadeade, regada toda pelo rio Cavallum.

A quinta murada, que é o centro da lavoura, compõe-se de pomares, hortas, vinhas, campos de *Centeio* e *Milho,* todos regados, jardins, mattas arruadas, e parques, com os seus respectivos celleiros, adegas, abegoarias e officinas de lavoura, tudo construido nas melhores condições, revelando-se, nas mais pequenas circumstancias, os vastissimos conhecimentos agricolas do seu actual proprietario.

A sua produção regula por 12:000 alqueires de *Milho* e *Centeio* e 80 pipas de vinho verde, afóra o rendimento dos prados ou lameiros, dos pomares e das mattas, que é muito importante.

Sustenta e engorda esta propriedade 120 cabeças de gado vaccum e outras tantas, talvez, de gado suino e lanigero.

A sua superficie regula por 6 kilometros quadrados.

Tem esta propriedade quarenta colonos ou caseiros arrendatarios de predios rusticos, e vinte de predios urbanos, como são: marchante com seu talho ou açougue, ferreiro, carpinteiro, alfaiate e jornaleiros, que alli vivem com suas familias.

São banhadas estas propriedades pelo rio Sousa, com o qual confinam, desde a ponte Cepeda, que liga o concelho de Paredes com o de Penafiel, até dentro d'esta cidade, isto pelo nascente, norte e poente, e pelo sul pelos ribeiros de Ajerella e Lavandeira.

É cortada a meio pela antiga estrada real, hoje municipal de 1.ª classe, que tem 8 metros de largura e é toda arvorejada de *Sobereiros, Acacias, Platanus* e outras arvores. Esta estrada é de muito transito, visto ser a que mais directamente liga a estação de Paredes com Penafiel. Junto a Penafiel, e no limite da propriedade, é dividida pela estrada real de Guimarães e Entre-os-Rios, passando logo ao sul a estrada real do Porto a Amarante.

Os pomares d'aquella propriedade são muito grandes e geralmente plantados ao longo das ruas, o que não só economisa terreno, mas produz magnifico effeito.

Os pomares, os jardins e a matta são dignos de ser visitados, já pela maneira como estão delineados, já pelos bellos pontos de vista que offerecem.

A avenida principal, que apresenta um bonito aspecto, é orlada de magnificas *Coniferas* e enormes *Sobereiros* e *Carvalhos* de porte magestoso. Ao fundo, duas nascentes de agua, tendo a um dos lados um enorme *Sobereiro,* convidam o visitante a demorar-se alli alguns minutos a gosar o lindo panorama que se lhe desenrola á vista.

Do outro lado completa o quadro um grupo de arvores collossaes, entre as quaes se destacam, pelo seu soberbo porte, dous exemplares de *Taxodium distichum,* alguns *Abies* e o mais bello exemplar, que temos visto, de *Dammara Moorei.*

Mais além, encontra-se um pequeno jardim com differentes *Palmeiras* e *Agaves,* já bastante fortes, e sobre troncos cortados a uma certa altura, para servirem de pedestaes, magnificos exemplares de *Dasylirium longifolium* e outras plantas ornamentaes, que, no seu conjuncto, produzem um effeito muito pittoresco.

Em seguida ha um grande exemplar de *Liriodendron tulipifera,* á volta do qual se vê uma pequena montanha, assentando-se sobre esta uma elegante passarinheira.

Caminhando d'aqui para a esquerda, encontra-se um grande lago situado n'um dos pontos mais bonitos. Este lago, que tem uma superficie de 866 metros quadrados, leva para cima de mil pipas de agua. Tem duas pontes e duas ilhas com grandes *Carvalhos*.

Além das muitas avenidas que a matta contém, como as ruas de um grande jardim de paysagem, e que seria prolixo descrever citaremos apenas a avenida que, partindo do lago, vae dar á casa de habitação. No fim d'esta avenida, que mede cêrca de 1:600 metros, encontram-se dous locaes surprehendentes pelos seus soberbos pontos de vista.

Um d'elles foi ha pouco tempo plantado com *Palmeiras, Fetos* arboreos e acaules, *Musas,* etc., etc., o que mais tarde deve parecer um bosque tropical. Não pude deixar de baptisar este sitio com o nome de Carmo Palha, em homenagem á esposa do snr. Manoel Pedro Guedes.

Em seguida encontra-se bruscamente uma especie de fundão, guarnecido de grandes *Carvalhos* de frondosas copas, á sombra dos quaes, já nos proprios troncos, já em volta d'elles, vivem, com todo o brilho de uma vegetação vigorosa, soberbas *Begonias* de folhagem ornamental e *Fetos* acaules e arboreos de rendilhada folhagem, suspensa sobre delicados fios d'ebano.

Alli podiam passar-se horas despercebidas a contemplar os encantos da natureza, combinados com a disposição artistica d'aquelles pequenos, mas elegantes grupos de plantas.

Tanto na escolha d'estas, como na sua disposição, quer nos jardins, quer na casa de habitação, onde se encontram numerosas e bellas plantas de sala, revela-se o bom gosto dos proprietarios de tão magnifica vivenda.

Terminando, não podemos deixar de sentir que uma propriedade d'esta ordem, com todas as condições necessarias para uma granja-modelo, cortada de estradas e a dous passos d'uma estação de caminho de ferro, não fosse a escolhida para a Quinta districtal, a qual, apesar de ter sido, como foi, installada em boas propriedades, não offerece as vantagens desejadas, attendendo a que fica muito distante do caminho de ferro, e, por isso, não satisfaz os fins para que foi creada.

José Marques Loureiro. *Jornal de Horticultura Prática.* 1882 Pages 206-208.

(On his visit to this estate, Marques Loureiro made special mention of the romantic ambience of the gardens and his description mainly concentrates on its trees and plants.)

THE PARK AND GARDENS
of the Quinta de Villar do Paraiso, 1873

Apesar da descrição não referir, os jardins foram desenhados por José Gomes de Macedo, com auxílio de seu filho Seraphim, para o Visconde de Proença Vieira. A atribuição é feita por Sousa Viterbo. (*A jardinagem em Portugal.* Coimbra 1906, pág. 78) a par de outros trabalhos de José Gomes de Macedo.

O leitor que ama do coração as flores deve conhecer, mais que não seja senão de nome, uma quinta de Villar do Paraizo pertencente ao nosso actual consul em França, o snr. visconde de Proença Vieira. Foi ahi que passamos o dia 26 de agosto.

O snr. visconde de Proença Vieira, cavalheiro sobremodo estimavel, ainda que pagão pelo culto que vota a Flora, depois de ter percorrido muitos pontos da Europa, onde a jardinagem é um elemento indispensável da vida recreativa, inoculou em si o germen d'este encantador passatempo que deleita a nós e a todos que nos rodeiam e vivem na nossa convivencia. Compenetrado d'isto, tendo gravado no seu intimo o ideial do bello, tractou de fazer d'esse valle de Villar do Paraizo uma habitação que nos recordasse esses castellos habitados por fadas e principes lendarios.

Um grande portão, que dá accesso á quinta e cuja architectura não nos é dado conhecer, denota desde logo que não será a vulgaridade quem nos ha de fazer as honras da visita.

Entremos porém nos jardins e ponhamos de parte a habitação. Em frente d'ella vemos bellissimas *Araucarias* de diversas especies, o *Capressus Lausoniana* com 7 a 8 metros de altura o *Thuiopsis borealis* com 4 metros, o *Anthocercis picta* com 7 metros, e entre muitas plantas curiosas e raras que estão proximas á casa acha-se um forte exemplar da *Wellingtonia gigantea* que mede cerca de 12 metros d'altura. Algumas *Cycadeas, Palmeiras, Dracaenas* e muitas outras plantas são tambem um dos principaes enlevos do jardim.

Pela esplendida avenida que nos leva do jardim ao lago cavalgava uma gentil castellã em fogoso bucephalo e o seu vulto gentil divisava-se phantastico entre a densa e variadissima folhagem do *Liliodendron tulipifera, Acer negundo, Celtis australis, Betula alba. Populus argentea, Paulownia imperialis, Platanus orientalis, Gleditschia triacanthos, Grevillea robusta* de 12 metros e de numerosas especies de *Acacias* e d'outras arvores que não nos recordam agora, onde se vogasse uma gondola, nos supporiamos em alguma d'aquellas esplendidas *villas* italianas, ou nas aguas da encantadora Veneza.

Desenhado pelo snr. Proença, é um dos lagos mais formosos que temos visto, reproduzindo exactamente a natureza que está aqui bem alliada á arte. De qualquer ponto que se olhe, não se encontra o fim. Sempre paizagem nova, sempre variados attractivos! Aqui um grosso tufo da *Banbusa arundinacea*, que pela sua vegetação luxuriante nos lembra a região tropical das Indias Orientaes, d'onde veio para a Europa. Acolá fortes tufos de *Papyrus antiquorum*, e mais além vigorosos *Caladium esculentum, Fetos, Salix babylonica, Populus canadensis, Populus alba* e outras arvores, cuja folhagem se estampa serenamente na superfície do lago.

Duas ilhas ornam a grande taça e estão, como as margens, guarnecidas com plantas formosas, sendo a maior parte de ramos pendentes.

Para o lado do poente vê-se uma assás extensa matta, que só o tempo, poderá tornar frondosa. Por enquanto, a não ser alguns *Pinheiros*, as outras arvores são todas de tenra edade.

No topo da collina ha um pequeno castello, d'onde se avistam os montes circumvisinhos e se gosa um espectaculo verdadeiramene grandioso.

Transcribed from the *Jornal de Horticultura Prática.* 1873. Page 214.

(This description gives us the evolution of nineteenth century landscape art in the north of the country and the way in which the gardens blended in with the surrounding landscape.)

NOTES

1 Laura Junot (Duchess of Abrantes). *Souvenirs d'une Ambassade en Espagne et en Portugal entre 1808-1811.* Paris 1837, page 360. (Author's translation.)
2 A. Rebello da Costa. *Descrição da Cidade do Porto.* 1789, page 66.
3 The rental contract between Devisme and Dona Francisca Mello e Castro was transcribed by Sousa Viterbo. *A Jardinagem em Portugal.* Coimbra 1906, pages 153-160.
4 Tollenare. *Notes Dominicales Prises Pendant une Voyage en Portugal et au Brézil en 1816, 1817 et 1818.* Paris, 1972. F.C.G., page 135.
5 Idem, pages 135-136.
6 Idem, page 136.
7 Idem, page 136.
8 Arquivo Pitoresco, 1858, page 364.
9 Idem, page 364.
10 Idem, page 364.
11 Jornal de Horticultura Prática, 1880, page 221.
12 Arquivo Pitoresco, 1858, page 364.
13 René Bazin. *Terres d'Espagne*, Paris. Page 209-210.
14 Princess Rattazzi, *Le Portugal A vol d'Oiseau*, Paris, 1893, page 241.
15 René Bazin. Ibid., page 214 (Author's translation).
16 William Beckford, *Diário de... em Portugal e Espanha.* Lisbon, 1983, page 162.
17 Sousa Viterbo. *A Jardinagem de Portugal,* Coimbra, 1906, page 114.
18 Idem, page 113.
19 Norberto de Araújo, *Inventário de Lisboa.* Part VIII, Lisbon, 1950, page 53.
20 Sousa Viterbo. *A Jardinagem em Portugal.* Coimbra, 1906, page 45.
21 Idem, page 77.
22 Idem, page 78.
23 Idem, page 68.
24 Arquivo Pitoresco, 1858, page 129.
25 Sousa Viterbo. Ibid. Page 47.

Notes on Illustrations

I. Arquivo Pitoresco. 1858, page 364.
II. Princess Rattazzi. *Le Portugal A vol d'Oiseau*, Paris, 1879, page 241.
III. René Bazin. *Terres d'Espagne*. Paris, page 212.
IV. Jornal de Horticultura Prática. 1882, page 1207.
V. Idem 1876, page 46.

THE NEED FOR A MORE PENETRATING LOOK

at the tradition of the Portuguese Garden

CONCLUSION

What has been said has been said. But what is perhaps important is not what has been said, but that other things can be written or done as a result of it. A book is more important for what it suggests, than for the information that has been set down on its pages. A book always needs to be followed by another; without this we have a closed system. What has been said is like something that has been done. It is past and will not be repeated.

This book also needs a garden. Not the garden of our memories, but of our dreams. We only really see what is in front of our eyes and so whenever we look at the past we run the danger of just remembering the picturesque and the stereotype. But the past is the past. It is up to us to construct the new, the original which has its basis in the past, and whose roots are themselves ancient. This should be the purpose of history. To help reconstruct the origins. Perhaps the Greeks were more concerned about preserving the myth of Troy than in reconstructing its ruins.

Gardens flourish each spring; when neglected they die. We have to remember that old gardens constitute our cultural heritage. When restored, there is the danger that they come to represent other memories than those which we remember, and if so they lose their original significance.

It is necessary to handle these historical and cultural memories carefully, without distorting their virtues, so that we can hand down to those who come after us a tradition that is free from confusion and which is, as far as possible, authentic.

Opposite page. *Summer house.*
Quinta da Assunção. Belas.

BIBLIOGRAPHY
Portuguese writers

Academia Nacional de Belas Artes. *Invetário Artístico de Portugal.* Lisbon 1943/1978.

Araújo, Ilidio. *Arte Paisagística e arte dos Jardins em Portugal.* Lisbon 1962.

Araújo, Norberto. *Inventário de Lisboa.* 12 instalments C.M.L. Lisbon

Arquivo Pitoresco. Lisbon 1856/1872.

Barbosa, Father Domingos Caldas. *Descripção da Grandiosa Quinta dos Senhores de Belas.* Lisbon 1799.

Barbosa, Ignácio de Vilhena. *Monumentos de Portugal. Históricos Artísticos e Arqueológicos.* Lisbon 1886.

Cadornega, António Oliveira. *Descripção de Vila Viçosa.* Introduction by Heitor Teixeira. 1983.

Calado, Father Manuel. *Valoroso Luciderno.* Evora 1648.

Camelo, Francisco Xavier Pereira. *Boletim de Trabalhos Históricos 1757/58.* Arq. Municipal de Guimarães.

Castelo Branco, Fernando. *Lisboa Seiscentista.* 3rd. ed. Lisbon 1969.

Castilho, Júlio de. *A Ribeira de Lisboa.* 3rd. ed. Lisbon 1948.

Castilho, Júlio de. *Lisboa Antiga.* 3rd. ed. Lisbon 1960.

Castro, Father João Baptista de. *Mappa de Portugal Antigo e Moderno.* Lisbon.

Chaves, Castelo Branco. *Guimarães em meados do séc. XVIII.* Braga.

Correia, Virgílio. *Azulejos datados.* Lisbon 1922.

Correia, Virgílio. *Uma Descrição Quinhentista do Mosteiro de Santa Cruz de Coimbra.* Coimbra 1930.

Côrte Real, Manuel H. *O Palácio das Necessidades.* Lisbon 1983.

Costa, Father António Carvalho da. *Chorografia Portuguesa.* Lisbon 1712.

Costa, A. Rebello da. *Descripção da Cidade do Porto.* Oporto 1789.

Craesbeck, Serra. *Memórias Ressuscitadas de entre Douro e Minho.* Manuscript 218 B.N.L. (Biblioteca Nacional, Lisbon).

Farinha, Father Manuel José dos Santos. *Subsídios para a História de Lisboa Antiga. O Palácio de Palhavã.* Lisbon 1923.

Figueirôa, Diogo Ferreira. *Epitome de Festas.* 1633.

França, José Augusto. *A Arte em Portugal no séc. XIX.* Lisbon 1966.

Góis, Damião de. *Crónica de El/Rei Dom Manuel I.*

Gonçalves, Father António Nogueira. *Casas Nobres do séc. XVIII.* Lousã 1950.

Guedes, Natália Brito Correia. *O Palácio de Queluz.* Lisbon 1971.

Jornal de Horticultura Prática 1873/1890. Dr. José Marques Loureiro.

Lucena, Armando and Belo, António. *Os Jardins do Paço Ducal de Vila Viçosa.* Calouste Gulbenkian Foundation 1955.

Machado, Cyrillo Wolkmar. *Colecção de Memórias Relativas às Vidas dos Pintores, Escultores, Arquitectos...* Coimbra 1923.

Machado, Diogo Barbosa. *Biblioteca Lusitana.* Lisbon 1752.

Madeira, Jerónimo Cabral. *Memória explicativa dos principais azulejos do Gimnásio do C. Militar.* Lisbon.

Marques, Isabel Maria de Sousa. *O desenvolvimento Urbano de Queluz.* Dissertation in Geographical Sciences submitted to the Faculty of Letters, Lisbon University. Lisbon 1960.

Meco, José. *Azulejaria Portuguesa.* Lisbon 1985.

Mesquita, José Carlos Vilhena. *O Palácio de Estói. Subsídios para a sua História.* Faro 1982.

Moser, Jorge de. *Boletim do M.N.A.A. de Lisboa 1949.*

Pereira, Gabriel. *Notas e Arte e Arqueologia.* Lisbon 1908.

Pires, António Caldeira (Pinho). *História do Palácio de Queluz.* Coimbra 1925/1926.

Queirós, José. *Cerâmica Portuguesa.* Lisbon 1907.

Rosa, Augusto Matos. *Lavoura Portuguesa.* April-August 1965.

Sabugosa, Count of. *O Paço de Sintra.* Lisbon 1903.

Santos, Reinaldo dos. *O azulejo em Portugal.* Lisbon 1957.

Sardinha, Francisco de Moraes. *Parnaso de Vila Viçosa.* Manuscript Collections. B.N.L.

Simões, João dos Santos. *Azulejaria em Portugal.* Calouste Gulbenkian Foundation, 1986.

Smith, Robert C. *Nicolau Nasoni. Arquitecto do Porto.* Lisbon 1966.

Sousa, Abade de Castro e. *Descripção do Palácio Real da Vila de Sintra...* Lisbon 1893.

Sousa, Dom António Caetano de. *História Genealógica da Casa Real Portuguesa.* Coimbra 1948.

Stoop, Anne de. *Quintas e Palácios nos arredores de Lisboa.* Barcelos 1986.

Teixeira, José. *O Paço de Vila Viçosa.* Calouste Gulbenkian Foundation, 1983.

Viterbo, Sousa. *Diccionário Histórico e Documental dos arquitectos e engenheiros.* Imprensa Nactional 1904.

Viterbo, Sousa. *A Jardinagem em Portugal.* 1st Series. Coimbra 1906.

Viterbo, Sousa. *A Jardinagem em Portugal* 2nd Series. Coimbra 1909.

Foreign writers

Al-Edrissi, Muhammad. *Descripção de Espana*. Madrid. 1901.

Bazin, René. *Terres d'Espagne*. Paris.

Beckford, William. *The journal of William Beckford in Portugal and Spain 1787-1788*. London 1954. Portuguese edition *Diário de... em Portugal e Espanha*. Translation and preface by João Gaspar Simões. 2nd ed. Lisbon 1983.

Carrère. *Tableau de Lisbonne en 1786*. Paris 1789.

Costigan, Arthur William. *Sketches of Society and Manners in Portugal*. London 1787. Portuguese translation *Cartas de Portugal (1778-1779)*. Translation, preface and notes by Artur Reis Machado. Lisbon 1946.

Corsini in *Viaje de Cosme de Medicis por Espana y Portugal (1668-1669)*. Translation and notes by Angel S. Rivero. Madrid. Partial translation into Portuguese in Revista Municipal by A.G. Madahill.

Courtils, M. de. *Une description de Lisbonne en Juin de 1755*. Lisbon 1965.

Dalrymple, William. *Travels through Spain and Portugal in 1774*. London 1777.

Flecknoe, Richard. Cited by Rose Macaulay. *Ingleses em Portugal*. Liv. Civilização 1950.

Gorani, José. *Portugal, a Corte e o País nos anos de 1765 a 1767*. Translation by Castelo Branco Chaves. Lisbon 1945.

Jantillet, Alexis C. de. *Horoe Subsecivoe*. Lisbon 1679. The part referring to the palace and gardens of the Marquises of Fronteira can be found translated [into Portuguese] in *Jardins e palácios dos Marqueses de Fronteira* by José Cassiano Neves. Lisbon 1945.

Junot, Laura (Duchess of Abrantes). *Souvenirs d'une Ambassade et d'un séjour en Espagne et en Portugal, de 1808 à 1811*. Paris 1837.

Lichnowsky, Prince Felix of. *Portugal Recordações do ano de 1842*. Preface and notes by Castelo Branco Chaves. Lisbon. Atica.

Link, Henry Frederic. *Voyage en Portugal depuis 1797-1799*. Paris 1803. Translation form the German.

Monconys, M. de *Journal des Voyages*. Lyon 1666.

Müncher, Jerónimo. *Itinerário do Dr. Jerónimo Müncher (Excertos)*. Translation from the Latin by Basílio de Vasconcellos. Coimbra 1931.

Murphy, James. *Travels in Portugal ... in the years 1789-1790*. London 1795.

Rattazzi, Princess. *Le Portugal à vol d'oiseau*. Paris 1879.

Rosmital, Baron Leo de. *Um viajante em Portugal há 393 anos*. O Mundo elegante. 1858. Translation by C. Castelo Branco.

Ruders, Carl Israel. *Viagem a Portugal, 1789-1802*. Translation by António Feijó. Lisbon 1981.

Southey, Robert. *Journals of a Residence in Portugal 1800-1801 and a visit to France 1838*. Oxford 1960.

Tollenare. *Notes Dominicales Prises pendant un Voyage en Portugal et au Brézil en 1816, 1817 et 1818*. Paris. Calouste Gulbenkian Foundation 1972.

Venturino, João Baptista. *Relato da Viagem do Cardeal Alexandrino*. Part translated by Alexandre Herculano in Opúsculos. Vol. VI. Lisbon 1884.

INDEX OF GARDENS ILLUSTRATED

INDEX OF NAMES